The Astronomer of Rousdon

Charles Grover 1842–1921

Barbara Slater

To my parents
Hazel Grover Sweetman
and
John Sweetman

Steam Mill Publishing in association with
Courseware Publications, Bury St Edmunds
The Steam Mill
Mill Road
Carleton Rode
Norwich NR16 1NQ

ISBN 1 898 737 30 4

Contents

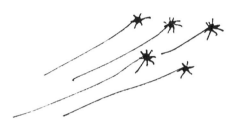

Australia: December 1882

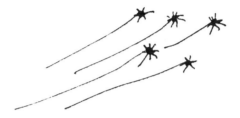

On the morning of 7 December 1882, five Englishmen and one Englishwoman rose before dawn and left an otherwise uninhabited mansion house on a huge and isolated sheep station on the Darling Downs in Queensland, Australia, making their way across the dry grassland to three portable astronomical observatories which had travelled with them on a 45-day journey by sea and then for almost another month along the coast and overland to their obscure destination.

In one of the observatories were a Captain William Morris of the Royal Engineers and a young man of the Marine Artillery known only as Gunner Bailey; in another were Lieutenant Leonard Darwin, son of Charles Darwin, and his wife Elizabeth; in the third was a young man, Cuthbert Peek, heir to a baronetcy, the son of the MP Sir Henry Peek, and his assistant, Charles Grover.

On behalf of the Royal Geographical Society in London, they readied their equipment, made the necessary measurements and adjustments and waited for the sun to rise and for their once-in-a-lifetime opportunity to observe a transit of Venus, an event that would not occur again until June 2004.

This is the story of Charles Grover, Peek's assistant. He began life in poverty, was almost entirely self-educated and became a scrupulous astronomical observer, specialising in observations of variable stars and gaining the respect of numerous well-connected contemporaries. He was one of a band of generally little-known and poorly-recorded working-class astronomers who emerged in the nineteenth century, determined and self-confident, overcoming the shortcomings of their education and often the beneficiaries of Victorian philanthropy.

His background would have made of Charles Grover a brush-maker. He himself had other ideas.

An Unremarkable Childhood

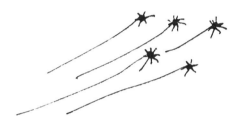

On 2 March 1910 Charles Grover celebrated his seventieth birthday at Rousdon in Devon, on the estate of the Peek family where he had been living and working for the past twenty-seven years, first as assistant to Sir Cuthbert Peek in his private observatory, then as observer in charge under Cuthbert's son Wilfrid. A photograph memorialises the occasion; a large cake, dressed in a old-fashioned fringed frill, is accompanied by a card which reads 'C. Grover, Astronomer, 70th Birthday, March 2.1910' and by a pamphlet which records the fortuitous return in the same year of Halley's Comet. The pamphlet was written by H. Perriam Hawkins and is illustrated with a sketch by Charles of the anticipated path of the comet.

The photograph can be read as paradigmatic of Charles's life: he was not seventy, the 2 March was not his birthday, and Halley's Comet has equal billing with his own apparent achievement in years. He records his date of birth as 2 March 1840 in his unfinished memoir of 1908 – '50 Years an Astronomical Observer' – whereas he was actually born on 7 March 1842. This is either a mistake, which is uncharacteristic, or the result of a deliberate adjustment; perhaps one made in childhood to facilitate other people's plans, although it is hard to see why in either case the day would have been confused as well as the year of birth. The only sure thing is that this seems to reflect an unconcern with everyday domestic life, the life that just 'is', as opposed to the astronomical side of life where Charles's observations – right from the start – are painstakingly accurate, where he does not make mistakes and will refer back over many years to early work with complete confidence in his own powers. In '50 Years' two-and-a-half paragraphs cover the years before Charles gets his first telescope. His memoir mentions neither his brother, his wife, formerly Elizabeth Birch, whom he married in the Lower Baptist Chapel, Amersham, in 1862, nor his children.

Charles Grover's is the story of a poor working-class boy who, through a combination of his own intellectual ability, a considerable degree of self-confidence and the typically Victorian philanthropic intervention of a number of well-known wealthy men, rose from the artisan status that his background would have ordained to hold a respected position in the Peek household and to have the value of his observations acknowledged by some of the greatest astronomers of the age. It is also the story of a man who was never educated to the degree that he perhaps should have been and who remained an assistant for many years when he almost certainly had the capacity to do more. He climbed about as high as it was possible to do in an intensely class-conscious society and experienced more than, as a young man, he could have dreamed of; but he was also a Victorian at heart, still a man of his time.

He seems to have been more than content with his lot, which was perhaps understandable given what he might have expected his life to be, and to share some of the snobbishness and prejudices of his age. His scientific and intellectual achievements raised him out of his place in professional terms; while the social and domestic side of life, the life that just 'was', remained unquestioned.

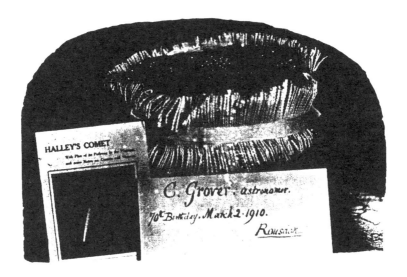

Photograph marking Charles Grover's 70th birthday, celebrated at Rousdon, Devon, 2 March 1910

He also demonstrated archetypal Victorian characteristics of self-discipline and self-reliance; 'self-help' was a nineteenth-century watchword. His life seems to have resembled more closely that of Allan Chapman's Scots' working-class astronomers, described in *The Victorian Amateur Astronomer*, who 'wrote with confidence to newspapers, passed on their observations to scientists of eminence, and did not see it as strange within the society in which they lived that men who worked with their hands could also have first-class minds which deserved to be taken seriously' than that of English observers working under the assumption 'that the manual working classes would keep their places, although great sacrifice and ingenuity might sometimes be deemed worthy of a modest present'.

Charles's father, John Grover, was a shoemaker. His mother, Eliza, formerly Eliza Benwell, was a shoebinder. In the census of 1841, shortly before Charles's birth, they are listed as living with Eliza's father, Thomas Benwell, aged 70, a shoemaker, and their four-year-old son George in Church Street, Chesham, Buckinghamshire. Thomas Benwell's wife Sarah had died fifteen years earlier in 1826, when her daughters Eliza and Sarah were aged thirteen and fourteen.

Eliza died shortly after the birth of her second son. Charles was around two months old; his mother would have been 25 or 26, his father John Grover was a few years older. At this point, Charles writes 'I was consigned to the care of my grand-mother and therefore saw very little of my father who died about 1850.'

In 1851 Charles is still living in Church Street, Chesham – the same street as the shoemaking Benwell household – his relationship to the householder given as 'grandson'. His maternal grandfather Thomas died in 1843 and it seems likely that Thomas would have been the householder and that his death would have left John and George Grover with no alternative but to find another home from which to conduct the shoemaking business. John Grover is listed as having died in Chesham. That he saw – apparently – little of his younger son suggests that he was living at some remove from him. Although since Charles was actually only eight when his father died he may simply not have remembered much contact.

The household at 37 Church Street, Chesham, in 1851 consisted of six people. The head of the household was Sarah Brown, a widow aged 61 and a lace maker. This was Charles's paternal grandmother, born Sarah Bunker around 1781, married to William Grover – who was almost exactly the same age as her – in 1809. As well as Charles's father John, she had another son,

William, and a daughter, another Sarah. After her husband's death, in 1833 Sarah Grover married William Brown, a shovelmaker, and by 1851 was widowed for a second time. With her lived her widowed sister Mary Statham or Stadham, aged 65, a lace maker; an unmarried 18-year-old lodger, Bridget Tofield, also a lace maker; another unmarried lodger whose occupation is not given in the census return, Selina Payne, aged 42; Susan Gennels (although her name is far from clear), a 15-year-old servant; and Charles, aged nine.

A brief outline cannot really convey the strangeness of the situation in which Charles found himself in comparison to more recent times. The loss of his mother in her twenties, his father in his thirties and his grandmother in her sixties, at which point, at the age of twelve, he is more or less thrown upon his own resources, and despatched as an apprentice to live with strangers, are inconceivable in the England of a welfare state and compulsory education; not to mention in a time when people are well-nourished, have good medical care and almost always come unscathed through the rigours of childbirth. Yet at the same time, it should be recognised that his background was not untypical by his own lights. He is certainly not given to self-pity.

In *The History and Antiquities of the County of Buckingham* by Dr George Lipscomb, published in 1847, the chief employment of the inhabitants of Chesham is described as being in 'the manufacture of coarse wooden-ware, the extensive cultivation of the beech-tree in the neighbourhood of the town, furnishing an ample supply of the necessary material. A number of operatives are likewise engaged in the shoe trade; and almost the whole of the female population, during many years, earned a good livelihood by lace making, and the production of straw-plat.' In their place too, Charles's family seem very typical. As an aside, Lipscomb also notes that there was an attempt after about 1820 to interest people in the health-giving properties of a local mineral spring, without much success.

Charles attended the British School in Chesham where he received a narrow education – 'Reading, Writing and the veriest rudiments of Arithmetic' – although he later revised this to include a little geography. There were two charitable organisations whose establishments formed the basis of British education through the first seventy-five years or so of the nineteenth century. The British and Foreign Schools Society, a non-sectarian Christian organisation, was established in 1808, and the Church of England National Society for the Promotion of the Education of the Poor in the Doctrine and Discipline of the Established Church, was established in 1811; its 'National Schools' set up in response to the fear that the young would otherwise be educated by dissenters (who supported the British Schools). Records suggest that Charles's family were Nonconformist. Both systems offered a very basic education in the 'three Rs' for a penny a week. Teaching tended to utilise the monitor system where slightly older pupils would lead or supervise younger ones (the blind leading the blind in many cases), although after 1846 the pupil-teacher system was introduced. This was more effective since the pupil-teachers were chosen with greater care and could be kept on in the school and trained towards a degree of qualification, although it was also subject to great inconsistency. In Charles Grover's time there was no compulsory school attendance – this was not introduced until the late 1870s – and rural children in particular were often kept home at busy times in the agricultural year.

Charles writes of a 'kindly schoolmaster' Mr Osborn (probably the William Osborne listed in the 1851 census as lodging with a saddler and his family in High Street, Chesham) who noted his interest in a drawing class and 'permitted him gratuitously' to join in. The system did not proscribe additional subjects, but they would generally have had to be paid for. Before Mr Osborn (or Osborne) left,

Charles had had three two-hour lessons in drawing: 'I remember him patting me on the head when he said goodbye and telling me to learn all I could. Those three simple lessons have always been invaluable to me and I could soon make an intelligible sketch of nearly anything.' When Charles first began observations of the stars and planets, astronomical photography was in its infancy and anyway far beyond the reach – technically and financially – of a working-class astronomer and it was standard practice to draw or paint observations. Some beautiful illustrations to Charles's observational record book bear witness to the confidence engendered by these few classes.

He remembers best among his fellow scholars a delicate boy of around his own age, Robert Barnes.

I have sat on the same form with him and watched with admiration the beautiful drawings he produced even at that early date, he rose to distinction, exhibited at the Academy in 1873, was a very constant contributor to the Graphic, and died in May 1895. He was particularly noted for his pleasing studies of children and scenes of happy domestic home life.

In spite of these achievements, like Charles Grover, Robert Barnes is now largely forgotten.

Charles notes that 'I never knew the time that I could not read or write', which suggests that these skills were acquired before he started school. It is unlikely however that, at home, he would have had access to any reading matter beyond a Bible, unless his grandmother was an unusually well-educated woman; and the description of the crowded household of piece-working lace makers does not suggest a context well enough off to include expensive luxuries such as books. Writing on his schooldays he notes that 'I read with eagerness any books that came my way.'

The question then arises of how he did come across reading material. There were the circulating libraries which began in Edinburgh in 1729 and whose reach was broadened in the 1840s by Charles Mudie (1818-1890). Some of the earliest circulating libraries were associated with Nonconformist chapels; chapels, churches and similar institutions also ran libraries on Mudie's behalf. Mudie was a bookseller and publisher – following in the footsteps of his father who was a second-hand bookseller who lent books to the public at a penny a time. In 1842 he bought large numbers of books, and using the expanding rail network would send boxes of books all over the country. Generally a small subscription would be payable against which the subscriber could borrow books from the library. Another source of books for working-class readers would have been the Mechanics' Institutes, which were fairly widespread and which also had Nonconformist connections. As with education, the established church quickly followed suit, setting up Church Institutes, with libraries. While still fairly young Charles would probably also have been allowed access to any local men's reading rooms; charitable establishments set up to allow working men places of relaxation in their leisure hours other than public houses.

The census of 1851 has Charles's correct age, so it is perhaps most likely that at some point after this date an adjustment in the date of his birth from 1842 to 1840 seemed useful or convenient. The grandmother seems the most likely perpetrator of this deception, which may of course already have been active at a local level even though the real date was written on the census return. Perhaps perceiving her grandson's sharp intelligence she thought he would be as well at school as at home and a couple of extra years would help in this. There was no formal starting age for school and he very likely began attending when he was – or was presented as – four or five. Maybe she saw it as a way of reducing her own burden of care. Charles himself notes ambiguously that 'My grandmother was so extremely kind (of course in a old fashioned and mistaken way) that had I long remained with her after my father's death I should have been good for nothing, but fortunately for my future welfare she also shortly died.' This is opaque in the extreme. Charles is not given to irony, although one might expect irony to be intended here, in the contrast between the extreme kindness of the grandmother and the observation that his own future welfare was better served by her death. It is also unclear at this distance of time – if it was ever clear – what he means by an 'old fashioned and mistaken way'. From a twenty-first century perspective, and perhaps from the perspective of the early twentieth century as well, 'old fashioned and mistaken' may well be taken to mean a fair degree of brutality, a fear of sparing the rod and spoiling the child. Equally, it is easy to see that he may have been much indulged in a household of widows and spinsters and have come to see this as an unfitting way for a boy to be brought up to the challenges and hardships that life was likely to offer.

In the end though the task of ensuring Charles's independence devolved to others. His father died when he was eight and his grandmother in 1854. At the age of 12 he would presumably have become the responsibility of other relatives – perhaps of his aunt Mary Statham if she was still alive. There seems little doubt that there would have been numerous relations around in the area, although their closeness to Charles – and indeed their willingness to take on another charge themselves – is debatable. His age may have been adjusted at this point. While it was by no means unusual for boys in rural areas to start work before the age of 12, it may have seemed preferable to present Charles as slightly older than he was in order to secure an apprenticeship. He was, therefore 'consigned to a Brush Maker to be initiated into the mysteries of that trade as a future living'. No doubt brushes were among the 'coarse wooden-wares' typical of Chesham manufacturing; the fact that the family were engaged in such very commonplace jobs emphasising the ordinariness of the background from which Charles came.

In the very small amount of more personal autobiographical writing that he has left, Charles twice refers to himself as 'consigned', more of a package than a person.

Brush-makers were fairly far down the ladder of rural industry. Charles may have been engaged in the simple manufacture of besoms – using timber and coppice wood – or brushes with drilled stocks, made using a pole lathe or possibly a treadle lathe, which was a technological advance, allowing for continuous working, and bristle heads. It was a doomed industry as well as a lowly occupation. By the early twentieth century it had almost died out altogether as a rural industry, taken over by mechanisation, and would have been dwindling in significance long before that.

In '50 Years an Astronomical Observer' his apprenticing to the brush-maker is the point at which Charles abandons any personal history. The auto-biographical fragment also starts to tell of his earliest forays into astronomy. The brush-maker to whom he was apprenticed and with whom he must have spent his working and at least some of his leisure time for at least 15 years – given a starting date of around 1854 and the date at which Charles left Chesham, which was 1869 – is not named at all. It is only from the 1861 census that we know that Charles (his name misspelled as 'Groves' and his age given as 21) was part of Henry Rose's household in Stratfords Yard, Chesham. Henry Rose is listed as a 'brush manufacturer', his wife Sarah and his 12-year-old daughter Elizabeth are 'brush drawers', Charles Grover is listed as 'lodger' and 'brushmaker'. A two-year-old boy completes the household.

Charles's background – the little of it that is known – does not sound conducive to the development of an emotionally rounded individual. Having effectively lost both parents, he then lost the person with whom he had known his whole childhood, and whether she had been good to him or not she would have been the only person with whom he had formed any kind of attachment or bonds of affection. While still a child he became a worker and a lodger. That he does not mention the brush-maker implies that the relationship was not an affectionate or significant one. It is hardly surprising then that all his passion was put into his studies and observations. It seems more surprising that he found the time to marry or to have children at all.

George Grover, his elder brother by four years, took the conventional course; something similar might have been expected for Charles. In 1864 George married Mary Sherriff at the Weslyan Chapel in Luton. George is noted as a widower – he married a Mary Philby in 1860, but she did not live long beyond the wedding and there were no recorded children from this marriage. He became a master shoemaker and in 1891 he and the former Mary Sherriff had nine children, all apparently still living at home in what had been Mary's mother's house in Great Missenden where all the children were born, William (aged about 25 – all the ages are approximate), George (23), Albert (19), Frederick (17), Lovell (14), Harry (12), Ellen (10), Emma (7) and Annie (3). While Charles may have seen little of his father he may have seen something of his brother at school (although the four-year age gap would have meant that their school years overlapped very little and George seems likely to have become his father's apprentice at an early age). A George Grover was witness at the marriage of Charles's only surviving son George Charles in 1886 and it seems likely that this was Charles's brother. Beyond this there is no evidence that the brothers remained in touch with one another at all.

Of his brush-making Charles notes only that 'my mind was not in this, and all my spare time was devoted to such books as I could get and the pursuit of general knowledge'. And so it might have continued and his intellect turned towards some other area of science or observation – because what shines through all his writing is a broad interest and curiosity in whatever is at hand – but for the appearance in 1858 of Donati's comet. This he watched night after night, tracing its path until 'October 5th saw it pass in splendour over the bright star Arcturus, and finally disappear from these latitudes. Thus the Great Bear, Arcturus and the Northern Crown (corona borealis) were the first constellations I recognised.'

He did not lose the habit of watching the sky and the following year, on 8 May, noticed a star close to the moon, which vanished only to reappear on the other side. 'Looking up in the almanac I found that this was an occultation of the planet Saturn, and then I found I must have a telescope'. There is an extraordinary sense here of compulsion. Charles was 17, a brush-maker's apprentice, with next to no money, a minimal formal education and little or no hope of escaping the path which fate seemed to have determined for him, yet he felt compelled to follow his interest into what was a truly exciting and constantly changing area of scientific observation and discovery. In his favour, throughout the nineteenth century astronomy remained largely the preserve of amateurs in Great Britain, although most of those who are remembered were wealthy men who were able to fund private observatories and pay professional observers and assistants to work in them.

So Charles bought 'an old ship's spy glass for 10/- and to me it was a wonderful instrument'. Using this he studied through the next year or so 'The satellites of Jupiter, the crescent figure of Venus, The Pleiades, the Cluster in Cancer and other wonders'.

Meetings with Significant Men

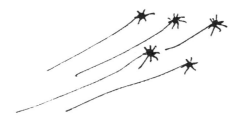

By 1861 – after two years' observing with the ship's spy-glass – Charles Grover wanted a more powerful telescope and, since there was no way that he could have afforded to buy such a thing, like many other working-class astronomers he set about making his own. Reflecting on the difficulty of such a project in 1908 he recalled that 'money was very scarce and cheap achromatic object glasses and fittings were not to be bought as they are now'. In 1861 a 'cheap' telescope would probably have cost around £3, a sum that would certainly have represented more than a month's wages. He therefore began constructing a non-achromatic telescope using a zinc tube and a double convex lens of three-inch diameter and five-foot focus. He noted that 'Much of the success of this kind of telescope depends upon the proper construction of the eyepiece, which should have a sliding cap with an eyehole at the exact focal distance from the lens; the entire field of view then appears very brilliant.'

Notable observations with the home-made telescope included the great comet of 1861. This was discovered by John Tebbutt (1834-1916) of New South Wales on 13 May. Tebbutt's observatory, equipped with a variety of instruments including a 4 1/2-inch Cooke refractor, was one of the first southern hemisphere observatories to specialise to a large extent in cometary work. (For a good deal of the information about Victorian astronomy in this chapter and elsewhere I am indebted to Allan Chapman's *The Victorian Amateur Astronomer*.) Tebbutt's Comet is probably better known from its appearance in 1881 – when it was also known as the Great Comet – but in 1861 it was the first comet through whose tail the earth had been known to pass. The second time that this has been recorded was with Halley's Comet in 1910. Charles describes his viewing of the comet in 1861.

it passed perihelion on June 11th and rising from the southern hemisphere became visible in these latitudes on June 30. The position of the comet and the peculiar broad fan shaped tails made it very probable that the Earth passed through the cometary envelope at that time, but beyond a peculiar yellowish haze noticed in one or two places, nothing transpired, and the alarming predictions of the destruction of the Earth, or of a Universal deluge as a result of a collision with a comet which so frightened the people of an earlier age were certainly not confirmed. My first drawing of the Comet, (Tuesday July 2 just before Midnight), shows a straight narrow tail of enormous length, about 70 degrees. On July 3 a drawing of the head shows two jets of light from each side of the nucleus, and a broad sector of light preceding. After this the brightness rapidly diminished and the comet was last seen on Thursday September 5 when it was an exceedingly faint object, having been followed two months and three days. Not a bad record for such an imperfect instrument.

The Pleiades, sketched 12 October 1866. The small circle with a dot in the centre indicates the position of the 'missing' star, which had been observed in 1861 and re-emerged to be faintly seen by 31 October

In the autumn of 1861 Charles made a chart of the Pleiades showing 52 stars which he kept and compared with observations made in 1866. He wrote that 'In 1861 I observed the cluster with a nonachromatic telescope of my own construction ... on comparing the drawing made then with the diagram on the preceding page [a drawing made 12 October 1866, observed with a four-inch reflector] I find many stars not marked on the chart of 1861, also their relative positions in some instances do not agree, this must be laid to my inexperience in 1861 being then but a beginner in the science.' However, he notes other discrepancies that he is not prepared to lay at the door of his own inexperience. There is a star marked on the 1861 chart which is not visible in 1866 even using a more powerful instrument, and he remembers quite clearly that this star did exist and also its position relative to others in the cluster. Consequently he continues to make observations of the Pleiades throughout October – a study which pays off in that the errant star is rediscovered, although rather fainter than previously noted – making a final drawing of the 'Pleiades for the Epoch October 31st 1866'. He notes further that 'at a future time the cluster will be re-examined with the view of detecting any change which may occur'. It is this patient, systematic observation, the painstaking search for changes and variations that will make Charles Grover such a good and accurate observer of variable stars.

While he notes that 'this simple form of telescope is by no means to be despised' it did not satisfy Charles for long, and in March 1862 he bought his first telescope, a purchase that must have represented a truly significant financial outlay, not least since at this time he must have also been courting Elizabeth Birch whom he married on 5 August that year.

With the new telescope came a new seriousness in record keeping. The first page of his observations book describes the telescope. It was made by Slugg of Manchester, with a focal length of 36 inches and an object glass two inches in diameter and was fitted with a pancratic eyepiece giving magnifications of x50, x65 and x80. Slugg, a

Fellow of the Royal Astronomical Society, also wrote a personal history of Manchester, *Reminiscences of Manchester Fifty Years Ago.* Charles made a drawing of this instrument and his excitement at its performance and at the opportunities which it plainly represented to him is evident: 'Though small in size this instrument performs well and the beautiful definition of its object glass cannot be surpassed. The appearance of Jupiter in this instrument with a power of 80 and a clear sky is truly beautiful the belts and cloudy spots being seen with great clearness. Double, Triple and quadruple stars are also very clearly seen.'

Charles Grover's sketch of the Slugg telescope: 2 and 3 show the construction of the eyepiece

Using this instrument Charles began systematic observations of the Sun, Moon, Jupiter and Saturn. His first recorded observations are of Saturn – the earliest of them from 25 March, which must have been almost the first night's observation with the new instrument – documenting the gradual disappearance from view of the rings. These observations are first noted in brief and then documented more thoroughly with reference to series of drawings.

There are notes on observations of Saturn made on March 25 and 31, April 3, 24, 25, 26, 28, 29 and 30, May 2, 14 and 31 and June 23. These are accompanied by ten drawings made at specific dates and times, so (1) is 10.00 p.m. on 25 March, (2) 8.45 p.m. on 3 April, (3) 9.30 p.m. on 30 April, (4) 9.40 p.m. on 2 May and (5) 9.30 p.m. on 14 May. These first five drawings follow the gradual disappearance from view of Saturn's rings, the next five date from later in 1862 and early 1863 and follow their reappearance.

A further set of drawings records observations up to 1876, and there are notes on observations into 1881. The later observations generally serve to confirm the earlier ones and Charles often refers to the diagrams that he made as early as 1862-63 as representative of later observations. At the same time he notes additional detail that can be seen as a result of using better equipment. His notes on 11 December 1880 credit the increased aperture on a 3 5/8-inch achromatic with bringing into view 'the inner dusky or Crape ring' which is 'perfectly seen within the ansae' (the name given to the ends of Saturn's rings projecting beyond the ball of the planet).

In 1862 Charles believed that the rings of Saturn were solid, although in 1852 a number of observers had noticed that the limbs of Saturn were visible through the inner dusky ring, itself only noted in 1850 by William Bond and George Bond, which made any theory that the rings were solid hard to sustain.

In 1856 James Maxwell deduced that the rings of Saturn must be made of 'an indefinite number of unconnected particles', and in 1895 this was confirmed by James Keeler and William Campbell's discovery that the inner parts of the rings orbit more rapidly than the outer parts.

What Charles Grover's notes and drawings from this period illustrate is a dedication and enthusiasm for the observing work that he was doing simply for the love of discovery and learning.

Charles Grover's paintings of Saturn, showing the appearance of the rings, 1862-1863

The dates for the Saturn observations suggest that he was out on most nights when the sky was clear enough for any observation to be done. He does not supply any indication of how the observations were made. It would have been dark at night even in Chesham in the 1860s (some of the later observations were made with other telescopes and in other places), but the view of the sky may well have been restricted by buildings. It is also unlikely that Charles would have had a sheltered place in which his telescope could have been left ready for use. While Charles would have had his nights free, his days would probably have started early. Sometimes he observed in the mornings as well: occasional observations are noted as having been made at 4.45 a.m. or 5.00 a.m. The detail of his drawings, which must have been made on the spot, suggests that many of these sittings were not especially brief and that he must have spent hours at a time, night after night, whenever it was clear enough, patiently observing at his telescope after a long dull day's brush-making and before rising early for another such day. He also found time in this period of astronomical self-education to study the sun. The observations here are almost always at 8.40 a.m. and 1.00 p.m. He observed and drew the changes in sunspots and in 1863 set out specifically to observe the period of rotation of the sun.

In deference perhaps to his newly-married status there are no observations recorded in August or September of 1862, but they recommence in October and are more or less unbroken (as far as is possible given the English climate) thereafter.

On 1 January 1865 Charles writes: 'Observing the Moon ... I saw on the dark part of the disc a bright spot like a 4th magnitude star to the naked eye, but rather larger, which I watched for fully 30 minutes. It was at the E foot of the Lunar Alps and about the same position in which a bright [spot] was observed in 1789 September 26.' He had a letter published on this in the *Astronomical Register* (3.255) – possibly the first of the many letters that were published in scientific journals throughout his life – and Charles's observation is further cited in an odd work, *New Lands*, by Charles Hoy Fort, whose idiosyncratic pursuits and varied interests gave us the term 'Fortean', bundling together wide areas of research to demonstrate what are known as 'anomalous phenomena'.

The *Astronomical Register* was first published in 1863 and its establishment almost certainly reflects an increasing interest in astronomy – certainly among the middle classes, for whom the publication would have been intended. 'The early numbers of the *Astronomical Register* (1863-1886), with their discussions of telescopes, observing projects, obituaries, accounts of lectures, and book reviews, convey a lively impression of the cultivation of astronomy amongst the middle classes, although one assumes from its tone that its readers were far from hard-up.' Allan Chapman further observes that the journal 'catered specifically for an amateur astronomical (but by no means poor) readership'. The journal would have been available to the working-class reader through libraries and other reading institutions.

More significantly for his astronomical future, Charles described the sighting of the 'spot' on the moon in a letter to Revd T.W. Webb (1806-1885), author of a well-known introductory work on astronomical observation, *Celestial Objects for Common Telescopes*, first published in 1859. In a 'reminiscence' of Webb added to the preliminary pages of the fifth edition of *Celestial Objects*, published in 1893, eight years after Webb's death, the author (probably T.E. Espin (1858-1934), who edited and enlarged the edition) described Webb as 'a father to all amateur astronomers'. He continues: 'the post brought an appalling amount of correspondence from them to Hardwick. All were carefully, kindly, and encouragingly answered in letters charming alike for their elegant writing, and the extraordinary amount of learning, and originality, and witticism.' Charles Grover was duly encouraged by his first astronomical correspondent whose 'kind and genial' reply to his letter 'was the beginning of an extensive correspondence continued almost up to the time of his lamented death'. Reinforcing Espin's comment on the elegance of Webb's writing, Charles remarks: 'He wrote a small and very neat hand and I have a considerable collection of his letters giving the most minute of practical instructions as to the mounting and adjustments of telescopes, diagrams of various celestial objects, etc.' Sadly it appears that this collection of letters no longer exists. In the fourth edition of *Celestial Objects*, published in 1881, Charles notes that Webb 'introduced many references to my observations as a proof of what was within the reach of small telescopes'. In the fifth edition, of which Charles had a copy, inscribed on the flyleaf 'Chas. Grover, 1894 Oct. 3, with kind regards, from H.R.', the early observation of the 'bright spot on the Moon is given on p. 104 of Vol. I and there are many other notices of my observations scattered throughout the work'. It is not known who 'H.R.' was, although he may have been Henry Chamberlain Russell, Government Astronomer at the Sydney Observatory from 1870·1905, who Charles would have met on his travels and with whom he very probably maintained a correspondence.

Although, as Espin notes, Webb was unfailingly courteous toward the amateur observer, it seems likely that he saw in Charles Grover something beyond the norm in terms of skill and intellect, since the correspondence seems to have led to other introductions and Webb gave at least one gift to Charles. Some drawings of Mars made between 7 December 1866 and 19 January 1869 were made using the 2-inch achromatic telescope with a 'single lens eyepiece power 200, presented to me by the Revd. T.W. Webb'.

Twice in 1865 – 5 June and 15 and 16 August – Charles was invited to Hartwell House in Aylesbury by the well-known astronomer and polymath Dr

John Lee (1783-1866), one of Allan Chapman's 'Grand Amateurs': 'Those independently wealthy individuals who took upon themselves the reform and advancement of British astronomy at the highest technical and intellectual level.' Lee's primary occupation was the law, and he was a close friend for many years of William Smyth, later Admiral Smyth, an enthusiastic astronomical amateur, and author of a notable work, the *Cycle of Celestial Objects*, published in 1844. Plans were made for an observatory to be built at Hartwell House in the late 1820s, and the house itself became a focal point for astronomical meetings and discussions. Charles described his visits:

> *On June 5 and August 15 1865 I went to Hartwell at the kind invitation of Dr Lee. The Hartwell Observatory, at that time one of the finest private observatories in the kingdom, was a fine building with a 16 foot revolving dome in which was the celebrated telescope used by Admiral Smyth in compiling his 'Cycle of Celestial Objects'. This telescope of barely 6 inches aperture, was nearly 9 feet focal length and was mounted as an English equatorial on a wooden polar axis, the hour and declination circles being each 3 feet in diameter. The definition was splendid, and I have a vivid recollection of the appearance of Saturn with a power of 240. I was particularly anxious to see the Pole Star with this telescope as I had been observing ? [sic] the small companion with my little two inch. One glance was sufficient to show me my mistake. There was the companion clear enough, but so small and so near the bright star even with this powerful telescope as to show that it was very unlikely to be ever seen with a 2 inch object glass.*

As well as his pleasure in using the very same telescope that Admiral Smyth had used, Charles was plainly delighted by other objects in Lee's library:

'An orrery moved by clockwork, and a similar machine showing the motion of Jupiter's four moons', also 'another machine showing the movements of Saturn's Ring and Satellites' and a seventeenth-century telescope, by Campani of Rome, dated 1650, with a 2-inch object glass and a 10-foot vellum tube. At the time of his visit, 'the great map of the moon projected by the British Association for the Advancement of Science (BAAS) was there in progress. This was to be 10 feet in diameter, and the lines of latitude and longitude were set out, some of the larger lunar formations were sketched in outline, and as one looked at this large scale chart the magnitude of the work was faintly realised.' The great lunar map was never completed. William Radcliff Birt (1804-1881) worked on it for many years, and the 'principal Lunar formations were laid down from Micrometer Measures with the Hartwell equatorial'. Charles says that Birt continued to work on the map – corresponding with observers and accumulating considerable material – even after the BAAS had abandoned the project, although the work gradually dropped away and the project ground to a complete halt at Birt's death. Also in the library was a lunar globe, about 2 feet in diameter and 'a fine collection of prints and drawings of celestial objects'.

In the transit room of the observatory Charles noted 'a transit instrument of 3 3/4 inch aperture and 5 foot focus, and a sidereal clock, both of these the best obtainable at that day, and each costing 100 guineas'. He writes that 'Dr Lee died February 25. 1866 at the good old age of 83.' Elsewhere he adds 'respected by all lovers of science'. 'The observatory was afterwards dismantled and I saw the transit instruments sold at Stevens Auction Rooms, King St., Covent Garden, July 2. 1880.' The great telescope used by Smyth also had a history worth noting.

The object glass was made by Tully about 1829.
The flint glass disc having been purchased by
Sir James South in Paris the previous year.
From 1830 to 1836 it was mounted in the
Bedford Observatory [of William Smyth] and
employed by Admiral Smyth in the compilation
of the well known 'Cycle of Celestial Objects'.
From this observatory it was transferred to
Hartwell where it remained about 30 years till
in 1866 on the death of Dr Lee this observatory
was dismantled. In 1882 I found it at the
Radcliffe Observatory Oxford, packed for
transmission to Bermuda for the observation of
the Transit of Venus, and in 1885 it was
transferred to the Hong Kong Observatory
where it has been employed by Dr Doberek in
measures of the planets Jupiter and Saturn.

The visits to Hartwell however were more than
opportunities for a poor amateur to admire the
equipment available to the wealthy or to peruse
instruments that had been a part of the making of
current astronomical knowledge. Charles writes
that:

The Dr. received me with the greatest kindness,
made the most minute enquiries as to my
circumstances, instrument, books etc. and
looked carefully through my manuscript
observations which I had been asked to bring
for his inspection, and before I left he
expressed himself as much surprised and
pleased at the accuracy of the work I had
accomplished with very small and limited
means, made me a liberal pecuniary present
and gave me a large number of books.

Among the presents given Charles after his visit to
Hartwell in August was a copy of Birt's
observations on the lunar crater Plato made in
April and May 1863 with the Hartwell telescope.
Charles's response to reading this was that 'I

resolved to attack this object with my small but excellent telescope of 2 inch aperture and 3 feet focal length.' Then follows some pages of notes, drawings and comments: 'there is a curious but very visible depression well shown in my drawings, but not mentioned by Mr Birt', and a low connecting ridge seen by Charles 'is not shown by Mr Birt but is drawn by the accurate Lohrmann on his map'. Wilhelm Lohrmann (1796-1840) was a German amateur astronomer who produced a fine lunar map.

A double page torn from a small notebook suggests that Charles remained among those amateurs who continued to correspond with Birt on the formulation of the lunar map and to send observations to him. The pages constitute a list of observations made by Charles on 9 July 1867, but written out in what must be Birt's hand, and including detail of only some of the observations made. The final paragraph reads:

> *I have particularised all those objects which Mr Grover saw <u>as craters</u> it being very important <u>now</u> that the present appearance of Linné as contrasted with its former appearance according to Lohrmann and Schmidt is becoming a subject of dispute to register from time to time the continued existence or otherwise of craters.*

The paragraph is dated 15 July 1867 and signed W.R. Birt. The underlining is as in the original note.

Charles was particularly taken, while at Hartwell, with the position micrometer with which Smyth had taken an extensive series of double star measurements. With his own small telescope Charles had been observing a number of double stars and dearly wished to be able to measure the observed distances between them 'but of course the position micrometer was out of the question for me'. So he set about devising a simple apparatus to this end.

A carefully divided cardboard circle was attached to the eye end of the telescope, the lines of 90° and 270° being horizontal and 360° and 180° vertical, the 180° being at the top. The index pointer which just touches the circle is attached to the eyepiece and revolves with it as it is turned in its tube, a little collar being put on so that it always keeps in focus.

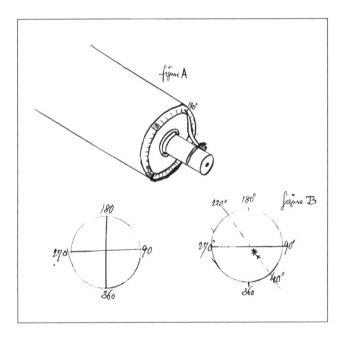

The whole arrangement will be readily understood from the annexed rough sketch, figure A. Now in the field of the eyepiece stretch a single wire as in figure B. So arranged that when the index points to 270° this wire is horizontal across the field, and therefore when the telescope is directed Southward and on the meridian the wire coincides with the path of a star as it moves across the field. Now bring in a pair of stars as in figure B and let the larger star of the pair

traverse the wire as it passes along. Note the degree on the circle, this should be 270°, now revolve the tube till the wire is parallel to the pair of stars and again read the circle which will show the index has travelled from 270° to 220° – but as the smaller star is in the opposite quadrant the reading must also be transferred and the position angle is 40°.

After some practice with this device, Charles reckoned that he achieved a good degree of accuracy in his measurements. It also constituted the subject of his first published article – 'Substitute for the Position Micrometer' – which appeared, with the assistance of Thomas Webb, in the *Intellectual Observer* for January 1866, and for which Charles received £1.5s (£1.25p) 'as remuneration'. Further, 'A table of the position angles of 16 well known double stars observed with this contrivance appeared in the "Astronomical Register" for November 1867.'The article in the *Intellectual Observer* was prefaced by the following remarks by the editor:

A strong interest attaches to the pursuit of science under considerable difficulties and we therefore depart from our usual custom by saying a few words on the author of this communication. He is an artizan – a brushmaker – fortunately possessed of a two-inch telescope, and doing such good work with it as to have attracted honourable notice from Dr. Lee of Hartwell House, Mr. Birt, and our own highly-esteemed contributor, the Revd. T.W. Webb, by whom this paper has been sent to us. The plan adapted by Mr Grover is certainly ingenious and may suggest to others, who like him cannot afford more perfect instruments, how much may be accomplished by ingenuity and perseverance. If a poor working man, subsisting and keeping a family upon slender weekly wages, can manage to make considerable progress in observational astronomy by the diligent employment of his leisure hours, what a wide field is open to those who can devote ample time and money to any favourite pursuit?

By this time, Charles did indeed have a family. Elizabeth gave birth to George Charles on 7 January 1864. The observations for that period include Jupiter on 6 January – one in a series of observations that began in 1862 – the 'Great Nebulae in Orion', a summary of observations accompanied by a drawing made in January 1864, and confirmation of earlier observations of Saturn, made on 1 February, that showed 'the outer edge of the ring was plainly seen to be much less bright than the inner'.

On 19 February 1866 Charles visited one James Buckingham 'and saw his great 20 inch achromatic telescope of 25 foot focus, at that time the largest telescope in England'. Buckingham was probably the contributor of 'Supposed Observation of Biela's Comet' to the *Monthly Notices of the Royal Astronomical Society* in May 1866. The telescope was in the open air at Buckingham's engineering works at Westmoreland Road, Walworth Common. 'The stand was on the German plan, and the polar axis was about 18 feet above the ground. The tube of iron about 30 foot long was cigar shaped, 3 feet diameter at the centre and two feet at each end and weighed nearly 3 tons.' In spite of the great size and weight of the telescope Charles was impressed with its manoeuvrability and even more with its light-grasping power. He writes that while he was with Buckingham a dense fog descended 'so thick that the moon about first quarter was quite invisible'. However, when the telescope was turned onto the sky where the moon was hidden behind the fog it could distinctly be seen, 'a striking proof of the light grasping power of such a large object glass'.

A duplicate lens for the telescope was being ground at the Walworth works using a steam-powered machine in which Charles was greatly interested, particularly 'in the complicated mechanism for altering the length and figure of the stroke and revolving the lens during grinding'. Steam power had first been employed for grinding large lenses by Lord Rosse, a very wealthy Grand Amateur astronomer, at his Irish country seat at Birr Castle. In this way he had had made a 72-inch mirror for a gigantic instrument of 52-feet focal length, familiarly known as 'Leviathan'. In some respects Birr Castle was an Irish equivalent to Hartwell House; Lord Rosse, like Dr Lee, being a passionate and wealthy amateur with interests and occupations that would have been distractions to observations, but that enabled them to be hosts and patrons and to extend the technology of instrument manufacture.

In his own way – as proprietor of an engineering works – James Buckingham was perhaps doing some-thing of the same, although inevitably on a smaller scale.

Charles notes that in a dome apart from the large telescope, James Buckingham had 'a beautifully constructed equatorial of 10 inches aperture ... also a transit instrument and sidereal clock'. Buckingham lent Charles a '4 inch Gregorian telescope by Short, on a massive brass table stand with which I made a great many observations'. Allan Chapman writes that James Short (1710-1768) was an eighteenth-century instrument maker who made numerous telescopes with 2 or 3-inch diameter mirrors and at least one large telescope, an 18-inch aperture Gregorian which is still in existence, in the Museum of the History of Science in Oxford. Short was also central to the calculations made following the transit of Venus in 1761 and was a member of the Royal Society committee on preparations for the transit of 1769. Although he died . before this date, instruments of his manufacture were used by Captain Cook aboard the *Endeavour.*

The telescope given him by James Buckingham was the instrument that Charles used in his 1866 observations of the Pleiades: 'The 4 inch reflector was preferred in these observations from its larger field and greater light – it operated beautifully on this object.' Although when he became the proud owner of a better telescope, it was the old 2-inch Slugg to which he bade his fond farewell. Perhaps he shared to some extent the view expressed by Allan Chapman that Short's instruments were 'replicable commercial artefacts ... with which to view one's estate or enjoy views of the lunar craters'.

Before moving on to Charles's next acquisition though, in November 1866 he reported his sighting of the Leonid meteor shower, possibly still among the greatest ever displays visible in England.

The great meteoric display of November 13. 1866 was observed at Chesham in Buckinghamshire. The sky was quite clear and so continued the whole night. About 9.15 p.m. a splendid meteor rose from the direction of the constellation Leo and slowly mounted to near the zenith where it burst with a shower of sparks, brilliantly lighting up the Heavens. Its path was marked by a beautiful blue track which remained visible for some time.

Meteors were seen at intervals, increasing in frequency, and by 11.30 the spectacle was very grand. By midnight bright meteors were shooting from the neighbourhood of Leo at the rate of 20 in one minute and this continued till nearly 2 a.m. on the 14th.

Many thousands of meteors must have been seen as for two hours they were so numerous as to be quite uncountable. A curious feature was a well marked tendency to flights in groups like a discharge of a number of rockets as shown in the annexed rough sketch. The longest tracks

*were those farthest from the radiant point in
Leo gradually shortening till near the radiant
several flashed up and faded away with scarcely
any visible motion.*

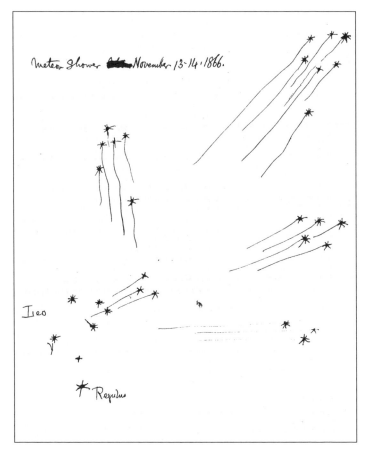

*Charles Grover's sketch of the Leonids meteor
shower 13-14 November 1866, showing the tendency
of the meteors to be seen in groups and the differing
lengths of the trails*

The description above is from Charles's memoir '50
Years an Astronomical Observer'. In a separate

brief report on the meteor shower, presumably made closer to the event and, judging from the more formal style of the piece, intended for publication, Charles describes the anxiety of waiting out a day of cloud and heavy rain that fortuitously cleared by sunset, and confesses that he himself did not see the first enormous meteor: 'Unfortunately I did not see this, but competent persons told me it exceeded in splendor [sic] any that afterwards appeared.' Writing up the meteor shower in retrospect, it is perhaps a forgivable lapse to claim – as well as a night's viewing of the longer spectacle – a sight of that first magnificent and unmatchable display of heavenly pyrotechnics.

Then, early in 1867 'the kindly help of several friends enabled [Charles] to set up a silvered glass reflector'. These friends were George With (1827-1904), who had made his first silver-on-glass mirror in around 1860 and was already receiving recognition for the quality of his work by 1863; the Revd Henry Cooper Key (d. 1880), whose parish was not far from Hereford and who had constructed a mirror-figuring machine based on that of Lord Rosse; and George Knott (1935-1894), an amateur astronomer whose speciality lay with double and variable stars.

George With gave Charles a 6 1/2-inch diameter mirror with a 5 foot 6 inch focus, and there is no doubt that he was extremely fortunate to come by such a fine piece of equipment. Allan Chapman writes that in Britain, With's mirrors 'became status symbols within the amateur world'.

Charles writes that 'with great frankness' With told him 'in one of his letters that he was afraid the gift would prove a "White Elephant" as so much of the success of this kind of telescope depended on the accurate mounting and adjustment of these specula'. However, he received advice from Cooper Key – in 'many kind and instructive letters' – and further assistance from George Knott. He writes that Cooper Key 'was the pioneer worker of silvered glass specula in England ... who had completed and mounted an 18 inch mirror of great excellence'. This may have been the mirror produced on Cooper Key's own mirror-figuring machine and mounted on a 2-ton Berthon stand. (The Berthon stand was designed by a Romsey clergyman, the Revd Edward Lyon Berthon, and was an equatorial, 'both compact and elegant'.) Cooper Key also gave Charles a 'good finder and some money help'.

In spite of potential problems, the telescope was soon completed, and the first observation was made on 11 April. Charles writes:

> *I very quickly mastered the details of adjustment, and found this mirror of great optical perfection. So that I at once took up a survey of some of the northern constellations and wrote a series of articles on the 'Wonders and Beauties of the Starry Heavens' in the Astronomical Register commencing in 1868. Mr With expressed the greatest pleasure at my success, and the Revd. Cooper Key and Mr Knott were kindly correspondents for a long time.*

In the second volume of *Celestial Objects for Common Telescopes*, introducing the section on double stars, clusters and nebulae, Thomas Webb writes:

> *it is to be hoped that some zealous lover of this great display of the glory of the Creator will carry out the author's idea, and study the whole visible heavens from which might be termed a picturesque point of view. This would involve nothing more than a sufficiency of optical power, of leisure, and of patience bringing with it its abundant reward. By a suitably arranged plan, every part of the sky might be swept over in succession, and the principal instance of intensity of colour, or elegance or singularity of grouping having been noted, the materials would be prepared for a most interesting work –*

a Handbook of the Wonders and Beauties of the Starry Heavens.

There is no doubt that at this time Charles Grover shared with Thomas Webb – and many other amateur observers – in tandem with the scientific curiosity that drove their researches, a contemplative view of astronomy, a sincerely religious sense of observation as, at least in part, a way of gaining a deeper understanding of the marvels of God's creation. Like Webb too he is involved with the beauty of what he perceives as well as with the science. His notebook combines accuracy with a fine aesthetic appreciation. 'Beautiful' is probably the most usual adjective, and he is concerned with accurate recording of the colours of stars – double stars in Ursa Major are '*A* orange yellow *B* decided blue perhaps violet type', '17 and 16 Draconis form in the finder a very pretty pair ... *A* pale yellow *B* lilac very prettily contrasted'. He concludes the observation of a lunar eclipse on 4 October 1865 with a comparison with an earlier eclipse, that of June 1863 'when the heavens were very brilliant and the smaller stars visible, this was a very striking celestial appearance. The gradual obscuration of the moon, the increasing darkness, and curious tints of surrounding objects were very striking to the attentive beholder.'

That Charles used for his series of articles – undoubtedly either at Webb's prompting or with his full agreement – the very wording suggested by Webb tends to reinforce the suggestion that Webb thought very highly indeed of this protege. It also demonstrates Charles's own self-confidence in his work and in his associations with men far better educated than he was and of far higher social standing.

Charles introduces the new telescope to his observation book with an acknowledgement of his debt to and affection for the instrument that he bought in 1862.

Thus I have to take leave of the small but excellent instrument with which I have diligently observed during the last 5 years, with what result the previous pages will show. And in thus entering on the use of a much larger and more powerful telescope I can but express the hope that the following pages will prove rich in practical results. The instrument which some kind astronomical friends have kindly furnished me with is one of the newly invented silvered glass reflectors, the principal mirror is 6 1/2 inches clear diameter mounted in a sheet iron tube 6 feet in length, the focus of the mirror being 5 1/2 feet, this is mounted in a very simple but efficient equatorial stand and when tried on the 11th & 12th of April showed splendid definition, with great light grasping power, two most important qualities in a telescope.

Charles uses the new telescope to revisit earlier objects. Of a cluster between Arcturus and Cor Caroli (a binary system whose name means 'Charles's Heart' and which was named in 1725 by Edmund Halley in honour of Charles II) he writes: 'This object has been repeatedly observed with the 2 inch achromatic and 4 inch Gregorian reflector in either of which it appears merely as a undefined shining mist without the least trace of a star.' Now it is 'a beautiful cluster ... a blaze of light at the centre, at the borders myriads of small stars.'

Charles also observes a great many double stars, comparing his observations with a number of sources including Webb's *Celestial Objects*, Smyth's *Cycle of Celestial Objects*, Dawes' catalogue – presumably a collected version of William Rutter Dawes' observations of double and triple stars published in the RAS *Monthly Notices* from 1831 – and something that seems to be called 'Mr Brothers Catalogue of Binary Stars'. (Mr Brothers may have been a regular correspondent to the *Astronomical Register*, so was probably another reliable amateur.) This method of comparison with the best available sources allows Charles to assess his own accuracy and also gives him confidence when his observations do not concur precisely with those of the published references. Of a pair of stars – 'A neat pair about 1/2° south following Cor Caroli' – he notes 'I cannot find it noticed'. Similarly he comments '*o Draconis* a very beautiful and easy object. Smyth ... remarks that this is probably a binary system, but does not appear to have given it any further attention since that epoch [1830, 1837]. It does not appear in Dawes or Brothers Catalogue, but it is undoubtedly a fine binary pair.'

Charles's sketch of the cluster between Arcturus and Cor Caroli observed 28 April 1867 with the new 6 1/2-inch silvered mirror reflector

Another gift presaged a major change in Charles's fortunes. In 1869 he was 'presented with a new plane mirror, Barlow lens & several achromatic eyepieces which considerably improved the performance of the telescope. These were supplied by Mr John Browning [1835-1925] who wrote me many kind letters, and lent me one of his 4 1/2 inch silvered glass reflectors of 5 foot focus, with which I did such good work that in December he offered me a position in his optical establishment at 111 Minories, and I finally left the country and came to London.'

Astronomical Adventures

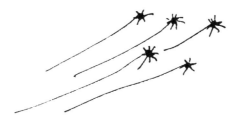

In 1869 Charles Grover was 27 (although presumably still believing himself to be 29), Elizabeth was 29, their son George was five years old. For the past fifteen years or so Charles had been working as a brush-maker by day and an astronomical observer by night. He had spent his whole life in Chesham – in the small area around Church Street and Blucher Street, where he was living in early 1867, and in Towns End Road, where he lived from later in 1867 until the move to London. His wife had lived in the same small area of Buckinghamshire for all her life. although increasingly Charles had travelled to visit various individuals concerned with astronomical matters. Charles's life had become a paradoxical combination of the mundane – the brush-making, which can barely have troubled his mind – with all the worldly and routine connotations of the word, and the transcendent; days in the workshop and nights gazing at the stars. He had developed an obsessive interest, and gained recognition for his skill and the friendship and approbation of some of the leading figures of the age in his chosen field. Small wonder then that he seemed to take the move to London absolutely in his stride. What Elizabeth thought of it is not recorded, but she was remembered as a strong-minded woman, with an independent spirit. She would most probably have been extraordinarily proud of Charles's success, grateful for the unanticipated improvement in her standard of living, but with little ambition on her own account, nor any particular expectations as to the nature of her marital relationship. In the context in which both Charles and Elizabeth were brought up, a 'good' husband was a good provider and a faithful man. Charles may have led a life in many respects independent from that of his wife, but he still fulfilled – well beyond expectations – the primary criteria.

John Browning was a successful instrument maker and a major customer for George With's silvered-glass mirrors. His business started in the 1860s and was thriving by the time that he employed Charles Grover, with a shop – trading as Spencer, Browning and Co. – at 111 Minories (near Tower Hill) that may, at that time, also have constituted the company's works, which were later situated at Vine Street, Southampton Street and William Street. The premises at the Minories were outgrown in the early 1870s and the shop moved to 63 The Strand. The company closed when John Browning retired to Chiselhurst in 1905.

In 1867 Browning had published *A Plea for Reflectors. Being a Description of the New Astronomical Telescopes with Silvered-Glass Specula and Instructions for Adjusting and Using Them* which was in part an advertising effort on behalf of his own company, focusing, as it did, on his own range of reflecting telescopes and how to get the best out of them. The book also included a number of testimonials from individuals expressing their great satisfaction with the instruments that they had purchased. Browning manufactured other instruments beside telescopes and was particularly known for spectroscopes.

In London, Charles 'used to go to business every day and at night did many hours observing' with Browning's 12 ¼-inch silvered-glass reflector set on a massive equatorial stand in the back garden of his house in Clapham which was close to the Grovers' lodgings at 1 Braywick Cottages, Prescott Place. In 1908 Charles recalls that behind the house 'was then all open fields but has long since been closely built over'. His notebook records observations made with Browning's large telescope: a 'fine powerful instrument which was of great excellence' – and he also devoted an article 'Observational Notes 1870' in the *Astronomical Register* volume VIII to work with this telescope – but his records also demonstrate that he still found time to make and record his own observations, usually using the 6 ½-inch reflector that came from With.

Charles writes that 'I found that the silvered glass reflector was just then being developed, several instruments of moderate size but great perfection had been made' and that his duties were:

> *to take and enter all orders for telescopes and astronomical apparatus, to measure the focus of all mirrors on the celestial bodies themselves, either the Sun by day or stars at night, and to set out working drawings for the engineer workman to construct telescopes of all sizes from 3 ½ to 18 inches diameter. I also tested all eyepieces and plane mirrors and other apparatus, and when completed packed and dispatched telescopes to all parts of the world. The silvering of specula was one of my duties in which delicate operation I became quite an expert.*

Charles also experimented with the polishing of glass specula, and recorded his technique in his observations book:

> *During the last three months of 1874 I carefully read over the processes of various experimenters in this matter and also Sir J. Herschel on the telescope, from the details of working there given and from the experiments of With, Purkiss, Calver, Cooper Key and others I carefully thought out a method combining what appeared to me the best features of the artists mentioned.*

The work of Purkiss is hard to trace. Calver (1834-1927), whose history bore resemblances to Charles's own – he was the son of a farm labourer, orphaned young, and apprenticed to a shoemaker before discovering his abilities in the silvering and grinding of mirrors – became a well-known telescope maker, working in Chelmsford, Essex, for most of his life.

The process adopted by Charles utilised a tool of 20-foot radius for the rough grinding of a six-inch glass disc. This produced a spherical figure with which he viewed the full moon of 20 January 1875, with which view he was sufficiently encouraged to continue, but with the radius of the tool reduced to 11 feet in order to shorten the focus of the intended telescope. The experiment was still continuing into March; on the 4th and 5th 'several stars were observed. The star discs were tolerably sharp but there was a considerable amount of false light.' The focus was further tested on a watch dial – this was a technique also used by With, who in turn inherited it from William Lassell: as Chapman notes, 'When he could see all of the details on the dial, in all parts of the reflecting surface, the mirror was ready for its warranty.' Charles concludes the description once he had attained a 'very distinct image ... the polish nearly extended to the margin'.

This was not a part of Charles's work, nor of Browning's business, but an experiment set up on his own behalf, no doubt in order to achieve a better understanding of the process of grinding and polishing, but also so that he would better be able to interpret faults and failings in mirrors that he would be testing or adjusting for others.

As well as reading Sir John Herschel on the telescope, Charles made notes (dated 11 May 1872) on Herschel's *Cape Observations* for 1834-1838, published in 1847. The notes suggest a particular interest in observations and discussions of annular nebulae. He also copies out an extract from a *Life of Faraday* (giving no more detail), describing Faraday's 1814 visit to 'the Academy del Cimento in Florence' where he saw Galileo's first telescope, 'a simple tube of wood and paper about 3 ½ feet long with a lens at each end … There was also the first lens that Galileo made. It was set in a very pretty frame of brass with a Latin inscription upon it. The lens itself is cracked across.'

The testing of telescopes also seems to make its way into the personal observation book as when Charles makes observations of the Sun on six days in June 1873: 12 June 'no spots on the Sun 6½ speculum'; 13 June 'the same 3 in achromatic'; 14 June 'no spots 2½ inch achromatic & 6½ speculum'; 15 June 'Disc quite clear with 12¼ mottling well seen'; 17 June 'Disc continues clear 4¼ achromatic 8½ speculum'; 19 June '3 are on the E limb – one was probably on yesterday 8½'.

Aided by the fact that the fashion for owning a telescope was not matched by the skills of many of the owners, Charles's ability to set up instruments added another interesting dimension to his working life, offering opportunities for meeting enthusiastic amateurs and making friendships (as he seemed very easily to do), as well as further observing opportunities with a variety of instruments. Neither is there any doubt that he relished the chance to enrol others into the astonishing world of astronomy.

Many of the telescopes were supplied to gentlemen in all parts of the United Kingdom and this led to many journeys to fix up and adjust equatorials etc. In the autumn of 1870 an elderly gentleman Mr. Frederick A. Eck, ordered an 8 ½ in silvered-glass reflector, and when it was finished and sent to his country house at Holly Bush near Ayr, he was quite aghast at the size and weight of such a telescope of the construction of which he knew nothing. So he wrote to Mr Browning and I was sent to fix this up. Leaving Euston by the night mail one Sunday in August I was at Carlisle at 4 a.m. on Monday and after a look at 'the auld Bridge of Ayr' and the quaint Market Place arrived at Holly Bush about 2 p.m. The telescope was set up by the evening, and that night for the first time the old gentleman saw some of the wonders of the Heavens. By the next night the telescope was perfectly adjusted, the details of the Lunar Mountains, the companion to α Lyrae, the double star ε Lyrae, the Ring Nebula in Lyra and many other objects were well seen, and I was going to return to London on the Wednesday but Mr Eck said 'nothing of the sort, now you are here I am going to make use of you to learn something of astronomy and I shall write to Mr Browning and keep you here till Saturday'. So I had a good week, by day I went long walks and saw much of beautiful Scotch scenery, for this house was on a hill overlooking the valley and the winding river Doon, on the opposite bank being the Burns mausoleum and many other places of interest, and each night was filled up with two or three hours astronomy. On Saturday I returned to London and Mr Eck wrote a most flattering letter to Mr Browning of my services and ability. When they came to London I was a frequent visitor to their house at 16 Stanhope Gardens W. and afterwards at 100 Cromwell Road. Mr and Mrs Eck continued my friend [sic] till his death 14 years afterwards, and he often said, my frequent letters on astronomical science which I wrote to him at his request almost weekly afforded him the greatest pleasure.

Among others Charles Grover adjusted telescopes for 'Mr G.W. Lea of Worcester and ... Mr W.D. Perrins of Davenham Bank Great Malvern', of Lea and Perrins Worcester sauce fame, both of whom had large equatorial telescopes. His travels do not seem to have taken him further north than Ayr, but they took him as far south as Jersey, to which he made two trips. The first was to set up a telescope in the usual way:

The owner being a gentleman fond of mechanics, we observed together many double stars and other things and he greatly admired the near well defined image of difficult pairs of stars. 'Now,' I said 'You see this is perfect, so be most careful and don't derange any of the adjusting screws'. Very soon letters came to Mr Browning complaining of imperfect vision, badly defined stars and so I had to write him many letters, and he confessed that the next night after I left he was working with the telescope & could not resist the temptation of just turning one screw, he then found matters worse & turned another and found the instrument hopelessly wrong. So I had another journey to put matters right, and I heard of him for some time as a successful observer.

Charles also struck up friendships while in London with N.E. Green, 'a most talented artist, & teacher of watercolour painting to several members of the Royal family', and W. Garrow Lettsom.

Green's studio was at 3 Circus Road, St Johns Wood and it is easy to see how attractive Charles found his combination of astronomical knowledge and artistic ability.

*He was an observer of many years experience
and many of his early drawings of Jupiter and
Mars made with small achromatic telescopes
appeared in the 'Astronomical Register'. He
had silvered glass reflectors of 6 ½, 9 ¼ and
others, finally in 1877 going in for an 18 inch
mirror, which I successfully silvered for him,
and he took it out to Madeira, and there made
the splendid series of Drawings of Mars which
are reproduced in Volume XLIV of the Memoirs
of the Royal Astronomical Society. It is not
often that accurate observational powers and
great artistic talents are combined in the same
individual.*

The significant factor here is that 1877 saw Mars in
opposition, and particularly close to the Earth.
Charles notes of Green's work that 'after watching
this planet at every opposition for nearly fifty
years, they are the most accurate drawings I have
ever seen'.

Lettsom's observatory was at Thurloe Place,
Lower Norwood. In July 1871 Charles went to adjust
a telescope for him – 'a 6 4/10 inch achromatic
telescope by Merz of Munich on an equatorial stand
by Cook of York' – and the several visits that were
required led to a series of invitations and a long
friendship. The visit to Lettsom suggests that
Charles was employed by John Browning in a wider
capacity than perhaps initially planned, working on
the adjustment of telescopes other than those of
Browning's own manufacture. There is little doubt
that Charles must have gained an enormous amount
of information about the telescopes being used by
amateur astronomers at that time. Of Lettsom,
Charles writes:

*He was a man of wide learning, had travelled
much, and as attaché of the British Legation
had lived in Berlin, Munich, Washington, Turin
and Madrid. He was also Charge d'Affairs to
the Legation at Mexico, where he was the object*

of an attempted assassination. He retired from the diplomatic service in 1869. The bullet which was intended to finish his career he often exhibited over the dinner table when recounting his many exciting adventures in foreign lands. He knew most of the eminent scientists of his day and had a fine collection of philosophical apparatus, and an extensive library. We did much observing together, among other things the transit of the shadow of Titan over Saturn's disc was well seen on December 9, 1877, and the transit of Mercury over the Sun's disc May 6, 1878.

Here in his memoir Charles departs briefly from a strict chronology and adds that the next time he viewed a transit of Mercury was with the very same telescope, but in the observatory at Rousdon, Devon, on 10 November 1894. 'This took place in the afternoon, and the planet was well seen for 25 minutes before sunset as a very black, circular, well-defined spot.' Charles seems to have written a report of this transit in the *English Mechanic* for 23 November 1894. The most striking feature of the Mercurian transit 'is the very small size of the planet in proportion to the Sun's diameter. It appears <u>so very small</u> that it is no wonder that beyond the exhibition of phases similar to Venus absolutely nothing is known as to the physical condition or time of rotation of this planet.'

One further interesting astronomical phenomenon discovered through his employment in setting up and adjusting telescopes and noted by Charles during his time in London was that it is possible to see numerous stars in daylight.

In the course of a long experience of adjusting equatorials I observed many stars by daylight, and it is surprising how many of the stars can be seen by day if only a moderate power is used and <u>most important</u> of all the eyepiece is <u>exactly in focus</u>. This should be insured by an *observation at night and then marking a well defined circle on the eye tube. With several silvered glass equatorials of 8 ½ inches aperture I have seen stars of 11th and 12th magnitude immediately after sunset, when the figures in the Nautical Almanac could be read and the circles set without difficulty by daylight.*

Charles's own observations from this period tend to expand upon observations made earlier, to reinforce them, occasionally to enlarge upon aspects less well understood previously or more clearly observed with better instruments. As with his reading, or with experiments in grinding mirrors, his primary ambition seems always to build up a truly worthwhile and competent body of knowledge and understanding of his subject. He is always scrupulous in detailing the particular instrument used. For example, the 6 4/10-inch Merz telescope that he adjusted for Lettsom is noted as that with which he observed Uranus in 1878 and Neptune in 1881, although he also made observations of Uranus with a 3 5/8-inch achromatic instrument. The transit of the shadow of Titan across Saturn on 9 September 1877 is recorded in some detail. A conjunction of Mars and Saturn in the same year, on 3 November, was observed using a '6 3/10 achromatic telescope by Goddard', which compares unfavourably with Lettsom's instrument: 'The object glass is not bad, but yet is not to be compared with the 6 4/10 Merz.' He was even more critical of an instrument by Horne and Thornthwaite (instrument makers to the Admiralty and based at 416 The Strand from 1876-1913; they were probably Browning's closest rivals, producing a very similar range of instruments to his own), which he went to see at the home of a C. Ryves, Claremont House, Bedford Hill, Balham. This was a 6-inch equatorially mounted silvered glass reflector with which Charles observed, among others, Venus and ∈ Bootis, Arcturus and α Lyrae –

'with the full aperture the performance with power about 150 was very bad on all these objects and so much loose light appeared around them that є Bootis and є Lyrae were hardly to be clearly separated – on Venus, Arcturus and α Lyra this loose light and want of definition was very painful ... on the whole the optical quality of this telescope is very inferior. Mr Ryves told me he had 3 different mirrors from the makers of this telescope but there was very little difference in their performance.'

Saturn and its satellites are a constant source of interest and fascination to Charles. His observations of them are barely broken and there are numerous sketches made of the rings as they change in aspect and of the satellites in different formations around the planet. He seems particularly interested in how much it is possible to see using a small telescope – perhaps for the series of 'Wonders and Beauties of the Starry Heavens' or perhaps as potential contributions to Webb's *Celestial Objects for the Common Telescope* – and many observations of Saturn and its moons are made with the 3 5/8-inch achromatic mentioned above. Many observations of Mars with the same instrument are also recorded and he continues to study and add to his observations of the Sun and the other planets, and of the constellations and double stars.

At least five articles in the series on 'The Wonders and Beauties of the Starry Heavens' were printed in the *Astronomical Register* between 1868 and 1872, and further articles may have been planned: the notes for an essay on the Pleiades exist in the observation book. In the draft article, Charles describes himself as 'assistant to J. Browning Esq. FRAS' – his official title in reports and articles after 1870 – and once again refers back to his 1861 observation with the home-made telescope, then to the drawing of 1866, made using the 4-inch Gregorian reflector, and compares these to observations of 1867-68 made with the 6 ½-inch silvered-glass speculum. He includes another drawing, apparently made initially from observations with the 6 ½-inch, but expanded following observations in October 1871 made using Browning's 12 ½-inch instrument.

The second article in the series, on 'The Constellation Cassiopeia', is followed by a brief editorial comment: '[Our readers will, we are sure, be much indebted to Mr. Grover for his careful observations of this constellation; but at the same time, the number of contractions in his MS. render it difficult to avoid errors in printing.-Editor.]' Subsequent articles do seem to have taken this criticism on board and are less packed with abbreviations and detail.

Charles also continued the interest in nebulae demonstrated in the extract copied from Herschel's *Cape Observations*, where he is obviously aware of recent developments in the field. These included William Huggins's 1864 observations of nebulae through a spectrograph and his discovery that while some nebulae have stellar spectra, others have spectra that could only be the result of gaseous composition. In 1870, 23 September, using an 8 ½-inch equatorial silvered-glass reflector belonging to a Mr Brindley, Charles noted that the 'Great Nebula in Andromeda' 'looks like what it is *supposed* to be, viz a mass of luminous gas', while the annular nebulae in Lyra 'shows clear signs of resolution notwithstanding its *suspected* gaseous composition' (emphases added). The annular nebula in Lyra formed the subject of the final article in 'The Wonders and Beauties of the Starry Heavens' in 1872.

A note in Charles's observation book shows that – probably at some time in his early years in London – he read Henry E. Roscoe's 1862 translation of Gustav Kirchoff's work on spectroscopy, *Researches on the Solar Spectrum and the Spectra of the Chemical Elements*, first published in 1861. This was plainly, at the time, a matter both of great interest and contentiousness.

Charles's notes on the book suggest that he is much taken with the ideas of spectroscopy, and with the way in which the technique was evolved: 'the exact and laborious labours of two German philosophers who quietly working in their laboratory [in] Heidelberg first made the wonderful discovery. This shows the value of quiet and painstaking study. It is not by hurried experiments or hasty conclusions that science is enhanced, but by the patient and slow processes mentioned.' Also a key part of Browning's business was the manufacture of spectrometers. But a conversation that took place on 20 March 1872 demonstrated that there was continuing opposition to the new theories, and that these were certainly not restricted to amateurs or people of little influence in scientific circles. Charles's conversation was with a Mr Vincent of the Royal Institution and his opinion – as reported – was that:

> *the inferences drawn from spectroscope observation would be received with great caution for instance Hydrogen gas gives 4 distinctly different spectra under different conditions or temperature and pressure and he believed that in many instances the spectrum of Hydrogen had been mistaken for that of Nitrogen and vice versa – he thought that very little was known regarding the constitution of the Sun and that eventually the theories now accepted would be found to be erroneous.*

While I think it is plain that Charles himself was convinced by the theory of spectrographic analysis as applied to celestial bodies, as far as the theory applied to nebulae, on 21 July 1872 Charles is still tending towards the idea, long-held by many astronomers, that all nebulae could be resolved into stars given high enough viewing power. Observing with the 6 ½-inch speculum, and almost as an aside to the primary focus of his attention at that date, which is double stars, he notes, again of the nebula in Lyra, 'about the minor axis the ring shows streaks of brighter light as if partly resolved. I cannot but believe this object to consist of stars.' However, only a month later, on 29 August, using Browning's 12 ½-inch instrument, he amends his opinion: 'the brilliancy of the ring which with moderate powers leads to the supposition that it is resolved disappears when higher powers are applied and with the highest power used on this occasion the light of the ring seemed more milky and irresolveable than ever although the minute stars near were sharply defined ... I closed this observation, the most favourable of this object I ever enjoyed with my faith in the resolveability much shaken, indeed the favourable view would lead me to be more inclined to believe the observations of Dr Huggins with the spectroscope showing the neb[ula] to be but gaseous.'

Charles was by nature an observer, a watcher of the skies rather than a mathematician, but he disciplined himself early on in the collection or analysis of data, and he records one use of a 'spectroscope', in the observation of sun spots on 26 January 1873. Here he was following in the footsteps of Joseph Norman Lockyer (1836-1920) whose main focus of interest was the Sun and who had for some time been trying to work out a way of obtaining spectra of solar prominences without having to wait for an eclipse. This was achieved in 1868 with a modification of the slit of the spectroscope – more or less simultaneously by Lockyer and a French solar physicist, Jules Janssen. Charles however did not see any prominences, but examined sun spots, having already observed through Browning's 12 ½-inch equatorial that there 'was a large spot near the centre of the disc ... as well as several smaller.'

The eyepiece was then removed and the spectroscope (a small miniature) was applied and the slit adjusted at a tangent to the solar limb ... the Sun's image was carefully focused

*on the end of the spectroscope and then
advanced across the slit ... the limb was
splendidly defined in the spectroscope and
several bright lines were seen in the chromo-
sphere near the limb ... the large spot was then
brought to bear near the centre of the slit by
observing the sun's image on the end of the
spectroscope and then with the eye at the
spectroscope, the spot was brought by the
tangent screw exactly on the slit, and being a
double spot, there were two broad dark bands
the whole length of the spectrum, bordered by a
lighter fringe corresponding to the penumbra
of the spots. Most of the lines were cut out by
this band, only the principal could be traced
across it.*

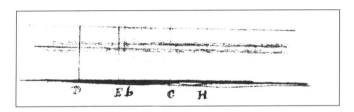

As with the experiment with grinding specula, this
reflects Charles's practical sensibility, an extension
of understanding beyond the mere reading of
somebody else's experiences into a comprehension
of the practicalities and problems involved.

Charles's imagination had first been fired by the
sight of Donati's comet in 1858. Now, during his
time in London, he was able – with the help of
better instruments – to observe several more
comets. 1874 saw the appearance of Coggia's comet,
discovered by 'M. Coggia of the Marseilles
observatory on the 17th April 1874'.

Charles followed the comet on the path
predicted by John Russell Hind (1823-1895) – the
son of a lace-maker who had worked his way
through astronomical circles from a humble clerical
position at Greenwich as a 16 year old to
superintendent of the essential *Nautical Almanac* –

observing it from 27 June until 15 July, when it fell
below the horizon, and sketching its progress
across the sky.

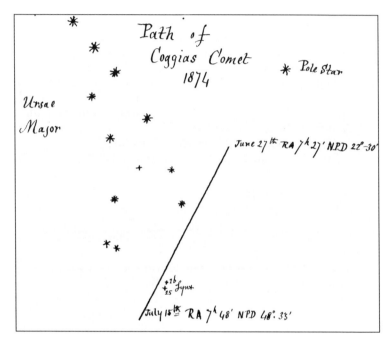

Path of Coggia's Comet, 1874

At its brightest Charles estimated Coggia's comet to
be a 3rd magnitude object, at the longest he
measured the tail at 'fully 15°'. In contrast,
Borrelly's comet, observed between August 15th and
22nd in the same year, was a 'faint, diffuse object
slightly condensed towards the centre, but without
any trace of nucleus of tail'. At his last sighting on
22 August 'the comet is really getting fainter'; after
a week's delay 'caused by moonlight and bad
weather' it is no longer visible using the 6 ½-inch
speculum.

Perhaps even harder to discern was Palisa's
comet, observed on 14 September 1879: 'It is a

degree or two preceding, a little north of the well known double star Cor Caroli. This comet is merely a very faint diffuse nebula with very little central condensation and no sign of a tail. It is not far from the small and bright nebula 94M – and anyone not familiar with this object might easily mistake it for the comet.' (Charles's 94M is Messier 94, a spiral galaxy in *Canis Ventici.*)

In 1881, Tebbutt's Comet returned. The 'Great Comet' as it was known, having been visible for some time in the southern hemisphere became visible in the north on 22 June although 'its elevation above the northern horizon was however so little on that night and the twilight so strong that only very few persons seem to have seen it'. Charles however was among those who saw the comet on the following night – when 'it was very generally observed' – and he tracked its path until 28 August.

Charles was fascinated by the way in which the appearance of the head of the comet changed and patterns of light and dark altered. He noted too the apparent thinness of the cometary material, the way in which as the tail moved across stars it barely dimmed their magnitude. At its brightest, on 28 June, 'the comet is so bright as to become visible to the naked eye before any star in this part of the heavens'. Still a naked eye object on 5 August, by 28 August it was 'a mere diffuse nebula, without tail or nucleus in the 6 4/10 achromatic'.

On 24 June, the Great Comet was photographed by two innovative astronomers, Andrew Common (1841-1903) and Henry Draper (1837-1882). While reasonable photographic images of the moon and objects within the solar system had been taken since the middle of the century, more distant objects still presented a challenge, and this represented a landmark. As the reach of photography expanded into the more distant areas of space it was also allied to spectroscopy. The accurate sketching of phenomena that had once been so important to the recognition and comparison of objects had been entirely superseded; and mathematicians could now begin to establish a new model of an expanding universe using photographic spectra. Charles's own beautiful drawings and paintings of his observations diminish to quick sketches that plainly function as personal aides-memoires, no doubt in deference to the fact that such a method of recording planetary and other astronomical phenomena has been rendered obsolete.

Charles came into contact with Common through the Revd Edmund Ledger, Gresham Professor of Astronomy from 1875 until 1908, who was in the process of purchasing a 5 ½-inch achromatic telescope on an equatorial mount from Common and asked Charles (whom he had met as a magic lantern operator for his illustrated lectures) if he would inspect and report on the instrument for him. Such a request testifies to Charles's growing reputation and expertise in the evaluation of instruments. He writes that:

> *This was many years before Mr Common became famous as the constructor of the 3 foot and the 5 foot silvered glass reflecting telescopes. The 5 foot speculum is still [1908] I believe the largest silvered glass reflector in the world ... this 5 ½ in equatorial was acquired by Dr Common in 1874 and with it he made his first attempts at astronomical photography, but it was soon superseded by silvered glass reflectors. But though he brought these to such size and perfection he unhesitatingly recognised the advantages of the refractor for this work, particularly as applied to the astrographic chart of the heavens.*

The 1881 appearance of Tebbutt's comet is also a useful juncture to consider changes in Charles's personal circumstances. One of the sketches accompanying the observations shows the position of the comet in relation to the star, capella, and the spire of St Barnabas church as viewed from 188 Wellington Buildings, between Ebury Bridge Road and Chelsea Bridge Road, in Pimlico, to which Charles, Elizabeth and George must have moved no more than a year or so before, since the block of flats was only completed in 1879.

It was a period of major expansion in London as the impact of the industrial revolution continued to be felt and the working-class population of the city rose. Villas were springing up in the suburbs to accommodate the growing middle classes, and Victorian philanthropy was concerned with the plight of the working classes, many of whom were forced by scarcity of property to live in poor quality housing, more often than not with shared and inadequate sanitary facilities. However, underlying many of the housing schemes that were established in the latter part of the nineteenth century was the idea that, by clever building and design and judicious setting of rents, housing for the poorer classes could still achieve a profit for the entrepreneurs who made the initial investments, albeit not a large profit, perhaps a return of 5 per cent or thereabouts. Effectively, this meant that those who benefited from such housing schemes tended to be the artisan classes. In the spirit of laissez-faire, it was hoped by some that this would decrease the density at which the poorest were forced to live and as a consequence lead to a slight improvement in their conditions as well.

Wellington Buildings was a part of what is now referred to as the Chelsea Gardens Estate. This is the name of the buildings to the front of the site, with Wellington Buildings behind. The blocks were built by an organisation called the Improved Industrial Dwellings Company, the brainchild of Sydney Waterlow (1822-1906), later a baronet, Lord Mayor of London and a noted philanthropist, who, together with three brothers, turned his father's stationery business into a successful printing venture which bears his name to this day.

Entrance to 177-188 Wellington Buildings. Access to all apartments was off a central open stairway with balconies onto the street to allow for fresh air and additional light within the building (photo 2001, Jerry Grover)

Waterlow's first building was constructed in 1863, entirely with his own money, in order to demonstrate that such a project could be commercially viable, and the company itself was established the same year. Wellington Buildings were built towards the middle of the company's life – it folded in 1892, when land was no longer available in areas where there was the greatest need for housing for poorer members of society, and when flats could not be rented in areas that were already saturated with such developments.

It seems most likely that the Grovers had a flat consisting of two bedrooms, a living room, a scullery or kitchen and a W.C. They may have had only one bedroom, or the arrangement may have allowed for two bedrooms and a larger kitchen cum living room. While we know little of their Clapham accommodation, and less of their living arrangements at Shiplake Cottages, Richmond, which was the address given in correspondence to the *Astronomical Register* for 1872 and the address on their son George's baptismal certificate (he was baptised at a late age for a period of high infant mortality; and in accordance with the Nonconformist principle that baptism should take place only once the subject is old enough to have some appreciation of the meaning of the ceremony), it seems highly likely that this move represented a fairly considerable improvement in their circumstances. And this in spite of the fact that Wellington Buildings are offered as a prime example of the 'effect of the increasing pressures upon the Company [in 1879].

The blocks were so closely spaced that it was necessary to use a white glazed brick for the lower floors in order to obtain even a reasonable degree of natural lighting.' In 1871, before the Grovers were at Shiplake Cottages, other tenants included two gardeners, each of whom was married to a laundress. Part of the attraction of Wellington Buildings may also have been that the six-storey buildings allowed roof access and a comparatively unobscured view of the night sky over an ever-brightening city.

Although the initial intention of the company was to provide affordable housing for those on lower wages, among the residents in the early 1880s were a solicitor, a civil engineer, an accountant, an architect, an analytical chemist and two theological students. Also in residence at that time was Rutland Barrington, a baritone soloist with the D'Oyly Carte Opera Company who played leading roles in many of the Gilbert and Sullivan operettas and was featured in Mike Leigh's 1999 film *Topsy-Turvy*. Barrington and his wife lived at 97 and 98 Wellington Buildings, which seemed to give them space enough to take a lodger. Charles may have been in residence there at the same time as Jerome K. Jerome, who wrote *Three Men in a Boat* (published in 1889) while living at number 104. From 1882 to 1894, Kenneth Grahame, who wrote *Wind in the Willows*, lived at number 65 (in the Chelsea Gardens block). The 1891 census indicates that he occupied four rooms, which would match the expected size of Charles's apartment and be comparatively spacious for a single man.

In February of 1881, Charles and Elizabeth had a second child – Charles Henry – born on Valentine's day. Elizabeth and Charles must have been stunned by the arrival of this second baby, when Elizabeth was already in her forties and their son George was 17 and already embarking on a career as a student teacher. The 1881 census, which is the only reason that anything is known about the infant, has the ages of both parents as 41 (Charles was actually 39 at the time the census is taken) and Charles's occupation as 'Opticians Assistant'. The baby died on 13 July 1881 aged just five months. On the night of the 13th, Charles was observing the Great Comet: 'The comet made a near approach to a bright star and at 11 p.m. the nucleus and star appeared as a double star in a good binocular glass...'

Does this demonstrate any particular callousness in Charles, or emphasise again how much he was a man of his time? It is quite impossible to second-guess the emotional states of individuals in different societies and at different times. In Victorian England men often had little connection with the lives of their children. Charles's busy life – with work and his own observation – plainly left little room for a wife either. The census indicates that two months after the baby's birth Elizabeth still had a nurse – a Mary Barnes from Chalfont, so possibly an old family connection – living with the family in Wellington Buildings. There is no doubt that the baby's birth would have been managed by its mother and the nurse; so too perhaps was its death.

The place of death is given on the death certificate as Belgrave, Middlesex, so the child may have been sick and in hospital. Quite near to Wellington Buildings, at 79 Gloucester Street, was the Belgrave Hospital for Children, formerly the Clapham Maternity Hospital, which was founded in 1866.

From 1870 to 1880 Charles was a regular attendee, with John Browning, at the monthly meetings of the Royal Astronomical Society, held in a small room in Kings College in the Strand – 'long before the present [1908] palatial home of the Society at Burlington House was even thought of'. They took with them 'micrometers, spectroscopes, astronometers and all kinds of astronomical apparatus for exhibition and description'. In 1870 the president of the Society was William Lassell (1799-1880), and over the years Charles saw there Warren De La Rue (1815-1889), G.B. Airey (1801-1892), J.C. Adams (1819-1892; president from 1874-1876), Charles Pritchard (1808-1893) and Richard Proctor (1837-1888), and numerous other well-known and highly-regarded astronomers of the day. It was a wonderful opportunity – of which Charles made full use – to listen to the papers and communications read at the meetings.

Occasionally, dull meetings would be enlivened 'by the wit of the late Captain Noble [1828-1904] who had a neat way of asking amusing questions'.

One night Prof. Pritchard had given a lengthy account of his wedge photometer as used at the University Observatory, Oxford. When after several comments from various gentlemen had nearly exhausted his patience, Captain Noble rose and with a childlike smile asked the Professor, 'Why do you slide the wedge in front of the scale?' Pritchard looked at him with angry scorn and thundered out, 'To extinguish the star, Sir.' And his looks plainly said 'as I should like to extinguish you'.

Captain William Henry Noble was to be the founding president in 1890 of the British Astronomical Association, which had as its remit, as Allan Chapman observes, that 'it was to be relatively cheap in terms of its subscription, open to both men and women, and catering for people who found the R.A.S. both too expensive and too technical'. Allan Chapman describes Noble as of 'legendary eccentricity'.

Charles also illustrated a number of papers read to the society by R.D. Proctor on the 'Projection of the Sphere', using the 'oxyhydrogen lantern'. (Lantern work figured quite highly in Charles's life in London, as the next chapter will show.) At that time, Proctor was publishing star maps and was also much concerned with the positioning of stations for the best observations of the transit of Venus in 1874 'on which subject he had great disputes with the Astronomer Royal'.

The transit of Venus brought much business in the way of telescopes, special eyepieces, dark wedges, etc, and many elaborate expeditions went to distant parts of the world for the observations. Some were defeated by clouds, and those who were most favoured by the weather were confronted with the unexpected difficulty of deciding what is real contact in the case of a black disc like Venus projected in front of a brilliant Sun, and the results differed so much among themselves that the transit cannot be held to have but slightly advanced our knowledge of the actual distance of the Sun from our earth. This led to almost endless discussions as the astronomical papers of that time show, and the matter was gradually shelved to wait for the next transit in 1882.

Lectures and Lanterns

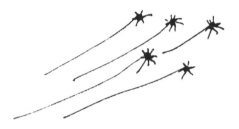

Public lectures illustrated with magic lantern slides were extremely popular in the late nineteenth century, drawing large audiences to numerous venues to hear talks on science or arts, for education and for entertainment, sometimes accompanied with spectacular sound and visual effects. They could provide an opportunity to hear some of the most distinguished people in the land tell stories of exploration and discovery, or they could be seen as an evening's entertainment, almost the forerunner of a night at the cinema.

Presumably as part of his work for Browning – the company manufactured magic lanterns as well as optical and astronomical instruments – during his time in London Charles Grover became a lantern operator and he assisted at many talks and demonstrations (apart from illustrating papers at the RAS) through which he came to meet a great many people. Although he doesn't mention it, it is likely that both Elizabeth and George would also have attended at least some of these evenings which were often family events.

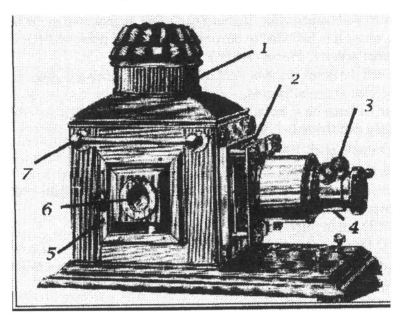

The main parts of a magic lantern: 1. Chimney – tall chimneys were used for oil-burning illuminants; 2. Slot for slides; 3. Focus knob; 4. Focus lenses; 5. Door – where adjustments to the illuminants were made; 6. Inspection window – often fitted with tinted glass to avoid glare; 7. Carrying rail.
(www.magiclantern14.btinternet.co.uk/diagram.html)

This part of Charles's story is best told in his own words.

> *During my 13 years in London I did a great deal of Lantern work, illustrating lectures for many well known scientific men. There was the late Dr. Carpenter who lectured on the bed of the Atlantic and other ocean depths. R.A. Proctor, astronomy and the star depths, Dr. Mann*

[presumably the author of a simple introductory volume, Guide to the Knowledge of the Starry Heavens, *published in 1856], Mr. E.B. Knobel [whose paper, according to* The History of the Royal Astronomical Society, 1820-1920, *in the* RAS Monthly Notices *of June 1880 commenting on a critical examination of Smyth's 'Double Star Measures of the Bedford Catalogue' by S.W. Burnham 'completely succeeded in vindicating Smyth's character'] and many others.*

I went to the Crystal Palace, Dulwich College, Shoreditch Town Hall, The Society of Arts, The Institute of British Architects and numberless others, and heard lectures on nearly every conceivable subject. There was much Sunday work in connection with the Sunday evenings for the people, when vast audiences were attracted to hear a lecture by some eminent scientist followed by a splendid musical performance. I went to the Dome at Brighton where a course of Gilchrist lectures were arranged, the first of which was by Dr. Carpenter. So it had to be given a good start, and I did a good show. The Mayor and Corporation attended and it was a brilliant affair. On another occasion I was illustrating a lecture on Spectrum Analysis by a young scientist, who struck a dramatic attitude and with uplifted hand commenced 'Light, Light, more Light'. There was a pause in which the audience audibly tittered. After struggling on some time and showing slides of spectroscopes & spectra he came to show the actual spectra of a few familiar substances and explained that spectrum analysis was so delicate that the 1/1000th part of a grain of sodium should be detected, and a friend of his who was assisting ? [sic] put on the electric light a very minute particle of sodium, which hardly showed a trace. I suddenly clapped in a _liberal_ supply of sodium – there was a cloud of smoke – a burst of flame, and a splendid display of spectral colours on the sheet, which were greeted by the audience with loud applause. When the lecture was over, he said 'that was a fine experiment'. I said 'Yes, these minute and exact things do very well in the laboratory but in the lecture hall you need something brilliant and striking.'

There were some very interesting lectures at the Society [of] Arts in Adam Street. One I remember by Dr. Perken on 'Aniline Dyes', when the lecture table was set out with a row of gas rings on which were placed a number of copper vessels and heated to a proper degree the process of dyeing was demonstrated before the audience. Another was on watches and watch making, when by means of an aphengescope [sic] on the electric lantern the various types of watchwork were shown <u>in motion</u> on the screen. The watch plates magnified to about 4 feet diameter. This was a very interesting exhibition.

About 1873 there was much discussion in the papers as to the work of Gresham College. The lectures delivered mostly in Latin failed to attract attention and frequently lapsed for want of an audience. The rules specified that if less than 3 presented themselves there was to be no lecture, but frequently 3 or 4 persons would arrange to be present to enjoy the fun of <u>making</u> the professor read his lecture. There were lectures supposed to be delivered on music, rhetoric, divinity, geometry and astronomy, and a salary was attached to each professor but little had been heard of them for many years. As the result of considerable agitation the establishment was reformed and new professors appointed, but it is only of the astronomy that I was concerned. The Revd. E. Ledger, M.D. was the new lecturer and I went regularly for some time to illustrate his Lectures with the lime light, they were made very interesting and the lecture theatre was often quite full, instead of the former array of empty seats.

There were a number of illuminants used in magic

lantern presentations: clearly, from what he says above, Charles frequently used electric lanterns, although in this instance lime would have been brought to a high temperature using combustible gas, probably hydrogen (although coal gas and ether were also used), together with oxygen. Once ignited the lime would give a brilliant light – so much so that it was also employed by the military for signalling across distances. This is the kind of projector that Charles also refers to as an 'oxy-hydrogen' lantern.

A brief article from the *English Mechanic* of 18 December 1908, written at the time that Edmund Ledger resigned the Gresham Professorship of Astronomy, reinforces Charles's doubtful view of the proceedings in the 1870s. A Mr Hollis writes that 'It is a well-known fact, which may be stated without any disrespect to the lecturers, that thirty or forty years ago the performance of Sir Thomas Gresham's will was in many cases a farce. Lectures were read, but there was no audience.' The article's main concern is the lectures in music, which obviously underwent a revival with the appointment of Sir Frederic Bridge.

It was in assisting at these lectures that Charles first met the Revd Ledger and, in consequence, came into contact with Andrew Common, the pioneer of astrophotography.

Some of the most complex and spectacular magic lantern shows were held at the Regent Polytechnic – the Royal Polytechnic Institution in Regent Street, founded in 1838. The screens here were huge – about 25 feet across – and the shows were accompanied by sound effects and music and utilised up to four or five large-scale lanterns to attain the desired effects. Charles writes that:

About 1874 to 1878 I was frequently at the Old Polytechnic in Regent Street, at that time a very popular place of amusement and instruction. There was the Diving Bell in which parties of about a dozen young people enjoyed

the novel sensation of being lowered to the
bottom of an 18 feet deep tank of water. The
great induction coil giving a four foot spark,
models of coal mines, Glass Blowing, and
machinery in motion. The lecture theatre was
fitted up with the finest and most powerful
lantern apparatus of the day. Some of the
condensing lenses were 9 inches in diameter
and the pictures were most beautiful hand
paintings on a 7 inch circle, and with a
combination of four lanterns most beautiful
effects were produced.

The lectures were mostly very clever, those on
science by Mr J.L. King especially so. But the
great attraction for several years was the late
Professor Pepper. He was the inventor of
'Pepper's Ghost' and many other strange effects
which always brought a crowded house and a
golden harvest whenever he was on the bill.
While as conjuror and sleight of hand
performer he was quite unequalled, and his
patter as a lecturer was wonderful.

Unfortunately differences arose between him
and the directors and the Professor resigned
with the result that the fortunes of the place at
once fell, money difficulties came on and there
was serious talk of the institution being closed.
I think it was December 1878 after a long spell
of empty houses the Professor took the
institution on his own account and agreed to
run the show for 6 weeks extending over
Christmas and the new Year, with the result
that the place was again crowded and hundreds
had to be turned away nearly every day.

Needless to say Professor Pepper's great
success aroused correspondingly intense
feelings of jealousy in his less fortunate
imitators. I was there one night of a most
crowded and enthusiastic audience, and the
Professor's tricks went off with remarkable
success, amidst loud cheers and applause, when
the sound of a few hisses were heard from the

back of the theatre. The old gentleman was equal to the occasion. Pausing in his performance he advanced to the front of the stage & said.

'Ladies & Gentlemen, I am very pleased at the hearty reception you have accorded me tonight, and your hearty applause is conclusive proof that my efforts to amuse you are appreciated. There are however a few discordant sounds coming from the back of this theatre the authors of which are perfectly well known to me. This exhibition is prompted by mean jealousy, and if I hear it repeated I shall name the authors and have them ejected, or if it will please them better they are welcome to come on to this stage and take my place tonight, and you Ladies and Gentlemen shall be the judges of the performance. We will now proceed.'

Needless to say there was no more interruption that night and the Professor's 6 week season was a great success.

After this final short season at the Regent Polytechnic, Professor Pepper took his show to America and Australia, where, in December 1882, Charles, travelling as part of the transit of Venus expedition, met up with him again at the Society of Arts in Brisbane: 'and very pleased he was to see me again and to talk over old times together'. Since Charles was plainly well known to Professor Pepper it is probably fair to assume that he was a participant in many of the shows featuring Pepper's Ghost and not just another member of the crowd. The Brisbane Courier of 9 December 1882 carried a report of what seems to be an inaugural lecture by Professor Pepper at the State School, South Brisbane, marking the fact that 'the School of Arts had secured the valuable services of Mr. Pepper as a lecturer on chemistry'. Another odd phenomenon that Charles came across during this period were so-called 'magic mirrors'.

In 1879 I had a lot to do with what were called the Magical Mirrors of Japan. These were metal mirrors of some alloy of silver, a plain mirror on one side, and on the reverse highly decorated with figures of flowers, birds, landscapes etc and some boldly polished Japanese characters. When a beam of parallel rays was thrown on the plain side of the mirror, the raised characters on the back were distinctly reflected on a white screen.

The late Professor Ayrton on his return from the Imperial College of Engineering at Tokio brought to London two cases of these mirrors. They had not been very carefully packed and were much tarnished by the sea voyage, and he consulted Mr. Browning as to whether he had anyone who could undertake the restoration of these mirrors and they were handed over to me. There were about 300 of them ranging from 3 inches to about a foot in diameter. When they were cleaned and polished the greater number showed no trace of this magical effect whatsoever and not more than 60 or 70 showed it at all well, while about a dozen were very perfect. Many experiments were tried with the *oxyhydrogen and electric lanterns, and lenses giving a parallel beam of light, but the best effect of all was obtained in a room with an open window facing the Sun. When the direct sunlight fell on the plane [sic] face of the mirror, the pattern and ornaments on the back were clearly projected on the white ceiling [see illustration].*

When these notes were written, in 1908, there were two of these mirrors in the Rousdon museum. Each was 9 inches in diameter; one showing no trace of the magical effect, the other working perfectly.

The following is a report of magical mirrors by 'orientalist' Paschal Beverly Randolph (1825–1875), 'Physician, Philosopher, world traveller, Supreme Grand Master of the Fraternitas Rose Crucis; Hierarch of Eulis and the Ansaireh, member of L'Ordre du Lis of France; the Double Eagle of Prussia, and Order of the Rose of England'.

In January, 1874, I received a few [Japanese magic mirrors] from Paris, and hung them on my chamber-wall to charge and fit them for their owner – a lady – and there they remained till the morning of February 8, when they became suddenly illuminant, and no grander sight ever was beheld by human eyes than was presented on that memorable morning; for the whole starry galaxies, rolling world-systems of nebulae, vast congeries of stellar constellations, cities afar off on the earth, and scenes never before beheld by eyes of this world, were displayed to such a grand, sublime, and amazing extent that the Soul panted with the weight of the transcendent Phantorama. Such mirrors as these – would they were mine! – if kept free from promiscuous handling, treated judiciously, and rightly used, are capable of more psychic marvels than all the mesmerists on the globe! Very few of any grade are imported,* *save when expressly ordered; the risk of breakage in crossing the seas and by inland carriage being too great to admit of larger consignments, even were it possible to have such, which it is not.*

* They are, every one of them, from the plain surface mirror, to the magnificent, golden-edged, Beauties, or the enormous 40-inch ones, fit for a Lodge, worth a king's ransom, capable of mirroring correctly, and before hand too, the Markets of the world. Here is a strange test, whose truth I solemnly avouch: A pregnant lady – and such are ever the most favored [sic] in all lines of celestial magic – on the morning alluded to above (February 8, 1874) gazed into one of the mirrors, and demanded to know the sex of her unborn child. The reply came instantly: 'A boy! And a great one! A vast Soul! The king-seer of Five Thousand years!' The result, so far as sex was concerned, was absolutely true; and there is but little doubt that the rest will prove equally so. This same lady was the only true mystic of her sex I ever saw in America. She was the best mirror-manipulator on the earth, and owned – still owns – all the genuine ones on the continent. Through her I have obtained specimens of such rare value, that to part therewith was like the loss of the right eye.

Professor Ayrton, the importer of the mirrors sent to Browning for restoration, was born in 1847 and died in 1908. A physicist and 'electrician', according to his obituary in the *English Mechanic* (18 November 1908), he studied electrical engineering under Lord Kelvin and worked on telegraph systems in Bengal and in England before taking up his post in Tokyo. After his return to England in 1879 he was Professor of Applied Physics at the Finsbury College of the City and Guilds of London Technical Institute, and then

Professor of Electrical Engineering at Central College. Charles's criticism of the packaging of the mirrors would have been soundly based in his own experience of packaging instruments for transit; it is echoed by the idiosyncratic Randolph; it may also have served as a reminder when he came to preparations for his own long sea voyage in charge of delicate instrumentation.

Shipboard Life

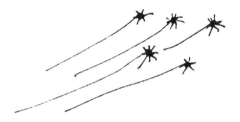

The 1874 transit of Venus proved a source of contention within the RAS: Mr Proctor (in 1873 Secretary of the RAS) having clashed on a number of occasions with Sir George Airy, then Astronomer Royal, over which of the two theories for observing a transit – Edmund Halley's or that of Delisle (see postscript) – would be most appropriate for the coming event, and over which locations in the still comparatively little-known southern hemisphere would best serve the planned teams of observers in their work. More amenable had been the decision to erect the monument to the memory and achievement of Jeremiah Horrocks; and more profitable – as Charles noted – had been the impact of the occasion on the astronomical instrument business.

Charles Grover could only have anticipated more of the same as the date for the next transit – December 1882 – approached: 'I little thought when busy with these matters in 1874 that I should be making a long voyage to observe the transit of 1882, but so it fell out.'

Among the many friends that Charles had made while working for John Browning was John Coles, 'at that time Keeper of the Map Room, and instructor in astronomy and surveying to the Royal Geographical Society'. Coles lived in Mitcham, Surrey, where he had a number of instruments, including a small silvered glass reflector (unusually Charles is not specific about the size of the mirror), and where Charles was a frequent visitor. Then: 'One day in June 1882 I got a note from him asking me to meet him at the R.G.S. and when there he told me that several expeditions were going out to various distant parts of the world to observe the transit, and one party was going to Brisbane, Queensland.'

The party was led by Captain William Morris, with Lieutenant Leonard Darwin as observer for the RGS and what Charles Grover describes as 'a young man of the Royal Engineers' – one Gunner Bailey, although as his rank suggests and Lieutenant Darwin confirms, he was actually a Marine Artilleryman – as assistant. Going out with the group as an individual observer, at his own expense, was a young man called Cuthbert Peek. Peek intended to observe the transit, then to continue his travels around Australia and on to New Zealand. He needed a reliable astronomical assistant for the transit work, and John Coles asked Charles if he would like the job: 'It was a great surprise to me and being as I was comfortably placed with Mr Browning it needed a little thinking over. However, the chance of a long sea voyage, and a visit to Australia and other places, and above all the opportunity of seeing the southern sky decided the case, and I signed an agreement for the expedition in July 1882.'

Cuthbert Peek, who was to remain Charles's employer until his death in 1901, was 26 when Charles signed up for the expedition, part of a large and well cared for household – consisting of his parents and himself, five in-laws and seven servants – on the east side of Wimbledon Common. In the 1881 census he is described as a 'Cambridge student of law'; he seems also to have been an enthusiastic student of astronomy and a keen traveller. According to his obituary in *The Observatory* for August 1901, which was written by Charles Grover, in 1881 he established a small observatory in the grounds of his parents' home in Wimbledon, where he worked with a 3-inch equatorial. Prior to this he made a journey to Iceland with John Coles (who brought Peek and Charles Grover together). In the chairman's note added to the report to the RGS of the expedition it is observed that 'Mr. Cuthbert Peek was one of the most promising pupils of Mr. Coles, the instructor in astronomical observations and surveying, under the system established by the Council two years ago for the scientific training of travellers. He went to Iceland as a promising field in which to test the value of the instruction he had received. So enthusiastic an observer, and one who had been so trained, would be sure to add something to the accurate knowledge of the geography of that island.' Coles published the results of the two journeys that the expedition made as 'Plan of the Great Geysir and Neighbourhood' in *Proceedings of the RGS* and 'Summer travelling in Iceland; being the narrative of two journeys across the island by unfrequented routes'.

Meteorological measurements were an important part of the work of the expedition, but Cuthbert Peek has something of his own to add about the Icelanders, of whom he admits to having been woefully misinformed:

With regard to the meteorology of Iceland, I may mention that our temperature observations varied from 80 F in the sun to 26 F at night. We experienced two severe snowstorms, but with those exceptions, the weather was magnificent.

The displays of the aurora borealis, too, were of the most brilliant kind.

In concluding, I should like to say a few words about the Icelanders. Before our arrival we had been led to expect to meet with an indolent dirty race, whose chief object would be to obtain as much money for as little work as possible, and who would spend all they earned in drink. I am glad to say we soon found we had formed a most erroneous opinion of the people. I think one might search the world over without finding three better guides than those we engaged. Cases of extortion were extremely rare, and we only saw one man at all the worse for liquor. The great majority of the farm-houses were very clean, and no matter what time we arrived, whether the farmer had gone to bed or not, all did their utmost to make us comfortable, charging most moderately for our board and lodgings.

Cuthbert Peek came from a very wealthy background. His grandfather, James Peek, was co-founder of Peek Bros. & Co. in 1821, then of Peek, Frean and Co. (of biscuit fame) in 1857; he lived in Devon at Watcombe Lodge, Torquay, from 1867 to 1879. Sir Henry Peek, Cuthbert's father, was a partner in Peek Bros., and was listed in the 1881 census as a 'tea, coffee and spice merchant'. The baronetcy was conferred on Henry Peek on 13 May 1874, and in 1881 his substantial new Devon mansion, at Rousdon, was under construction. Sir Henry's wife, formerly Margaret Maria Edgar, was the second daughter of William Edgar of Swan and Edgar's department store, so would herself have been a woman of considerable wealth.

The first task of the transit expedition in 1882 was to equip Cuthbert with a suitable telescope. He wanted to buy a second-hand instrument, so Charles suggested Lettsom's 6 4/10-inch aperture telescope, which stood in his Lower Norwood observatory. This had two advantages: first, that

Charles knew the instrument well, having himself made numerous observations with it, and second (advantageous for transportation purposes) it had an unusually short focus, of 74 inches. Charles was also aware that Lettsom wanted to change this telescope for one with a longer focus and that he would not be loath to part with it.

This telescope survived the sea voyages and in 1883 was transported to Rousdon where it was used in the observatory until Charles's death. It resurfaced in 2001, during the redevelopment of the mansion, in pieces, but still identifiably the same instrument and is now stored at the Science Museum in London.

The remains of the Merz telescope on a Cooke equatorial base taken to Australia in 1882 to observe the transit of Venus (photograph 2001, Dominic Sweetman and Carol O'Brien)

One of the problems that had emerged after the transit of 1769 had arisen from what is called the 'black drop' effect, which increases the difficulty of measuring the exact moments of ingress and egress. As the planet approaches the face of the sun it appears to elongate, resuming its correct shape only once it has passed in front of the sun's face.

The clockwork motor (photograph 2001, Dominic Sweetman and Carol O'Brien)

This effect and the penumbra visible around the planet serve to blur the instants so vital to calculations. To overcome this and to ensure that all the expeditions setting out to observe the 1882 transit would be working along the same lines, the expeditions, together with their equipment, spent three weeks at the Radcliffe Observatory in Oxford. Here was constructed an ingenious 'model transit of Venus'. As described by Cuthbert Peek:

> *This contrivance consisted of a metal plate, in which was cut a triangular opening, the two sides of which were curved to represent the Sun's limb. In front of this aperture a little black disc of proportional size to represent the planet Venus was drawn from side to side by*

clockwork with a velocity apparently the same as the planet. Thus the mechanical effects of the transit could be studied whenever desired, the model for this purpose being placed on the gallery surrounding the tower of the observatory, so as to be in full view of the telescopes of the expedition which were erected in the grounds below.

The equatorials belonging to the Brisbane expedition were set up exactly as they would be in Australia, including the erection of the temporary observatory buildings in which they were to be housed. Far enough apart that they would not be overheard by one another, they practised timing moments of ingress and egress against the mechanical transit, comparing and tabulating results until each pair of observers was noting events as closely as possible to the others. They also practised the use of graduated tinted wedges to reduce glare and enable more accurate observations when the Sun was close to the horizon and most subject to atmospheric distortion.

Cuthbert Peek writes of 'many long and heavy nights' work got through with the altazimuth and transit instruments' in determining accurate longitude measurements 'so that it frequently happened that when the morning hours were chimed out in the still air and the stars looked down on the quietly sleeping city, the glimmer of lamps in the portable observatories showed the astronomers still at work'; and of sleep sacrificed to 'the monotonous and troublesome calculations of the computing room'. For Charles such hours probably more nearly represented life as normal.

Charles notes that E.J. Stone (1831-1897; then director of the Radcliffe Observatory and a winner of the RAS Gold Medal in 1869 for his work on the solar parallax) 'was quite satisfied with the qualities of the instrument, and I had about three weeks very pleasant time at the observatory. There was much of interest there, notably the well known

Oxford Heliometer of 7 ½ in aperture and 10 foot 4 inch focus, and the Carrington Transit Circle of 5 inches aperture, and many other instruments.'

When the time arrived to pack up all the instruments for transportation to different parts of the globe the paraphernalia of all the expeditions was laid out in the Great Hall of the Radcliffe Observatory, which 'was nearly filled with the accumulation of astronomical apparatus thus brought together'. It has already been noted that among the instruments gathered together there was the Hartwell telescope used by Admiral Smyth in the compilation of his *Celestial Cycle*, Cuthbert Peek adds that also of historic interest was 'the Reade Equatorial ... for many years the working instrument of the late Revd. J.B. Reade [1801-1870], of Stone, near Aylesbury, Bucks'. Reade was a regular visitor to John Lee at Hartwell and, according to Peek, 'an active worker in Astronomy, Optics, Photography, and the Microscope [and] one of the pioneers of Celestial Photography. His earliest efforts were an attempt to get a picture of α Lyra with this instrument in 1845.'

As well as the Merz telescope, Peek's equipment included a position micrometer, three diagonal eye-pieces, a pair of tinted wedges, a low power Kellner eyepiece of very large field 'which was found a specially useful addition to the telescope', two chronometers, a sextant, artificial horizon and 'a good portable telescope'. Added to this list was a selection of 'appropriate astronomical texts, writing and drawing materials, stationery, notebooks, etc.' – 'so that my equipment was tolerably complete'.

On 24 August 1882, the expedition boarded ship at Tilbury in the Port of London on the Steamship *Liguria* of the Orient Line. Charles's Second Saloon ticket indicates that he was to be in berth 145 and that the cost of the passage was £41.11s. The ticket has been amended from the *Orient* to the *Liguria*. According to Lieutenant Darwin, writing to his mother on 31 August: 'If it had not been for the Egyptian transports we should have gone out in the

"Orient" and probably come back by the "Austral", two of the finest ships afloat, and both with the cabins in front of the engines.'

The *Liguria* was built in 1874 by John Elder & Co., Glasgow, and was a ship of the Pacific Steam Navigation Company under Orient Line Management from 1880. The ship travelled between London and Australia from then until 1890, when it reverted to its original South American route. It was a vessel of 4,666 tons and carried 600 passengers in first and second class and in steerage.

The design of the sister ships Iberia *and* Liguria: *the* Iberia *was built in 1873*

According to Lieutenant Darwin, the cargo included 700 tons of railway iron. The *Liguria* was designated as a steamship and had two funnels, but also carried sail; the yards were removed in 1893 and the ship was finally broken up in 1903.

Cuthbert Peek's account of the embarkation and the first night aboard gives an idea of the atmosphere that would have surrounded such a ship at such a time and it is as well that such an account exists: in '50 Years an Astronomical Observer' Charles's recollections of the voyage move at once to the first astronomical event of interest. Peek records:

Charles's passenger ticket from Gravesend (London) to Melbourne and Sydney on 24 August 1882

*A fine bright morning, a crowded Railway
Station, Heaps of luggage of the most
miscellaneous description. Porters staggering
along with Portmanteaus, Boxes & Parcels
followed by importunate travellers anxious to
see their belongings safely put in the train,
above all a babel of voices from the six hundred
passengers who were waiting for the 'special'
which was to convey them to Tilbury where the
Liguria was lying out in the river. This was the
scene at Fenchurch Street on Aug 24th 1882. All
the anxious glances at the great clock over the
platform did not for an instant retard the flight
of those last precious moments when friends
have always something to say which until that
time they have quite forgotten. So at 10h 15m
a.m. came the last shake of the hand, the last
kiss, the shrill whistle and we were off, rattling
along at such a pace that Tilbury was soon
reached. Here we had a repetition of the former
confusion while the Luggage was transferred to
the tender ... as the tender drew up under the
shadow of her lofty sides the vast magnitude of
the hull, above which towered the gigantic
funnels and tall masts and yards, was
strikingly apparent. Looking to the immense
strength and solidity everywhere apparent it
seemed impossible that such a structure could
be tossed about like a cork on the tempestuous
ocean, and the comfortable and luxurious
appearance of the internal fittings favoured the
illusion, which as will be seen later on was at
times rudely dispelled. [Peek's journal was
written up after the end of the voyage, at
Jimbour on the Darling Downs, the site chosen
for the transit observations.]*

*Fancy six hundred persons just arrived at the
door of some great hotel, at which they have all
bespoke accommodation. Fancy the endless
enquiries for room no. so and so, the rushing to
and fro along corridors nearly blocked up with
luggage among which some were helplessly*

*lamenting the loss of something they just
wanted, while others were struggling along
with their possessions and asking all sorts of
questions of everybody which nobody seemed
able to answer and you can form some notion
of the confusion during the first few hours on
board. Gradually however things settled down,
and the deep note of the steam whistle from the
tender which had remained alongside, warned
all friends of the travellers to depart, and
crowding over the side they took leave with
more handshaking and farewells and with a
parting cheer we were left to ourselves, when
after stowing away our effects we had time to
look around and inspect our floating home, in
which we were destined to live nearly two
months.*

In the event, the *Liguria* was not fully loaded in
time to sail on the 24th, and the passengers spent
their first shipboard night still securely moored in
the Thames. The steerage passengers (who could
anticipate the least comfortable voyage in the most
overcrowded conditions on the ship which seemed
so well-appointed to the first-class passenger
Cuthbert Peek) took advantage 'of this quiet
evening on the river for a little amusement'.

*It was soon discovered that among the motley
assemblage berthed forward musical talent
was not wanting, and very shortly a violin, a
concertina, and the Bagpipes made their
appearance, a squeal on the latter not very
melodious instrument soon drew a crowd round
the foremast and when this artist had
performed to his satisfaction the other two
came in for their share of attention. The violin
however appeared the most popular
instrument, and seated on an inverted pail the
catgut scraper was soon the centre of a number
of young couples who footed it on 'the light
fantastic toe' in energetic style. Neither was*

vocal ability wanting for when the dancers were tired, roars of laughter were excited by a comic Irishman fresh from the 'Emerald Isle' who sang of his courting adventures and their successful termination to an appreciative and admiring audience.

The several hundred steerage passengers – some emigrants, others returning home to Australia from visits to the 'old country' – endured cramped and unsanitary conditions even in the 1880s, by which time some of the misery and discomfort of the voyage, even for the poorer passengers, was supposed to have been overcome. Passenger lists generally did not name steerage passengers, but listed them only by numbers: so many men, women, children, infants. They slept in dormitory-like conditions, on small bunks. Marginally more allowance was made for married couples, children had smaller bunks and infants were not provided with individual spaces. Single men and single women were kept strictly apart. In some ships the steerage passengers spent a great deal of the voyage below decks. When the weather was bad they could be in constant gloom, with hatchways and portholes covered and few lamps, and in constant danger of being drenched by incoming water. While the first-class and saloon passengers were served their meals in surroundings of comfort, if not luxury, the steerage passengers were given an allowance of food that they could prepare for themselves. The passengers were divided into 'messes', each mess having a captain who was responsible for collecting the mess rations. If the system worked as it should there would be plenty of food to go around, but corrupt officers could ensure that people went short of food. A woman called Anna Cook, shipping out to Australia with her husband and three children, one still a baby, in the same year as the transit expedition, on a ship called the *Scottish Hero*, noted that, 'We went on very short allowance for a little while, and there was a bonny fuss. All the men went to the Captain and demanded their weight. They said the Purser was robbing them to line his own pockets at the other end, because whatever is left is sold by auction, and a commission is given to the purser.' (This quote and others that follow are from Lucy Frost's *No Place For a Nervous Lady: Voices From the Australian Bush*.)

The diet was not varied, but it was adequate:

> *Sunday fresh meat soup, and fresh tinned meat – not corned beef but actually roasted. We get that about 11 o'clock and I generally make a nice meat pie, and they are good too, and if we want any potatoes we only have to put boiling water to them and mash them with butter, pepper and salt. Every other Sunday, and every other Thursday we can boil a pudding. The single men take the other turn but we can always bake. After dinner the men wash up – all at one trough, pipes of hot water leading from the condensing house. Tea is fetched in the same way. All toast is made half an hour before tea. Monday pea soup and pork, very good. Tuesday fresh meat and soup. Wednesday pea soup. Thursday fresh meat. Friday pea soup. Saturday salt beef. Bread and water is served out every day before breakfast.*

There was always illness among the steerage passengers. The great fear was that typhoid or cholera would break out in the unhealthy and overcrowded conditions. When infectious diseases were suspected the steerage would be emptied of passengers and fumigated 'with brimstone and sulphur, the hatchways were closed as soon as the fire was put to it. The men ran like mad or they would have been smothered.' Disinfecting powders and fluids were used on a daily basis in an attempt to keep sickness in check.

Deaths were commonplace among the steerage passengers. On the voyage recorded by Anna Cook, a young man disappeared overboard, believed to have killed himself, and a number of babies and children died. Measles was a problem – 'a little girl died ... and since then her little brother has died, so now the poor woman has lost both her children, but is expecting another shortly'. People also died because of seasickness and the consequent dehydration.

Class divisions were strictly maintained. Cuthbert Peek may have observed that boarding ship was 'like six hundred persons just arrived at the door of some great hotel', but once everyone had settled into their quarters he would have seen little of the majority of those boarding, for whom the months that were to follow would prove harder and more squalid and uncomfortable even than the lives of hard toil and making-do that many of them were hoping to leave behind.

Cuthbert Peek's journal of the 1882 expedition has long been in the hands of Charles Grover's family. It was written up at Jimbour in Australia, the site chosen for the transit observations and appears to be in Charles Grover's handwriting, more particularly it resembles his writing of the early 1880s. Obviously different historical times have idiosyncratic handwriting styles, but it is in the detail – in the crossed 't's of 'that', where one line suffices for both 't's, in the apparently random use of capitals (generally reproduced throughout this book), or the use of lower case letters for the start of sentences (not reproduced here), or the use of a dot for all forms of punctuation – as well as in the more general appearance that the similarities lie. A series of letters written from Australia and, later, after Charles had returned to England, to his parents from New Zealand, offer example of Peek's own handwriting for comparison. It is important to remember that at the time of the voyage to Australia Charles was employed as assistant to Cuthbert Peek, and may well have fulfilled the broader duties of an amanuensis on occasions, such as writing up his employer's notes, or even taking dictation from him. A further peculiarity of Peek's journal is that the astronomical observations are written in almost exactly the same words that Charles uses in his own recollections in 1908. In one case, which will be looked at later, Peek's notes on the great comet refer to a figure that does not accompany the notes, and is in fact a figure drawn by Charles and published in *Astronomical Notes*.

However, the genesis of the astronomical observations in Peek's journal doesn't undermine its value as a record of the voyage, although evidence that the journal was dictated to Charles or written up from his employer's notes does underline, in case there was a danger that it might be forgotten, that while he certainly wasn't a steerage passenger, neither was he one of the 'gentlemen' aboard ship.

And while these gentlemen frequented the saloon and partook in entertainments, and the steerage passengers below lived a wholly different life, Charles seems to have taken up with the crew and followed his interests in all things mechanical.

> *The Commander Captain Coulan was a most genial gentleman, and his chief officer Perry and the rest of them were good fellows and I had a fine time with them, being much on the Bridge and seeing a good deal of the working of the ship. The chief engineer Sparks was also a very genial man who allowed me to go below in the Engine room, Stokeholds etc. and along the Screw alley so that I saw much of the machinery in which I was greatly interested.*

The *Liguria* left her anchorage at breakfast time on 25 August, moving off down the river under power: 'Many were the lingering glances directed to the many well known spots by some of our passengers who in all likelihood would never look on these familiar scenes again.' Nearing Dover, 'a fresh breeze made the ship rather lively and developed among some of the weaker of our passengers the usual unpleasant sensations'. The leisurely pace of the ship meant that the Isle of Wight was not reached until 6.30 in the evening, its green hills luminous in the low light and the Needles lighthouse brightening as the dusk deepened until it appeared as a brilliant star shining out across the water.

In the morning of the next day, the ship arrived in Plymouth where some additional passengers 'who had put off the evil day of embarkation' came aboard, as well as 'a quantity of mail bags, several cattle, and a supply of vegetables'. The carrying of live animals to be slaughtered for food en route points up something of the complex logistics of a long sea voyage for a large number of passengers in the days before reliable or mobile refrigeration. They left Plymouth at 2.30 p.m., and moving out of the shelter of the harbour 'soon found ourselves in rough water again, and getting up full speed the land rapidly dwindled to a shadowy line on the horizon and vanished. Night coming on we found ourselves not very cheerful company and turned in early.'

The route of the *Liguria* passed Madeira, then took it to the Cape Verde Islands. The ship should then have stopped at Cape Town to take on final supplies for the remainder of the voyage to Melbourne. However, an outbreak of smallpox in Cape Town meant that additional supplies needed to be taken on board in the Cape Verde Islands and that the ship was unable to dock in Cape Town. Instead it moored offshore near Simons Bay and a very few provisions were sent across in small boats. From Plymouth to Madeira the weather was capricious:

Sunday August 27th was a most miserable day – we were crossing the Bay of Biscay. The weather was dull & cold with a lead coloured sky overhead and a lead coloured sea below, in which the vessel rolled so heavily as to seriously try the stability of those amongst us who had not yet found their sea legs, at noon we were in Latitude 46°10'21" north, Longitude 7°21'15" west, having run 282 miles in the preceding 21 ½ hours. The evening came on wet and thick with every sign of a dirty night and we turned in duller and more miserable than usual.

Position measurements and predictions of the miles travelled seem to have been a constant feature of the voyage, essential for the ship's crew and useful practice for the expedition members. Charles notes that:

Mr Peek was an adept with the sextant, and each day at noon I took up the sextant and chronometer to the bridge when the usual observations of the Sun were taken. There were generally four observers. The 1st and 2nd officers, Mr Peek and a youngster, and immediately after the observation all would retire to work up and then compare results. When the position of the ship at noon was posted up, there was always quite a little crowd to see this, and the usual bets were always made every morning after breakfast as to how many miles we had made since yesterday's noon. We made about 350 miles a day.

Lieutenant Darwin mentions other regular measurements: on 31 August he noted that 'For the last two or three mornings we have been at work practising sending out telegraphic signals between 2 cabins, comparing the two chronometers; we shall have to do this work at Brisbane. The officers of the ship have lent us their cabins for this purpose, as they are so much quieter than ours; they are just a little in front of the engines, nearly in the middle of the ship.'

Very little seems to be known of Captain Morris – William George Morris (1847–1935) of the Royal Engineers – but there is more information on

Lieutenant Leonard Darwin (1850–1943), the eighth child and fourth son (the third to survive) of the great Charles Darwin (who died earlier in 1882, on 26 April). Prior to the expedition to Australia Leonard Darwin was teaching at the School of Military Engineering in Chatham, Kent; he served in the Intelligence Division of the Ministry of War between 1885 and 1890, was MP for Lichfield in Staffordshire from 1882–1895 and became President of the Royal Geographical Society in 1908, resigning the post in 1911.

After the end of his term with the RGS, Leonard Darwin's life took a less attractive turn as he allied himself with the protagonists of eugenics (the philosophy so admired by Adolf Hitler, among others), becoming President of the Eugenics Society from 1911–1928 and Honorary President from 1928–1943. He was made a life Fellow of the society in 1937, and wrote a number of eugenicist tracts between 1913 and 1942, among them, *Eugenics and National Economy* (1913; originating as a Presidential address to the society) and the even more dubious sounding, *Mate Selection* (1923). Eugenics could, I suppose, be seen as a manipulative descendant of Darwinism.

In an article in *Eugenics Review*, 'Race Deterioration and Practical Politics', in 1925/6, Leonard Darwin wrote of 'permanent detention of all confirmed habitual criminals ... To save the race compulsion would be necessary in many cases ... Compulsion is now permitted if applying to criminals, lunatics, and mental defectives; and this principle must be extended to all who, by having offspring, would seriously damage future generations.' Despite marrying twice, Leonard Darwin himself had no children.

Darwin wrote regularly to his recently widowed mother both during the voyage and from Jimbour. If he saw anything in his fellow travellers to excite admiration he certainly did not feel it worth writing down, although he does – writing on 31 August – extend our knowledge of the party: 'Captain Morris,

Miss Morris his sister, Miss Porter, a friend of Miss Morris's who is going with her to Australia for amusement, Mr Peek and ourselves; that is six in all.' Darwin's 'ourselves' includes neither the Marine Artilleryman or Peek's lowly assistant; apart from the men of the party it includes his new wife, formerly Elizabeth Fraser whom he had married in July; one would imagine in order that she could accompany him. The expedition may well have been in the nature of a honeymoon tour. It is also, as is clear from his letters, intended to benefit Elizabeth Darwin's poor health; something about which he writes a great deal to his mother. He continues:

> *Capt. Morris is a queer tempered man, but I think I shall get on with him all right, as he is very fond of his work, and will listen to reason when I differ from him as to how things are to be done. He is very energetic and is always at work at something ... He has got a microscope, and works at that all day long, except when we are working at some practice observations with chronometers. It is a great blessing for him that Mr Peek has joined the party, as he would be very dull without some companion, and I don't see much of him all day long. Mr Peek is a fat, good-natured looking man; he is not clever, but I think he has got a nice mind, and the mere fact that he is spending his money on this sort of a trip shews that he is not an average specimen ... He is an only son and his father is very rich; a merchant I think, and Bart. M.P. Lady Peek was a Miss Edgar of Swan and Edgar ... Miss Morris and Miss Porter are average young ladies; not interesting in any way that I can see.*

A couple of quiet days brought the *Liguria* within sight of Madeira. Days when, as Peek observed, 'fine bright sunshine and a sea as smooth as the Thames at Gravesend put everybody in good humour. The vacant seats in the saloon began to get filled and conversation began to get general and lively, whilst on deck the beautiful deep blue of the ocean and the graceful gambols of shoals of porpoise or the passing of distant sail were watched with interest.'

Madeira was passed at close quarters because the ocean is so deep even near in to the steep cliffs of the island. Signals were exchanged, and from the *Liguria* the passengers could observe gardens and buildings and people taking the air, which Cuthbert Peek described as having a 'soft balmy feeling, a sort of hazy humidity and warmth which one could well understand makes this a favourite spot for those who are suffering from, or in danger of consumption'.

More calm weather, with the voyage enlivened by the occasional sight of a sail or a shoal of flying fish, carried the ship on to the Cape Verde Islands, where it docked at Saint Vincent, the little port unusually busy because of a combination of factors – 'the troubles in Egypt which deterred many vessels from going through the Suez Canal, and the epidemic of small pox by which they are prohibited calling at the Cape of Good Hope.' The *Liguria*'s owners had sent a telegram to Saint Vincent to the effect that the ship should not land at Cape Town and should therefore take on sufficient fuel in the islands for the remainder of the voyage to Melbourne.

Two days were spent in Saint Vincent. Cuthbert Peek seemed more impressed with the approach to the town than he did with his experience of it at closer quarters.

> *The view of the town and harbour opening as*
> *you proceed like a beautiful panorama,*
> *prominent in the middle of the bay is the very*
> *curious 'bird rock' on which is a very white and*
> *solid looking signal station, from this a flight*
> *of steps leads up to the foot of a most lofty and*

*elegant lighthouse perched on the very pinnacle
of the rock ...*

*The white houses of the town look very pretty,
with the background of mountains, one of these
prominent among the rest has a divided summit
and is called the 'double peaked mountain'. The
tops of these are often enveloped in cloud. On
landing the first thing to arrest attention is the
utterly barren appearance of the surrounding
country. Nothing but rocks covered with sand
in which the foot sinks at every step is to be
seen. The rainy season is said to be from July
to November, but though the date of my visit
was about the middle of this period,
appearances showed none had fallen for some
time, and on enquiry I found it was very
uncertain and no rain had been known for the
last five years.*

*The principal square is ornamented with a
Town Hall, and a Catholic Church, in which a
few candles are always burning on an altar
decorated with a little tawdry gilding. A few
general stores are near this, but nearly
everything exposed for sale is of European
manufacture, and no more than can be seen in
London. Some large palms in this square are
the only vegetation visible. The rest of the town
is so irregularly built that nothing worthy of
being called a street exists and the houses and
shops are of the rudest description. Many of
the windows are without glass, the doors are
destitute of locks and bolts and the furniture is
limited to a rough stool and table with a few
domestic utensils of coarse brown earthenware.
In some of the smaller shops abundance of
Oranges, Bananas and Pine Apples are offered
for sale, grown on the adjacent island of San
Antonio, the valleys and low lying ground in
the interior of which are very fertile, thus
belying its forbidding aspect as seen from the
sea. The inhabitants are mostly negroes, mixed
with mulattoes the descendants of the*

Portuguese to whom these islands belong. Their habits appear very indolent. The children run about naked till they are about 12 years of age. They follow the travellers in swarms begging for money in a most importunate manner. Whilst here a company of Portuguese soldiers marched into the Grand Square. Their awkward gait, slovenly uniforms and dirty arms were in striking contrast to the smartness of our troops at home.

A massive 1500 tons of coal were taken on board the *Liguria* in Saint Vincent. During this day long operation all the portholes and hatchways on the ship had to be kept closed to minimise the invasion of the whole boat by coal dust: 'not only were the bunkers filled but a considerable quantity had to be stowed on deck. Coal and coal dust were everywhere.' It is not clear whether the steerage and second saloon passengers were below in the suffocating heat. For the first-class passengers 'the only part of the ship bearable was the stern',

Here beneath an awning to protect from the fierce tropical sun was quite a little market of Bananas, Oranges, Pine Apples, Birds etc which a crowd of small boats had brought off from the shore, and quite a brisk trade was carried on with a great deal of chatter and gesticulation. Much amusement was caused by the wonderful performances of the diving boys, who came off to the ship in great numbers, paddling along in rude little boats made from the hollowed out trunk of a tree. These young urchins seem to be perfectly amphibious and as much at home in the water as the fishes. They eagerly watch for the sixpences tossed over the side by the passengers, and four of five of them instantly follow the coin as it enters the water which is so clear that they can be plainly seen diving and struggling for its possession far below the surface. I never saw them lose a coin.

It is certain to be caught, placed in the mouth and brought up to be exhibited in triumph. I got some of them to dive under the ships keel and although she draws 27 feet of water it was done without difficulty. I then tried to persuade one or two of the best divers to get up a stone from the bottom, but as there is here a depth of 60 feet, this proved too much for their powers.

From the Cape Verde Islands to Simons Town – to the east of Cape Town, where the ship was allowed to anchor offshore – the voyage was largely uneventful. For many of the passengers there was their first sight of a volcano on the southernmost of the Cape Verde group, Fago. A peak of 9175 feet (according to Cuthbert Peek), where 'a column of smoke gently drifted with the wind and was soon

Charles Grover's sketch of 'Bird Rock' at the entrance to St Vincent Harbour, Cape Verde Islands, 3 September 1882

lost in the distance'. There were splendid sunsets, flocks of birds that followed the ship and never seemed to need to land, flying fish that could be watched in the clear water 'vigorously struggling up from the depths below, leaping from the water and skimming along before the ship a little way and dropping back exhausted'. The *Liguria* deviated a little from her course in order to greet and exchange signals with the clipper *Le Hogue*: 'the sailors mounted the rigging, and exchanged ringing cheers, when with a mutual dipping of the ensign we stood on our way'. Sunday was marked by services in the 'First and Second Saloons and also in the Steerage' and Cuthbert Peek found it 'gratifying to observe how heartily all classes joined in the religious observances of the day ... There was something very impressive in seeing the assembled passengers reverently bowed in prayer and listening to the strains of the well known hymns, a sort of strangely familiar sound when heard on the broad ocean.'

While the sailing was easy an entertainment was improvised. On the quarter deck, 'under the direction of the Captain and Officers a very comfortable theatre was rigged up with the aid of a few old sails.'

The stage was made to present a very gay appearance illuminated by numerous ships lamps, and tastefully decorated with an abundance of brightly coloured flags, the Union Jack forming an appropriate background. Neat little handbills were circulated announcing a performance at the 'Liguria Theatre Royal' on Wednesday evening, and on the morning of that day considerable amusement was caused by several amateur sandwich men parading the deck bearing boards displaying bills of the play humorously illustrated by the skilful hands of some of the first class passengers. On entering the theatre programmes likewise comically adorned were distributed by a black servant well got up for the occasion. The first part of the entertainment consisted of Songs, Recitations, and Pianoforte solos, received with great applause by the numerous audience. In the interval refreshments were handed round by the Stewards, after which followed a little farce entitled 'Who Speaks First' provoking roars of laughter. Our good Captain Coulan then came to the front and in a neat and genial speech expressed the pleasure it afforded him to see his passengers enjoying themselves. He hoped they would all have a safe and comfortable voyage, and announced the determination of himself and his officers to do the utmost to make everybody happy. It need hardly be said that these sentiments were cheered to the echo and after they had been emphasised by the musical assertion that 'He's a Jolly Good Fellow' the National Anthem concluded a very enjoyable evening.

Another entertainment was given the next night at which the farce of 'Little Toddlekins' was performed amid roars of laughter to a crowded audience. The well known ditty 'The Crew of the Nancy Bell' was then recited by the Chief Engineer in such splendid style as to bring down the house.

Entertainments do not feature in Charles's description of the voyage. From Peek's memoir, it seems probable that they were restricted to the first-class passengers. Anna Cook's letter home mentions just one entertainment, a New Year's Ball, held in the 'single men's apartment'; and refreshments served by the stewards hardly sounds like second saloon treatment, let alone the masses in the steerage. Plainly the captain and crew were adept at setting up and taking part in theatricals when conditions allowed.

Lieutenant Darwin was less enamoured of the voyage from Saint Vincent to Simons Bay finding fault with the food (which he seems to have found exceptionally bad) and with the captain. In a letter dated 17 September he complains to his mother:

> *Have I ever growled at the feeding on board before? It is the worst that I have ever come across on good ships; the meat is raw and awfully tough, and they serve very few simple dishes; curried 'internals' of different sorts is the favourite dish. The tea and coffee are both undrinkable ... we are bound to take in provisions here [Simons Bay] by some rule of the Board of Trade; otherwise [the captain] would not call at all. But there will be as little communication as possible with the land; no one will be allowed to land, and no one come on board ... the Captain is very civil, and so are the officers; he is an excellent navigator, but a man with an unpleasant temper ... Consequently no one likes to complain about the food, and we shall have to grin and bear it the rest of the way.*

As well perhaps that Leonard Darwin was not eating the food available to the passengers below. From Charles's point of view the really exciting part of the voyage began on this leg of the journey with the first appearance of a comet, observed on 14 September by the officer of the watch, but this will be looked at in detail in a later chapter.

On 17 September the ship rounded the Cape of Good Hope, giving fine views of Table Mountain, and anchored in Simons Bay. There is a nostalgia for land in all the descriptions of Simons Town, lying beyond the bay and disallowed to all but the travellers who have reached their destination. Cuthbert Peek observes that:

> *Simons Town ... is a very pretty place, the houses have an unmistakable English air of comfort about them, they are all whitewashed and spotlessly clean and embosomed as they*

are in the most luxuriant vegetation it looks a
very desirable spot. There are two or three
churches, some forts and a cemetery in which
we can plainly see the crosses and monuments
in memory of those who sleep below. The regret
is universal that in this homely looking place
we are not allowed to land.

Peek notes that 'some absolutely necessary stores
are taken on'; still longing for better food,
Lieutenant Darwin was less impressed by a gift
from 'the Admiral ... a beautiful basket of wild
flowers ... with "the result of a morning's walk" on
it. It was a kind thought, sending it to a ship load
of people longing for something to remind them of
dry land. But if the truth be told, 1 pat of fresh
butter would have been infinitely more acceptable;
butter and cream is our idea of perfect bliss at
present.'

A small boat drew alongside with David Gill
(later Sir David Gill), astronomer at the Cape Town
Observatory, and a few other gentlemen, and a brief
discussion regarding the transit and the work of the
expedition was held with Captain Morris and
Lieutenant Darwin over the ship's side. They were
not allowed even to shake hands.

Lying close to the *Liguria* was *HMS Boadicea*,
flagship of the Simons Bay naval station: 'at 8 a.m.
her flags were run up and commencing with the
National Anthem the band on the quarter deck
discoursed sweet music for one hour to our great
delight'.

Some of the passengers amused themselves with
fishing, although notices posted around the ship
warned them against eating unknown and
potentially poisonous varieties. Among these 'one
of the most remarkable is the "Toad Fish" so named
from the back being beautifully spotted like a large
Toad. The belly is silvery white with very pretty
fins, they are about 8 or 9 inches long with a large
chubby head, and so virulent is the poison that on
eating it death is certain within a few minutes.'

Several of these terrifying monsters were caught and displayed to general enthusiasm in a bucket.

Simons Bay marked an approximate halfway point in the voyage. They had been 24 days at sea, and would reach Melbourne, without further landfall, in another 21 days. It also marked a change in the weather, which no longer remained calm, but veered between severe storms and gales and rolling seas and days of dazzling tranquillity. Cuthbert Peek records some turbulent days – perhaps we should spare a thought for the second saloon and, above all, for the steerage passengers, for whom conditions were undoubtedly still worse:

No sooner had we left the friendly shelter of Simons Bay than we discovered that we had also left fine weather and smooth water behind. During the night the vessel rolled so heavily that it was difficult to keep in bed, and in the morning the performance of the usual toilette required a deal of patience. I struggled on deck to find the ship going through a gale, with a sea mountains high – the huge mainsail had been split by the force of the wind and it was impossible to replace it by another till the weather moderated, every few minutes enormous waves would dash over the bows carrying everything moveable before them. Wednesday was no better, water poured in everywhere, and about midday one of the massive cattle pens secured to the deck by thick ropes fastened to heavy iron ring bolts and containing several pigs, was lifted as easily as a piece of cork, the ropes torn away like so much thread, and carried bodily overboard. Thursday was but a continuation of misery, the waves flew to the top of the funnels and washed halfway up the main mast. It became positively dangerous to remain on deck so we were reluctantly compelled to go below, where in a state of semidarkness and suffocation we had to drag out the day – reading was nearly impossible from want of light and violent motion. And at meal times the saloon looked more wretched and cheerless than ever. Many vacant places are seen at table and those who do manage to put in an appearance look more or less ill and wretched. In fact it is almost a farce to attempt to eat under these conditions for it requires a considerable amount of management to get through a meal while you hold onto the table with one hand and secure your plate with the other, meanwhile the knives, forks and spoons are travelling in all directions and you are fully alive to the danger of being deluged by a tureen of soup or something equally savoury and convenient.

On Friday September 22nd the wind abated, the sea went down and to everybody's great delight we could walk on deck in comfort enjoying the fresh air and sunshine. Observations at noon showed we were in Latitude 38°12'3" South, Longitude 37°29' East. After sunset the moon shone with great splendour for about an hour when heavy clouds came up with vivid lightning and a torrent of rain which continued with but little intermission the whole night. About 2 a.m. the darkness was intense, the sky was literally black as ink, not a glimpse of sea or horizon was visible except when a flash of lightning showed for a moment the angry seething waves clear as noon day – to be instantly lost again in the blackest night. The thunder rolled long and loud and with the wind and waves made such a terrible din as to nearly drown the voice of the Captain who was on the bridge, the shouts of the sailors, the clatter of chains and the roaring of the wind through the rigging – put all idea of sleep out of the question, by 9.30 a.m. the thunder was muttering on the distant horizon but it had left behind a gale of wind and cold again with a tempestuous sea which increased in violence as the day wore on until *the ship had one side under water, and at night we have to make ourselves secure in our bunks to avoid the unpleasantness of being somewhat rudely deposited on the cabin floor. Next morning we got another brief lull, the wind and sea quieted down and we could walk around and see the evidences of the storm by broken ropes, split sails, a large piece of the bulwarks torn away, and the saloon skylight smashed in.*

Monday September 25th bears a sad memory in the records of this voyage. The weather was very squally and uncertain – now an hours beautiful sunshine – then in a few minutes black clouds, wind and a deluge of rain. In the afternoon some of the sailors were busy getting up one of the new sails, when by some means the running gear got foul and a seaman went out on the boom to get it clear, while doing this a sudden squall sent it over to one side with great violence and the Captain observing this from the bridge sung out to the men below to hold on to the stays to keep it steady. By some means his orders were misunderstood or not promptly obeyed and the rising wind jerked the boom over with such force that the poor fellow could hold on no longer, but was flung clear over the side into the water. He instantly rose and struck out bravely and several life buoys were at once flung over towards him, but the vessel going at full speed he was quickly left behind. The cry of 'Man overboard' was raised and the second officer Mr Taylor jumped into a boat with eight volunteers, and impatient at the delay in lowering the ropes were cut away, the little boat tossing on the waves like a cork. Meanwhile the engines were stopped and the ship brought around broadside to the wind. Hitherto we had been going with the gale and therefore had not felt its full power but now feeling the full force of wind and sea she heeled over to an alarming extent. The Captain, hoarse with excitement, shouted to his men to let go the sails, but those who best understood this duty were gone with the boat and the men on board getting bewildered he ordered them to cut away which they did with a will, some of the sails tumbling on deck and others flying loose in the wind, snapping with a tremendous noise. The vessel eased of the pressure began to right herself. Still the engines being stopped she rolled like a log in the trough of the sea and heavy waves swept clean over her carrying everything before them. The passengers, who on hearing the alarm, had rushed on deck were soon made aware of their danger by being dashed in a confused and half drowned heap against the side of the ship and several nasty falls took place and a general scene of confusion ensued. However, we were all anxious for the fate of the brave fellows who were now out of sight, and the Captain from the bridge failing to discern them we ran up the signal of recall. For some time we all looked in vain. At last we could just catch a momentary glimpse of the boat like a tiny black speck on the crest of a wave, then lost to sight again as it descended the deep hollow between to presently appear again on the top of the next and so on. Gradually they struggled nearer until within shouting distance when a loud cheer was raised on the supposition that they had picked up their unfortunate comrade, but this was not the case, the poor fellow was never seen again. The boat managed to get on the lee side of the ship but so violent was the sea that it was impossible to come close to the side and ropes were at last flung over by which the men were hauled on board half drowned and exhausted. The brave second officer being the last to be pulled on deck, our good Captain Coulan was so overcome that he embraced him and wept like a child. The boat was allowed to drift astern and the engines being started was smashed up by the propeller.

Man overboard. Charles's sketch of the loss of a seaman off the Liguria *on 25 September 1882*

The vessel was again put on her course and for the next few hours all hands were busy clearing the deck of the litter of Ropes, Oars, Sails and so on, while the doctor was engaged below administering restoratives to several ladies who had fainted with fright, and dressing the wounds of those who were unfortunate enough to require his services. A movement was soon made to reward those who had so bravely done their duty, and about £60 was collected for this purpose, when after a respectable sum had been placed to the credit of each seaman, it was decided to present the officer with a massive gold Maltese cross, engraved with a suitable inscription, to be purchased on our arrival at Melbourne.

The cross was purchased and the presentation made. In 1987 it was sold in a Christie's sale of militaria, together with a Mercantile Marine Service Association silver medal that had been awarded to the same officer. The inscription on the Maltese cross read: '*P.S.N. Coy's "S.S.LIGURIA" presented to J. Scott Taylor. 2nd Officer By First & Second Class Passengers in recognition of his bravery in attempting to rescue a shipmate on 25th September 1882*'. (The Christie's catalogue of the sale has the date as 1862, but I doubt that the medal is wrong, perhaps just not very legible.)

The medal in gold with rose diamonds presented to J. Scott Taylor by the first and second class passengers on the Liguria

Lieutenant Darwin gives his mother a restrained picture of the storms, in a letter dated 1 October: 'I could not sit it out at dinner for three or four nights ... whilst at the beginning of the voyage I was sometimes the only one at our table for dinner.' For this moderation his wife criticises him and he writes that 'Bee [Elizabeth's nickname] says my description of the storm is washy in the extreme and does not give the faintest notion of what we went through. It [the sea] washed an iron ventilator overboard, and the water flowing in through the hole in the deck swamped the steerage passengers; one or two pigs were washed overboard, and the cattle pen was broken in.'

Two days of better weather brought the *Liguria* within sight of Amsterdam Island, a barren, uninhabited island with a central peak rising to 2500 feet. Together with its neighbouring island, St Paul, it comprised the only land sighted on the journey from the Cape to Melbourne. More importantly perhaps on such a turbulent voyage, it marks approximately the halfway point. Charles was much impressed by the navigational skills of the First Officer who confidently predicted the time that the island would be sighted, as was Cuthbert Peek.

The remainder of the voyage seems to have passed with a combination of entertainment and storms. The first class saloon was the venue for a performance by the 'World Renowned Ligurian Christy Minstrels', featuring the songs 'Dem Golden Slippers' and 'Silver Threads among the Gold' and a degree of merry banter, including specially tailored jokes. On the chief engineer, imaginatively known as Sparks, and a man known for his ardent recitations:

> 'What would most surprise the passengers on the *Liguria*?'
> 'Why, to see sparks come out of the funnel and give a recitation on the quarter deck.'

And on the comet (interesting this, in the relationship between the comet and a spirit – albeit the alcoholic kind in the joke – unquestioned in Peek's retelling of the tale, and begging questions as to what the non-astronomically minded passengers made of the phenomenon – were they relating it to the dreadful weather, for example, the loss of the man overboard?):

> 'Suppose the comet broke his tail. Where would he get it mended?'
> 'Why, in a London gin palace, for there spirits are re-tailed!'

This was presumably for first-class passengers only, but the concert of comic and sentimental songs held two days later in the Second Saloon, seems to have been for first and second class travellers. The featured performer on this occasion was a young Welsh woman in traditional dress 'singing two songs in a manner that showed musical talent of no mean order'. Meanwhile 'our fellow voyagers in the steerage were vigorously footing it on deck just above our heads to the squeal of the Bagpipes or the scraping of the Violin so the evening seemed going in merry style.'

It was as well to take pleasure when it was offered. The next day – 3 October – saw a return of bad weather.

heavy clouds came on, the wind rapidly increased in violence till in the afternoon it was a fierce gale. Heavy seas flew high over the funnels and fell on deck with such force as to made the big ship tremble like a little boat and some tons of water found its way down the stoke hole from which rose clouds of steam. It was impossible to remain on deck so we were again compelled to go below and even here the water followed us, flowing through every crevice of the skylights and ventilators. The ship rolled so heavily that we could hardly manage to take tea and this night surpassed all our previous experience at sea. I only kept in bed with the greatest difficulty and as to sleep that was out of the question. The noise of the steering engine, the racing of the screw, boxes and everything moveable flying all over the cabin, and the sound of smashing crockery, together with the wind and waves made that quite impossible. No wonder that many seats were vacant at breakfast next morning, and complaints were general. Several had been thrown out of bed and one or two cabins were unfortunately flooded with water which found its way into the saloon in considerable quantities.

By 6 October the weather was once again warm and calm, and there was a land breeze beginning to be evident. Captain Morris gave a talk to passengers on the transit of Venus 'and the method of turning this interesting phenomenon to account in determining with increased precision the dimensions of the Solar System'. Presumably some curiosity had been aroused as to the purpose of the expedition members among the passengers.

The final entertainments of the trip included a magnificent 'Fancy Dress Dinner' in the First Saloon.

Here was a well got up Father Neptune, with the flowing robes, long beard, glittering crown and trident of the aquatic monarch, accompanied by the Queen of the Waters, robed in ocean blue. His majesty with aid of his speaking trumpet addressed the assembly – welcoming them to his watery domain and expressing a hope that they had enjoyed themselves whilst passing his dominions. He announced his intention of very shortly introducing his hearers to the New World of Australia – where he hoped they would long live prosperous and happy. These sentiments were received with hearty cheers and the piano struck up the lively tune 'A Life on the Oceans Wave'. His majesty turned to his queen and the stately pair led off the dance, followed by a glittering crowd of Chinese, Circassian Chiefs, Spanish Brigands, Negro Gentlemen, Ladies in quaint and elegant costumes, Red Riding Hood and numerous others. The beautiful illuminations of the Saloon, the rich dresses and sparkling jewellery made up a scene of splendour not easily forgotten.

One has to admire the grit of people who can be menaced by the sea one day – thrown out of their beds through long, frightening, sleepless nights, soaked by the penetrating seawater – then get out the fancy dress costumes that they packed before they left, just for this one on-board occasion, fasten their jewellery, and set off for a party. Whether or not the steerage passengers found it as easy to bounce back after bad weather would be hard to determine.

The last night saw a final concert and a valedictory speech by the Captain. But on 8 October, the expedition members were up early, looking over the ship's rails for the first sight of the Australian coast, for the first landfall since the Cape Verde Islands, for the first glimpse of a long low outline of the land on the horizon that would become home for many of the passengers that had travelled with them from England on the *Liguria* and for Charles Grover would represent the site for an experience of a lifetime.

The Great
September Comet

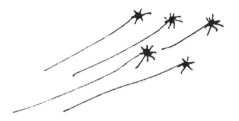

For both Charles Grover and Cuthbert Peek, one of
the great pleasures of the voyage to Australia was
the opportunity to watch the southern skies.
Charles had taken with him several star atlases and
a 'pair of good large binocular glasses' and notes
with particular interest the appearance of α and β
centauri and the Southern Cross; Cuthbert Peek
lists more stars seen as the *Liguria* continued
south, perhaps because he had a portable telescope
and Charles did not, but in both Peek's journal and
in Charles's 1908 memoir it is the appearance of
the comet – Comet C/1882 R1, the Great September
Comet – that dominates.

The first sighting of the comet by an astronomer
was that of W.H. Finlay at the Cape of Good Hope
on 8 September. Being unable to compare
observations of the comet with the very men who
first sighted it must have been a further
disappointment to the shipbound expedition unable
to land at Cape Town and forced to lie offshore only
ten days later. On the *Liguria* the comet was
sighted by the officer of the watch just before

sunrise on 14 September. The next day, the astronomers on board were up early to make their own observations.

It is at this point that the journal of Cuthbert Peek and the memoir of Charles Grover appear to intersect. What are ostensibly Peek's journal observations of the Great September Comet refer to figures that are not included in it in words that are almost precisely echoed in Charles's – later – memoir, '50 Years an Astronomical Observer', where they are accompanied by a series of sketches. However, one of Charles's sketches was published in 1882, and it seems most likely that his description of the comet in '50 Years an Astronomical Observer' was collated from his own contemporaneous notes and drawings, either subsequently discarded or, more likely, comprising the astronomical element of what passes at this point as Peek's journal.

Essentially, while the history of the voyage seems to have been dictated by Cuthbert Peek, the astronomical observations appear to have been written up almost entirely unaided by Charles Grover in his capacity as astronomical assistant. The journal's record of a visit to the Melbourne Observatory where the author 'had the pleasure of looking over the notes and drawings of this object made by Mr Turner [who was in charge of the Great Telescope] ... The resemblance between that gentleman's drawings and my own was so remarkable that they might almost have been supposed to have been executed by the same hand – whilst our remarks on the structure and appearance of the comet are expressed in nearly the same words', is one point at which the first-person of the voyage – Cuthbert Peek – is substituted by the first-person astronomical observer – Charles Grover. However, Peek's sketches – if they ever existed – no longer do so; and later evidence – the publication of *Observations of Variable Stars made at the Rousdon Observatory, Lyme Regis* under the name of Sir C.E. Peek, Bart., M.A. – suggests that the assistant's role was to observe on behalf of his employer, without expecting to receive the credit for the work: perhaps much as the copyright of an invention or creation devised as part of employment today belongs to the employer rather than to the employee. So if Charles sketches the comet, or writes a description of it, as part of his employment by Cuthbert Peek, under Peek's instruction or by his request, that is to all extents and purposes, the work of Cuthbert Peek; while Charles's letter to his friend Lettsom, containing much the same information and the drawing published in 1882, can be attributed to himself, because it is outside his employment. That the journal comprises Charles's astronomical recollections also explains why he retained the volume.

On 15 September, Charles writes that 'at 4.45 a.m. a magnificent comet was visible in the east. The tail rose nearly vertical about 40 minutes before the Sun, and when the nucleus suddenly appeared it was certainly brighter than Sirius and the tail 8° or 9° long.' Peek's journal records 'the horizon being perfectly clear, I saw [the comet] rise in great splendour about 40 minutes before the Sun. The nucleus was certainly brighter than Sirius, and the tail 8° or 9° in length, and so brilliant that it rose above the horizon as a bright beam of light followed by the nucleus which continued visible till the approach of daylight and a few clouds blotted it out.'

On 16 September the comet had approached so much closer to the sun that it did not rise until the light was sufficiently advanced to have obliterated the stars. It also remained visible until the sun was well above the horizon. On 17 September, Charles notes that 'at sunrise the comet is again well seen. It is evidently nearing the sun, and the tail points exactly straight away from that luminary.' The journal adds, 'It continued visible until the Sun was half an hour above the horizon.' Also on 17 September, A.A. Common, pioneer of astronomical photography and the man from whom Charles had helped the Revd Edmund Ledger purchase a telescope, observed the comet in a routine search around the Sun from his observatory in Ealing. On 18 September the *Liguria* was anchored in Simon's Bay and conditions were ideal for observing the comet as it rose 'just before the Sun with a brilliancy like a little moon and remained visible the whole day. At noon it was about 1°30' North a little West of the Sun, by just shading the Sun with the hand the comet was quite distinct, and its rapid motion was very striking.' The journal notes that 'At noon, and within little more than a degree from the Sun's limb it appeared as a very bright star with a short but distinct tail. It was evidently moving around the Sun with great velocity and the change of position was apparent from hour to hour.'

The journal notes a search for the comet on the following morning, using the naked eye and a 'good binocular glass', but that it could not be seen. (Charles's memoir confirms that the comet was not visible again until 27 September due to the terrible weather; frequent references to observations with the 'binocular glass' tend to confirm that the experiences recorded were those of Charles Grover rather than of Cuthbert Peek, who had a portable telescope for observations at sea.) Later, the journal records:

I was surprised to observe Venus looking very ruddy and more like Mars than the usual silvery evening star and the sky being clear and free from mist I could not for some time comprehend the cause. Till as the evening wore on the red colour gradually disappeared and the planet resumed its usual whiteness I found the illusion was an effect of fatigue of the eye from continued gazing on the brilliant Sun in my search for the comet.

On 27 September, at 4 a.m. the comet rose 'tail first above the E by South horizon'. Charles continues:

> *it is a magnificent object and in brilliancy far exceeds any comet I had previously seen. When well above the horizon the tail is about 10° long. The preceding side is remarkably brilliant and sharply defined. Slightly curved in a direction following the nucleus. And on the following side not so sharply defined and fading away gradually, a dark cone shaped channel or shadow is visible down the middle of the tail and can be traced with the binocular glass as a fine line nearly to the nucleus, which though intensely bright does not show the appearance of a planetary disc as it did on September 18th when so near the Sun. Sirius, Canopus and α Centauri, with the comet at the lower left hand corner form a gigantic square.*

But the most interesting observation, and the one that was published at the time, was made on 28 September.

> *With the binocular glass the comet is seen enclosed within a longer and fainter envelope, the boundary lines of which are distinctly straight and do not coincide with the curved figure of the comet within, so that at the points A & B it projects some distance in front and on either side of the nucleus. At B this straight edged envelope is very plain and at both A and B it ends in a point as drawn. The enclosed sector between A & B looks quite black. In fact as if a quadrant shaped shadow was projected in front of the nucleus. Probably in a powerful telescope this space would be filled with luminous matter, the illusion would then be complete of a brilliant comet enclosed in a much larger but less bright envelope of cometary matter.*

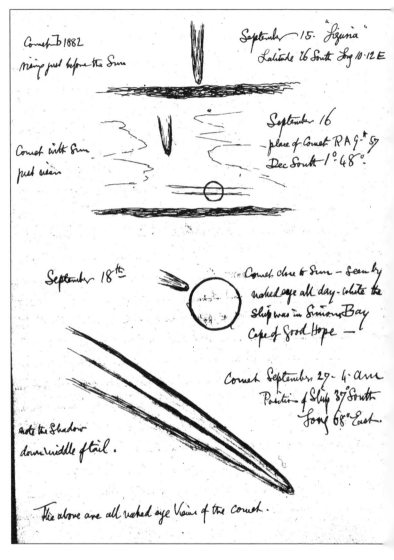

Comet b 1882
rising just before the Sun

September 15. "Figuria"
Latitude 26 South Long 10·12 E

Comet with Sun
just risen

September 16
place of Comet R A 9·ʰ 59
Dec South 1°·48°.

September 18ᵗʰ

Comet close to Sun — seen by
naked eye all day — while the
Ship was in Simons Bay
Cape of Good Hope —

Comet September 29 — 4· a.m.
Position of Ship 37° South
Long 68° East.

note the Shadow
down middle of tail.

The above are all naked eye Views of the comet.

*Charles Grover's sketches of the 1882 September comet,
15, 16, 18 and 27 September*

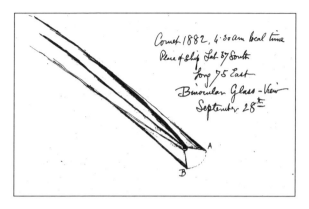

Comet 1882, 4·30 am local time
Place of Ship Lat 37 South
Long 75 East
Binocular Glass - View
September 28th

The Great September comet on 28 September 1882. This illustration is from Charles's memoir, although it closely resembles the one published in AN, 12 December 1882, pp. 59-60

It was this phenomenon that Charles described to his friend W.G. Lettsom, enclosing a sketch with his letter. Lettsom, in his turn, wrote to *Astronomische Nach-richten (AN)*, also *Astronomical Notes*, founded in 1821 by H.C. Schumacher, a respected German astronomer, and still going strong. Lettsom was responding to an earlier edition of the publication in which 'J.F.J. Schmidt describes and illustrates by lithograph a nebulous body perceived, sketched and measured by him, upon the 9th, 10th and 11th of October, in the vicinity of the Great September comet.' He suggests that Schmidt's observations can be seen as confirming those made earlier by Charles Grover 'who is well known among us as a trustworthy observer'. Lettsom quotes Charles's description of the phenomenon, and encloses the sketch – 'I made a sketch of the Comet, as seen from the bridge of the Steamer.'

Charles notes that from then onwards the motion of the comet was very slow and that by 17 October – by which time the expedition had made its way to Sydney – it was no more than a 5th magnitude object with all signs of sectors and envelopes gone, although it then developed a 'singular appearance

... down the centre of the tail where before there had been a dark channel visible even to the naked eye, there is now a bright streak of light and toward the end of the tail this can be clearly seen half a degree beyond the fainter portion giving the comet a very curious appearance compared with September 12 & 28. It is as if the comet had turned 1/3rd round on an axial line up the tail.'

The journal has entries relating to the comet on the 3rd, 7th, 9th, 10th and 12th October, and an almost exact duplicate of Charles's description of it on 17th October – down to the time of day of the observation, 3.30 a.m., confirmed on the sketch accompanying Charles's description.

In London Charles had attended RAS meetings with John Browning and had talked on equal terms with well-educated and wealthy gentlemen. The rigid class divisions on board ship may have proved less than comfortable and reinforced his role as assistant to the much younger Cuthbert Peek whose social status gave him a position that was denied Charles, despite the latter's substantial astronomical skill and knowledge; although Charles does seem to have forged a remarkable bond with Peek, both over the period of the voyage and more so in following years. Charles is himself prone to generalisations on class and race that mark him out absolutely as a nineteenth-century figure, but on the *Liguria* his subservience was underlined by his accommodation, which ensured physical separation from the first-class passengers and by the attitudes of some of the 'gentlemen' themselves, and for the first time in very many years he seems not to have had a telescope for consolation.

Freed from the restrictions of life on board ship, Charles once again becomes informative. He has a great deal more of his own to say about Australia.

From Melbourne
to Brisbane

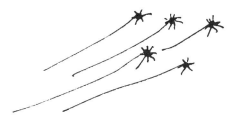

The first fleet carrying transported convicts to
Australia arrived in Botany Bay – later Sydney
Harbour – in January 1788. Transportation to the
east coast was suspended in 1846, and the final
convicts landed in Sydney – to considerable protest
from the population – in 1849. The system
continued on the west coast until 1868. Convicts
served their sentences under a system of 'assigned'
labour, working out the term of their sentence
under a master rather than in a penal institution.
Once the time of assignment was up, the convict
was a free man – a ticket-of-leave man – able to
work for himself, set up a home and raise a family.
Only sixty years after the arrival of the first fleet,
in 1848, the white population of New South Wales
was 187,000, no more than 11,000 of them convicts
still under sentence. Many of them were the
descendants of ticket-of-leave men and women,
many others had set out from England with few
possessions and only a determination to take their

chances in the new world, and they were all free Australians.

Emigration was further boosted by the discovery of gold in Australia in 1851, and, according to Robert Hughes in *The Fatal Shore*, by 1871 there were some half a million Western settlers living in New South Wales, 730,000 in Victoria – almost a tenfold increase over the twenty gold-rush years – 189,000 in South Australia, and 122,000 in Queensland.

By 1888 – the centenary of the new nation, and only six years after the RGS transit expedition travelled across the country – Australia was looking firmly forward, and had turned its back on what was seen as its murky past. By that date, the percentage of the population that had arrived as prisoners would have been negligible.

The RGS party (with perhaps the exception of the sometimes hard-to-please Lieutenant Darwin) found it an exciting place to be and admired its youth and vigour. Charles himself – had he been younger or just perhaps unencumbered – may well have been tempted to stay. From his own descriptions it seems as though he felt at ease in Australia in a way that he never felt at ease aboard the ship.

The *Liguria* arrived off Melbourne on 8 October, although there was a delay at landing, again due to the smallpox scare that had followed the voyage. After forty-five days at sea, the only sight of land since Simons Town the barren rock of Amsterdam Island, and not so much as a sail to remind the passengers of the existence of other human beings, Cuthbert Peek's journal records:

We all rose betimes to see the first glimpse of the new world and very refreshing was the sight of the long low outline of the land on the horizon ... The coastline as we steam towards the entrance of Hobsons Bay is not broken by any tall mountains, a succession of headlands of moderate elevations come into view affording a continual change of scene as we move along and the dark blue of the Indian Ocean is now replaced by a sea of delicate green, flecked with the gentlest ripples. Queenscliffe with its tall white lighthouse lies on our left. The neat white villa residences of this celebrated watering place, which is to Melbourne something like what Brighton is to London, could be distinctly seen in the Sun. On the other side of the entrance is the quarantine station, a series of buildings charmingly situated amidst the most luxuriant vegetation, the beautiful green lawn in front sloping down to the water was quite refreshing to our sight after the long sea voyage, but as we noticed the yellow flag on the flagstaff we recalled the famous line of 'Campbells', 'Thus distance lends enchantment to the view' as very applicable to this, for in consequence of the scare about small pox we were fearful of detention here longer than agreeable especially as there was a rather doubtful case of sickness on board. No sooner had we dropped anchor than a boat left to fetch the health officer, and when after some delay that official made his appearance on deck quite a flutter of excitement was caused by the announcement that all on board would have to undergo an examination to ascertain if they had been duly vaccinated. This took place in the saloons. The ladies first and then the gentlemen passing the doctor's scrutiny with very amusing results. For while those on whom the marks of vaccination were apparent were jubilant, others who had got to undergo that simple operation looked as serious as if some serious amputation was in prospect.

In a letter from the Melbourne Quarantine Station on 9 October, Lieutenant Darwin wrote of 'beautiful fine weather and a smooth sea to pack up in ... We got into harbour about 4 ... and the Health Officer came on board; we all had to show our arms, and everyone who had not a mark of vaccination was told that he would be vaccinated at Melbourne. We hear that they are terribly afraid of smallpox in Australia, because the disease is almost unknown there, and they have just heard of how bad it is at the Cape; consequently they will be very hard on us, and will not let us go so long as there is the faintest possibility of smallpox.'

Fortunately for the expedition and for the other passengers on board ship the precautions taken were evidently deemed adequate and the case of sickness diagnosed as other than smallpox and, after a short further delay for various formalities, they continued on their way:

As we moved up to our anchorage opposite Melbourne the water was smooth as a mirror and the innumerable lights of the city were reflected like stars in the depths below. Another large steamer of the Orient line the 'Catopaxi' was just moving out on her homeward voyage. The two vessels passed within a few yards of each other, Red and Blue lights were burnt and the passengers of both ships crowded the sides and exchanged hearty cheers which only ceased as the huge form of the 'Catopaxi' faded away in the darkness. Scarcely was this little excitement over than our ears were greeted with the familiar strains of 'Home Sweet Home' beautifully sung in unison and softly wafted across the still water. As the melody drew nearer we found it came from a steam tender coming out to meet us crowded with the friends of the returning Australians eager to welcome them on their return to the land of their adoption. No sooner were they made fast than our deck was crowded with a motley assemblage chatting, laughing, Crying, Hand-shaking and every expression of Joy. The Saloons soon presented a lively scene filled with animated groups of friends eagerly recounting to each other the numerous events of interest to each during the period of their separation, and under the influence of liberal supplies of Champagne etc. the welcomes extended far into the small hours of the morning, and as long before the departure of our fellow passengers and their friends the steam winches were at work taking out cargo on one side and taking in coals on the other, sleep was out of the question.

This was 10 October, and others, including Lieutenant Darwin, had already disembarked. As he wrote on 15 October, from the comfort of the Menzies Hotel: 'we were both very glad we had come ashore, if only for the sake of a comfortable bed in place of a narrow bunk with a steam winch over our heads'.

Cuthbert Peek and, presumably, Charles Grover, came ashore on the following day, Wednesday 11 October:

The sun rose without a cloud and the view of Melbourne from the sea was very beautiful. The numerous shipping in the harbour, the Turret Ship Nelson with other men of war at anchor and numerous little steamers puffing to and fro with passengers and stores made a very animated picture. Landing at Sandridge Pier, the Railway Station is close at hand, and a few minutes ride brings us to the Melbourne Town Station, on seeing which with its Bookstalls, Daily Papers, Wall Advertisements etc. exactly like those at home we find it hard to believe that we are on the other side of the world. There is however one slight difference here in that the uniforms of the officials all bear the initials V.R. the Australian Lines being under state control.

A good walk through the principal streets of Melbourne excites feelings of the greatest wonder when we recollect that 50 years ago a few rude wooden huts were the only buildings on the site of what is now a splendid city. The

streets are fine and wide, running at right angles to each other and perfectly straight. The principal buildings are of noble proportions and imposing architecture, and in many instance ornamented with a profusion of statuary and decorative sculpture equal to the finest specimens of street architecture to be seen in our own metropolis. Great enterprise is displayed by the tradesmen here in the fitting up of their respective establishments, and in the splendour of the exterior and in the elegance and costliness of the goods displayed within they fairly equal their friends at home
...

Melbourne is situated on the Yarra-Yarra River, which is however so shallow as not to allow of vessels exceeding 200 tons coming up to the city. Larger vessels lie out in Hobsons Bay or come up alongside the Pier of Williamston [sic] which is in connection with the railway by which goods and passengers are conveniently conveyed. The growth of this city received a great impetus after the discovery of Gold in the colony in 1851 – and among the principal sights may be named the Cathedral, the Governors Residence and the new Museum and Picture Gallery.

Charles notes that 'a stay of several days was spent in a good look around what may be called a little London of the southern hemisphere. Where the Buildings, Streets, Shops etc. are singularly like the British capital, and one does not feel the least like being on the other side of the world.'

Lieutenant Darwin was less impressed with his first landfall since leaving the Cape Verde Islands:

[Melbourne] is a disappointing town after all one has heard about it; two or three long broad streets with some 'fine' buildings separated by rather shabby ones form the heart of the town. Then the suburbs seem to stretch for some

miles, and consist of abominably dusty and badly made roads, with poor untidy one or two storied villas dotted about ... it covers an immense amount of ground, and there are three times as many people in Melbourne as in the rest of the Colony of Victoria put together; but it is a most un-interesting place.

Charles Grover's sketch of Melbourne Observatory, 13 October 1882

In Melbourne Charles seems to have been able to embark once again on a more independent life. He 'called on many people [he] had met in London' and he visited – on his own as well as with Cuthbert Peek – the Melbourne Observatory. This 'is situated in the Botanical Gardens, on a considerable elevation about two miles out of the City. From the top of the tower is a magnificent panorama of the surrounding country, with the domes and spires of the various buildings, the docks, crowded with shipping and beyond all the wide expanse of Hobsons Bay which is indeed of such extent as to almost [appear] a little landlocked sea. From this tower a time ball is dropped at 1 p.m. as at the Royal Observatory Greenwich.'

Peek's journal lists some of the equipment of interest at the observatory:

An 8 inch equatorial by Cooke, of the usual form with the ordinary clock movement, a new driving clock has been constructed in the observatory workshop with Grubbs Electrical Pendulum which carries the telescope so accurately as to keep a star bisected by the micrometer wire for two hours. There is another equatorial here of but 4 ½ inches aperture but of such great accuracy that it has been employed by Mr. White (the first assistant) to fix the position of the great comet now visible. A Photo-heliograph is also kept at work and during 1882, 217 Pictures of the Sun were obtained. The transit is not more than 4 inches aperture of old form and construction but the necessary funds have been voted for a new transit circle of modern form and of dimensions sufficient to cope with the present requirement in meridian work.

But of course the instrument that really drew the visitors' attention was the observatory's large telescope. Known as the Great Melbourne Telescope, it was built in 1868 at a cost of £5000 by the instrument makers Grubb of Dublin. The company was founded by Thomas Grubb (1800–1878), who was joined by his son Howard (later Sir Howard) Grubb (1844–1931). The Grubb electrical pendulum listed approvingly in Peek's journal was designed by Howard Grubb and represented a new form of telescope drive controlled by electrical impulses from a pendulum clock. It was hugely successful and was still being used, relatively unchanged, as late as the 1930s.

The telescope itself was examined by an RAS committee who found it to be 'a masterpiece of astronomical mechanism'; they were Lord Rosse, who had constructed the gigantic 'Leviathan', Dr Robinson, Ireland's Astronomer Royal, and Warren de la Rue, pioneer of astronomical photography. The telescope's giant tube was partly made of solid iron plates and partly of a lattice of steel bars, which was extremely strong and stable and reduced the overall weight of the instrument. Nonetheless transporting the instrument and setting it up in the Melbourne Observatory added something between a further six to eight thousand pounds to its cost. When the telescope began operations it was the largest steerable reflecting telescope in the world. Allan Chapman notes that 'This was the last major speculum mirror telescope ever to be built, and the first major instrument of that class not to be in the hands of a Grand Amateur. And almost from the start, the skeleton-tubed Melbourne reflector was found to be a disappointment.'

The role of the Great Melbourne Telescope was to have been one of observing and revising nebulae and clusters, to update and extend Sir John Herschel's observations from the Cape of Good Hope in 1834–38, but the telescope had inadequate definition and was vulnerable to the motion of the wind to which it was exposed during observations. Drawings were made by Grubb for a dome, but none was built. Neither was it a useful instrument for photographing objects such as nebulae and clusters, although a great deal was achieved with it in the latter part of the nineteenth century in the way of lunar photography.

Cuthbert Peek's journal and Charles Grover's memoir confirm both the mechanical brilliance of this huge instrument, and its technical weakness. Charles writes that on 13 October 1882, at 3.30 a.m.

I went with Mr. Peek to see the great reflecting telescope. The steel tube of this monster is 40 feet in length & 5 feet in diameter (I found I could almost stand upright inside the end of the tube) ... Suffice to say it is a model of what a great telescope should be. The movements are smooth & easy. The circles large & distinctly divided. The focussing arrangements and

> *Clamps are conveniently placed, and the clock movement very accurate. In fact it is without a doubt one of the handiest of Great telescopes.*

Mr Turner, who was in charge of the telescope at that time, directed it first at 'the great nebula surrounding η Argus' then at the 'grand cluster ω Centauri'. The journal records that in the first case, while 'the field was very brilliant, there was however a want of proper definition of the numerous stars included and no amount of careful focussing gave them the neat appearance they present in any good moderate sized telescope. The wonderful nebula which spreads in complicated folds over this region, appeared very conspicuous but confused, ill-defined and certainly very unlike the drawings by Sir John Herschel in his "Cape Observations".' Charles had read the *Cape Observations* in 1872, and made a few notes on them in his own observations book on 11 May that year. The journal continues with the observation that the appearance of this nebula through the 6 4/10-inch achromatic set up in the temporary observatory in Jimbour in November more closely resembled the 45-year-old sketches of Herschel than did even the most recent drawings from Melbourne.

Of ω Centauri the journal notes that 'this gorgeous cluster of stars appeared so brilliant as to strike even a practised observer with astonishment, but there is such a want of accurate definition that the closer stars run into each other and the separation of the individual stellar points is impossible.'

> *Jupiter was intensely brilliant, but on attempting to focus his belts the same defective defining power was apparent and no more could be made out with this giant, than is equally well if not better seen with an 8 inch achromatic. The Satellites did not show the*

neat circular figure which they present in many a small telescope.

Saturn appeared no better, the same bad definition prevented anything like detail being seen. The Satellites looked very bright but ill defined. I looked carefully for the two inner moons, Mimas and Enceladus but failed to find them.

Mr. Turner has attempted to remedy this want of definition, by the application of a metal plate, pierced with a number of small apertures of varying diameters which is made to slide in front of the eyepiece, and thus limit the amount of light which reaches the eye of the observer – by thus applying a very small aperture a decent image of Jupiter or Saturn could be obtained, but so much of the effective aperture of the Great Telescope had been sacrificed in this manner that the resulting image was no brighter than I had been accustomed to see with a 10 or 12 inch silvered glass reflector, and even then the definition of the details on these planets and the discs of the Satellites was nothing compared to what I afterwards saw with my own 6 4/10 in achromatic when erected at Jimbour.

These observations are sufficient to show that so far as definition is concerned this telescope is a failure, and surpassed by many instruments so much smaller that the comparison is simply absurd. The enormous aperture has allowed the observers to pick up many of the smaller and fainter nebulae which are invisible with lesser instruments, but even this is a doubtful advantage, since the definition is so defective with the full aperture that we can never feel sure that what is seen is seen correctly, for instance a small star may be described as Hazy and Diffuse, or such objects as the Satellites of Jupiter and Saturn might be credited with the possession of an atmosphere all arising merely from instrumental defects.

However, there was one area in which the Melbourne telescope did seem to excel and that was in the realm of lunar photography. 'Anyone who is familiar with the productions of De La Rue in England and Rutherford in America, knows to what perfection this art has been brought, but the later Melbourne pictures are without doubt far and away the most beautiful and perfect photographs of the moon that have ever been obtained.'

This is the point at which Cuthbert Peek's journal comes to a close. Since it was dictated and written up and the astronomical elements also added at Jimbour this was perhaps because the expedition's stay there had come to an end and the parties were dispersing. Charles's memoir however has a great deal more to say about Australia and the process of setting up for the observation of the transit.

Later on the same day on which he had accompanied Cuthbert Peek to Melbourne observatory to see the telescope, Charles returned to see Mr Turner and to compare their notes and sketches of the comet: 'The agreement was remarkable, the drawings were so much alike that they might have been done by the same hand, and the notes on the structure and detail are expressed in nearly the same words.' He also looked at Turner's notes and drawings of the southern nebulae and at the other instruments held at the observatory. He renewed acquaintance with the 'genial Director Profr. R.J. Ellery, whom I had met in London on several occasions' and who 'was very pleased to see me again, and we talked over many matters.'

He thought it quite a pity I was returning to England after the transit, as he said handy scientific assistants like me were much wanted in the colony. He first went to Australia in 1851 and two years later superintended the building of a small observatory in Williamstown, which was followed by the present Melbourne observatory in 1863. He was for many years the Chief Scientific man of the colony of Victoria, and President of the Royal Society of Victoria for 23 years. He continued director of the observatory till his 68th year and died January 14th 1908 in his 81st year.

Ellery's area of expertise was positional astronomy with refractors.

The Great Melbourne Telescope was broken up towards the end of the 1940s and some elements of it – the polar axis, half of the declination axis and the mirror cell – were re-used in the construction of a 50-inch reflecting telescope at the Mount Stromlo Observatory in Canberra. This instrument was in use through the 1990s in the MACHO (massive compact halo objects) project, using an optical technique known as gravitational micro-lensing in the search for the 'missing mass' of the universe. Along with a number of other historical instruments and a quantity of irreplaceable library records this instrument was destroyed in a massive firestorm which swept through parts of Canberra on 18 January 2003, destroying 500 homes and damaging many more and killing four people.

The following day, 14 October, the expedition left Melbourne for Sydney. The only surviving description of this leg of the journey is that of Leonard Darwin, who records a trip by train in typically negative style (it seems likely that Charles travelled on the *Liguria*, which was still carrying the expedition equipment – he notes that the trip took 48 hours, while Darwin's journey was considerably shorter – and it remains uncertain as to how the remaining members of the passengers travelled) – but even the irascible Lieutenant was seduced by the beauties of Sydney. He was, however, unable to resist a negative shot at Captain Morris. Darwin was writing on 25 October aboard the SS *Katoomba*, which took the party on the next leg of the trip, from Sydney to Brisbane:

We left Melbourne on Monday afternoon about 3 by rail, reaching Albury at 11 that night. Slept at Albury, and went on Tuesday afternoon at 3 and reached Sydney at 7 Wednesday morning ... It was a very monotonous journey, as the train only goes at about 25 miles an hour, and the scenery is almost exactly the same the whole way. An open wood of gum trees, four out of five of them being killed in many parts by a ring being cut in the bark; and occasional pasturage for the sheep; ... the villages are very few and far between, and the country has the appearance of being utterly uninhabited ... Mr Russell, the Astronomer there [in Sydney] was most civil, and organised two very pleasant excursions. The first was a trip round the harbour in a steam launch one afternoon, winding up with tea at their house. I think the Harbour is quite worthy of its reputation, and of all the sites for a great city, Sydney is undoubtedly the finest I have ever seen. It consists of a perfectly land locked inlet of the sea, not very many miles in length, say 15, but with such a complication of winding creeks and bays that there are 120 miles of coast line in all. Some of the inlets are very like Scotch lochs, well wooded down to the sea; many miles are built over, closely or with villas and gardens; in grounds ... The streets are not quite straight, and the situation being very hilly, it will in time be a wonderful city. The other expedition was to the Blue Mountains ... We started out from Sydney by rail, and after about 40 miles the railway went up the 'first zigzag'. The country is crossed by a steep line of hills about 500 feet high, up which no incline could be found, so the railway is taken up zigzag; in the middle part the train goes engine behind. It is a curious bit of engineering. After getting to the top the railway keeps rising for 40 miles, till at Mount Victoria it is 3500 feet above the sea. Here we ... found a comfortable hotel ... On Monday morning we went on in the brake van of a luggage train to the second zigzag, which is much the same as the first, only down a rather more precipitous hill, which leads to the plains below. We only went to the bottom of the zigzag and then had to return by train to Sydney ... [the country] consists of a complicated network of valleys and hills, which is difficult to understand as there is no good map. In the sides of all the valleys there is a deep cliff, sometimes many hundred feet deep; the cliff with the hill above and below it makes a very deep valley, and from the railway one caught glimpses of a wooded country not far off, but very deep below us, and stretching away far into the distance ...

I find at starting I did not know Capt. Morris a bit, and that on the whole he does not approve on acquaintance. He has some nice qualities as he is sympathetic, but yet selfish. He has a greater power of making himself unhappy than anyone else I ever saw, as he always expects the worst to happen, and is always conjuring up possible or impossible catastrophes ... Mr. Peek is disgustingly contented: nothing ever goes wrong with him; he can sleep anywhere, and through any conceivable noise, and can digest anything. He is not an interesting man, but is a good hearted man on the whole ... Miss Morris and Miss Porter have not developed any interesting qualities nor are they likely to do so according to Bee.

It is not clear whether Captain Morris and his sister and her companion or Cuthbert Peek accompanied Lieutenant and (presumably) Mrs Darwin on their outings. Charles certainly seems to have had a great deal of freedom in which to explore the city and to take up old contacts and to make new ones. His memoir refers to 'us' on a visit to the Sydney observatory, which certainly suggests that this was one trip he made with Cuthbert Peek, and possibly other members of the party as well.

Like Lieutenant Darwin, Charles is overwhelmed by Sydney – 'The scenery around the harbour is magnificent' – he is also taken by the way in which the deep water of the channels allows 'large men of war [to] lie at anchor within a stones throw of the sea wall of the Botanic gardens' and with the fact that 'crowds of ships of all nations are lying at the wharves'. He likes the contrast with Melbourne, and his description of the city and some of its facilities demonstrates just how far Australia had come from its sorry beginnings:

[Sydney] is built on very hilly and irregular ground, in fact so steep in places that the houses look almost one on top of the other, the streets run in all manner of directions and are altogether destitute of the order and regularity which characterizes the plan of Melbourne. The reason is not difficult to learn. Sydney was one of the earliest founded of the Australian cities, and passed through many rough and trying years when the earlier settlers faced enormous difficulties. But Melbourne fell on happier times and was a comparatively new city with all modern improvements. The Sydney Botanical Gardens is a splendid place. Here is a museum & picture gallery, also a collection of wild animals. The school of arts has a fine library & reading room and although a notice tells you it is only open to members the courteous attendant at once gave me permission to make free use of it during my stay in the city and assisted me in many ways. There is a laboratory, a studio, and a commodious Lecture Hall with lectures every Saturday evening. This Saturday October 21 the subject was comets. [Charles does not note whether or not he attended the lecture.] From the School of Arts to the Natural History Museum in Hyde Park is but a short walk. The collection is housed in a noble building in front of which stands the statue of Captain Cook,

which I at once recognised, having seen it standing on a temporary pedestal in Pall Mall some time before it was sent out to the colony. I found Mr. Ramsay the Curator busy in his office but he received me with the greatest cordiality and had an hours chat. Natural history was well supported, and he said the authorities were very liberal to the museum which is not cramped for want of funds, and the result is very visible in the superior manner in which the numerous specimens are arranged and exhibited.

The public library is one of the finest I ever saw with an enormous collection of books, the catalogue filling two thick volumes. The reading room open from 10 am to 10 pm is most comfortable and the attendants most obliging.

On Monday October 23 [when Darwin, and perhaps the other gentlemen of the party, began the trip to the Blue Mountains] I called on Dr. G.A. Wright of Wynyard Square, who I knew by name as I had some time before when at Brownings sent him an 8 ½ inch Silvered glass Reflecting telescope. He was delighted to see me, and I found the telescope in perfect order. He is one of the leading amateur astronomers of the City, and also possesses some valuable microscopes and other instruments.

At this point in his description of Sydney Charles writes of a trip to the Chinese quarter of the city around which he was conducted by an individual who is not named, but from whom I suspect he derives at least some of the opinions that he expresses. He finds the Chinese quarter 'remarkable not only for its quaint appearance but for its pungent smell', and goes on to define the dangers not only to health and welfare, but also 'the menace to fair English trade and commerce' consequent on the increasing numbers of Chinese, living in cramped conditions, conducting business from their homes, and undercutting prices.

This is one of those occasions in which Charles, who is at ease among professional astronomers and scientists with whom he has intellectual interests in common, but who does not seem to chafe at his position among 'gentlemen' – accepting without a murmur of complaint his second-class saloon and second-class passenger status, his role as assistant to the much younger and less knowledgeable Cuthbert Peek and, later, the subsuming of his years of observations under the Peek name – and who, while no doubt according appropriate traditional courtesies to women, would be unlikely to concede that a woman could be a man's intellectual equal or that a female was anything other than an altogether weaker specimen than a male, displays equally typical nineteenth-century ideas and values regarding 'foreigners'. These are attitudes that are indefensible in the twenty-first century; but they were ingrained in earlier generations and their existence needs to be admitted for a full picture to be drawn. (I would note that while the Chinese in Sydney and the Aboriginals around Jimbour are mentioned – if disparagingly at times – by Charles in his memoir, no woman at all rates a mention; neither are women mentioned in more than the odd passing remark in Cuthbert Peek's diary. This is as it was. There is no point apologising for it now, but a lack of apology doesn't signify any kind of approval.)

In nineteenth-century imperial Britain, foreigners were there to be conquered and colonised, not to do the colonising. And they were not to be equated with the English in any way. So Charles can observe at first-hand the unwholesome and overcrowded living conditions of the Chinese emigrants in Sydney without apparently drawing any parallels with the position of the working classes in London of not so many years before (taking the generous view that things had much improved since the middle of the century) – the vast problem of unsanitary slums heaving with the poorest people of the city that his own London home was built to help alleviate – and he can interpret the situation wholly in terms of national failings (or indeed something altogether more sinister) in the Chinese and not in prejudice in the host country. There has to be some unspoken and worrying intent in the determination of the Chinese to huddle together – no suggestion that they might be greeted with hostility away from the protection of their own community.

However some – just a little – ambiguity enters Charles's description – as it does later when he writes about the Aboriginal people; 'remarkable for its quaint appearance' is not a negative response, and the danger to English trade comes from 'cabinet makers turning out most beautifully finished furniture at little more than half English prices'.

We are back on much safer ground with the proto-British institutions.

The Post Office is a magnificent building, quite as grand as that at Melbourne. A great feature of the Colonial Post Offices is that they are not merely places for the receiving and dispatch of letters, papers, etc., but they are made the great centres of general information. Here are displayed notices of the weather, arrivals and departures of shipping, summarys [sic] of important telegrams from all parts of the world, and an alphabetical list of unclaimed letters, telegrams, etc. This last is a feature of special importance to the traveller whose friends at home may have written him at some place where he is not to be found, and as he casually looks down the list and lights on his own name he often secures a welcome letter. The arrival of the English mail is always a time of great excitement. People flock into the town from many up country stations, and the vicinity of the post office is crowded.

The Sydney Observatory is splendidly situated on a headland projecting into the harbour, and is in fact surrounded by water on three sides. The view of the city and harbour from the top of the central tower is grand, a time ball is displayed here exactly as at Greenwich and being 213 feet above sea level is well within view of the docks and shipping.

The largest telescope here was a 11 1/3 achromatic Equatorially mounted by Schroder of Hamburg. This telescope stands under a dome of Muntz metal [a copper alloy, green in appearance] 22 feet in diameter, and though weighing more than two tons, rotates on five canon [sic] balls so easily that a good push sends it half a revolution.

Charles Grover's sketch of Sydney Observatory, 18 October 1882

There is also a 7 ½ inch achromatic equatorial by Merz under an 18 feet dome of Muntz metal, which revolves almost too easily for it is sometimes turned by the wind. The transit room contains a fine transit circle with 7 inch object glass by Troughton & Simms, with chronograph, sidereal clock etc. Mr. H.C. Russell, the government astronomer, was most obliging and showed us the action of a Polarising eyepiece on the Sun, with the 11 1/3 telescope stopped down to about 7 inches. The definition was most perfect, as I had found with similar eyepieces made at Browning years before. Mr. Russell is a many sided man and besides the astronomical work has organized a most extensive and complete weather service, and publishes elaborate annual reports on the Rainfall and Meteorology of the Colony. He has also done much in investigating Ocean Currents, a most important but little known branch of research. He gets bottles (prepared and weighted so as to sink vertically to the neck in water) thrown overboard from vessels in known positions. These bottles contain a card requesting the finder to post it at the nearest post office after writing on the date and place where found and his name and address. A small reward is then given. Some of these bottles have been picked up after 15 months immersion and travelling several thousand miles, and the collective results have shown the existence of permanent ocean currents in some cases reaching several miles per hour, a knowledge which is of the greatest importance to shipmasters and a possible explanation of the mysterious occasional losses of ships through getting set out of their correct course.

There is a workshop attached to the observatory in which have been constructed several simple equatorial mountings for 3 or 4 inch telescopes designed by Mr. Russell for use at the transit of Venus in 1874. These were now being improved and other apparatus made for use in the present transit of 1882. Electricity was much in use for controlling the driving clocks of the equatorials, chronographs, etc., and Solar Photography was carried on with a photoheliograph on the new model. This instrument was intended to be used at the approaching transit.

The meteorological work of Mr Russell in Sydney may have been a further inspiration – following Cuthbert Peeks' meteorological surveying in Iceland – behind the establishment of the meteorological station at Rousdon from which continuous measurements were taken over many years.

Charles was also occupied, during the week that the expedition members spent in Sydney, in supervising the landing of the transit equipment from the *Liguria* and its reloading onto the SS *Katoomba*, 'a small twin screw steamer of the Australian Steam Navigation Company', for the short voyage to Brisbane. While the gentlemen had been comfortably lodged ashore, in a letter to his father, dated 22 October 1882, Cuthbert Peek observes that 'Since we have been in Sydney [Grover] has been living on board but has now had to move to a Temperance Hotel as the ship has left dock.'

Charles Grover's sketch of Brisbane Observatory, 1 November 1882

The expedition left Sydney at 5.30 p.m. on 24 October and arrived in Brisbane at 8.15 p.m. on the 26th. Charles noted that 'at 6 pm on October 25th we passed the Solitary Islands with its lighthouse, and the next morning at 8 am we were opposite Point Danger with another lighthouse, above which tower the colossal crags of Mount Warning', then on the approach to Brisbane, arriving 'off Morton Island. Turning the north point of which we steamed across Moreton Bay, and on the western Horizon see the gigantic summits of the glass house mountains, although at a great distance these present a very remarkable appearance, two of them look exactly like a large & small pyramid and the other four make up a remarkable group.' Charles was impressed with the notion that all the geographical features and major landmarks of this short trip, together with the coastline, had been recorded 'with wonderful correctness' in Captain Cook's charts of 112 years previously. The day after the *Katoomba* anchored at Brisbane, the expedition's equipment was landed and put into the customs shed for storage while the party's destination was finalised.

Charles does not record any impressions of Brisbane at this stage in the journey, but he did manage a sketch of the observatory – looking very much a smaller relation of those in Melbourne and Sydney.

As Lieutenant Darwin observed on 28 October:

Here we are at last ... though we have not come to rest yet, and shall not do so until we have decided whether to fix our headquarters here, or up country ... On Monday we are going 100 miles inland to look at possible stations as almost everyone says we shall have finer weather there. We have been offered a very nice house according to report, but with no servants, and that is rather a difficulty here ...We shall have to manage it somehow between us if we go.

Jimbour and the Transit of Venus

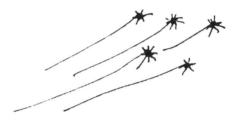

The name Jimbour – otherwise known as Jimba and Gimba – derived from the aboriginal word for good pastures. The first white man to explore the area was Alan Cunningham who is credited with the 'discovery' of the Darling Downs in 1827. He reported vast expanses of fertile countryside, at that time supporting a wide variety of grasses and wild flowers and providing habitats for varied colonies of wildlife; by 1842 a Scottish settler, Richard Todd Scougall, had applied for and received a licence to take up land beyond the presently settled area, and had established 11,000 sheep and around 700 head of cattle at Jimbour.

In the following year Scougall began to get into financial difficulties, which later resulted in his becoming bankrupt, and he sold the station on to Thomas Bell of Sydney. Bell was of Northern Irish descent and had come to Australia in charge of convicts. He had three sons and two daughters and had settled in the country in around 1829. The price that he paid for Jimbour – including all the stock – was £3200. Initially Bell left the management of the estate to Henry Dennis (who had sought out the land for Scougall), but after Dennis drowned in the sinking of the *Sovereign* in Moreton Bay in 1847 Bell took over the running of the estate, establishing a partnership consisting of himself and his sons.

In 1844 the explorer and natural scientist Ludwig Leichhardt stayed at Jimbour where he assembled his party of nine and organised the animals and supplies for his expedition to find a new route to Port Essington, near Darwin. On 1 October the party left, apparently full of enthusiasm for the adventure ahead: 'After having repaired some harness which had become broken by our refractory bullocks upsetting their loads and after my companions had completed their arrangements in which Mr Bell kindly assisted, we left Jimba and launched buoyant with hope into the wilderness.'

The nine men were accompanied by 17 horses and 16 bullocks, and the supplies included 550 kg of flour, 90 kg of sugar, 40 kg of tea and 10 kg of gelatine. Leichhardt does not seem to have been either an especially competent navigator or an inspiring leader. The 3000-mile journey took 15 months and by the time the remnants of the party arrived in Darwin they were exhausted. Two men turned back soon into the journey and a third was killed by Aborigines. The party was frequently lost and constantly short of food although they ate a wide variety of native creatures – including lizards and flying foxes. Once when they dropped and broke a bag of flour the men swept it up – dust, leaves and all – and made it into porridge. Nonetheless, Leichhardt and his party did arrive at their destination, and on the way they noted and named – among others – the Dawson, Mackenzie,

Isaacs, Suttor, Berdekin, Lynd and Mitchell rivers and the Expedition Range and the Peak Range. Leichhardt over-extended his skills when he attempted to cross the whole continent. An expedition started out in 1846 from the Darling Downs with the intention of reaching the Swan River in Western Australia, but was forced to turn back, defeated by heat and by the lack of water. A second expedition, consisting of Leichhardt and seven others, two of whom were Aborigines, which intended to travel from Brisbane (Moreton Bay) to Perth, set out in 1848 from a sheep station and were never heard of again. The party was ill-equipped because Leichhardt believed that they would be able to live off the countryside, and inadequately provided with horses.

Stories and legends abound as to the fate of the party: that they simply died of thirst, that they were caught in flash floods and drowned, or killed in bushfires. One tale has it that the party mutinied and murdered Leichhardt and that all but one of the remaining members of the expedition were killed by Aborigines; the survivor, Adolf Classen, it was believed, lived on and remained with the Aborigines.

Besides making the expeditions for which he is probably best known, Leichhardt collected numerous botanical specimens and aided in mapping the flora of the new nation, and his enthusiastic reports on the richness and the potential of the countryside beyond the Darling Downs drew large numbers of squatters to new stations in central and northern Queensland.

In the same year as Leichhardt set out for Port Essington the property at Jimbour was reduced in size – down to an area approximately 22 miles by 15 miles, of over 211,000 acres – and in a commissioner's report of 1845 the name is spelled 'Jimbour' for the first time.

A book on the history of Jimbour, written in 1955 by Charles Russell whose family owned the house from 1923, records that in the early days the sheep were on unfenced country, tended by shepherds housed in huts about four miles apart. Because of fears of the 'wild blacks', the more distant huts were each home to two shepherds and a 'hutkeeper'. Russell believed that 'it can be said that the blacks of this area were more sinned against than sinning' but,

> *In common with most of the natives of Queensland, the Downs blacks were cannibals, and no doubt some of the early pioneers and employees at Jimbour were afforded the opportunity of tasting human flesh ... slain enemies were eaten and, as a tribal custom, deceased members of the tribe were partaken of in order that their good qualities would be absorbed by their living kinsmen. The gins [an Aboriginal word for a woman, which later gained derogatory connotations] were allowed the scraps only, but, on occasions, when the men were away from the camp, an elderly gin was quietly tapped on the head and afterwards cooked and eaten by the sisterhood.*

Russell observes, without further comment, that 'in their natural state the blacks were, physically, a fine race of people, being free from disease and vice ... Contact with the whites brought a rapid deterioration in both health and habits and early in the [twentieth] century the last of the blacks disappeared from the Dalby district.'

The Aborigines were considered 'not conspicuous for bravery' but 'crafty', less inclined to organised attacks on the better protected homesteads, but a greater danger to those in isolated outposts: 'All over the Downs there are many nameless graves of their victims.'

When the Bells took over at Jimbour they lived in a wooden house that had been erected by Scougall and that had, in turn, replaced the original primitive hut built by Henry Dennis. In 1867 this house burned down and the family erected a two-storey house in stone and cedar in which they lived until the large house was completed. The work on this mansion began in 1874 and it took two years to complete, employing an army of builders and craftsmen: including all those involved in quarrying, cutting and transporting timber and handling other raw materials there were around 200 labourers employed in the basic construction, as well as around ten stone-masons and nine carpenters. Most of the raw materials were acquired locally – timber, stone and sand – and the lime was burned on-site from local limestone. The slates for the roof, in contrast, were imported from Wales. There are no extant plans of the site and some disagreement as to the chief architect of the project. Charles Russell writes that 'Many people think that the architect was F.D.G. Stanley of Brisbane, who was Colonial Architect from 1873 until 1880. He was the architect for the Queensland National Bank building at the corner of Queen and Creek Streets [Brisbane]. However, later evidence suggests that the architect was Joseph Warren, who was associated with Stanley in various construction projects.' It is also possible that the architect was 'Richard Suter, of the firm of Suter and Voysey. He was a prominent architect of his day, having designed major buildings on the Darling Downs ... as well as extensions for the Queensland Club of which Joshua Peter Bell served as President.' Thomas Bell died in 1874 and it was his son Joshua Peter who took over the management of the estate and was the prime mover of the construction of the new house.

The mansion had gas and water laid on; the gas was generated on the estate from locally-mined coal, and the water was pumped using the first windmill erected in Queensland. The construction cost £30,000, and there were 24 rooms, but, oddly, neither kitchen nor staff facilities were included. Instead these were situated in the old house, at some distance from the new one, which must always have been an inconvenient arrangement.

In 1881 Joshua Peter Bell formed the Darling Downs and Western Queensland Pastoral Company with other landowners. Bell's co-directors were Sir Thomas McIlwraith (who was then Premier of Queensland, having gained the position in 1879), J.C. Smyth and W.V. Ralston. Then, on 20 December 1881, Joshua Peter Bell died, quite suddenly and unexpectedly at the age of 54 in a cab on Queen Street in Brisbane. Early the following year his widow left for England in order for her children to complete their education, and the family did not return until 1889. Sir Arthur Palmer was appointed as General Manager of the company.

Subsequently the company ran into financial difficulties and by 1892 the whole estate was in the hands of the Queensland National Bank who now controlled the Darling Downs and Western Land Company. Lady Bell was given entitlement to live in the house for her lifetime. In 1908 the greater part of the land was acquired by the Crown, the bank retaining the house and 100 acres, which remained the home of the Bell family. The family's financial state worsening, Lady Bell moved to Brisbane, where she died in July 1912. Following her death a sale was held of all but the family's most prized possessions and the mansion was left bereft of its former grandeur. Two men, Mr Ryder and Mr Thomas, both with families, were the putative new owners of the house and intended each to occupy part of it, but they failed to complete the sale and ownership reverted to the bank. The next owner, a Mr Whippell, continued to neglect the house which was sold to Wilfred Adams Russell, father of Charles Russell, in 1923. At this time only a few ground floor rooms had been in occupation and the whole of the upper floor was closed off with a partition. It was the Russells who renovated the house and laid out the grounds. Jimbour is now listed with the Australian Heritage Commission and considered to be one of the finest houses in the country.

The transit of Venus expedition members therefore arrived at Jimbour during a state of transition for the mansion, with Joshua Peter Bell dead for less than a year, his wife and children returned to England, and the estate in the hands of the company that had been established only months before Bell died. There were still Aborigines living in the area and they co-existed in a slightly suspicious but generally reasonably harmonious relationship with the whites. According to Lieutenant Darwin's letter of 8 November the offer of Jimbour as a place to live and from which to observe the transit was made by Mr McIlwraith – 'a man I met in New Zealand, and travelled with him for two or three days; I liked him then, but when I saw him here I was rather disappointed' – although 'He did not tell us ... that Sir Arthur Palmer had more to do with the house than he (McIlwraith) had'.

Captain Morris and Darwin travelled up to Jimbour ahead of the rest of the party in order to check out the suitability of the establishment. They seem to have been accorded almost VIP treatment. Writing from Brisbane on 3 November, Darwin notes:

On Monday [30 October] Morris and myself started by rail up country in order to see if this place would do. We started at 6 am in a special train and found a nice breakfast waiting for us at a station 3 hours on the line ... After that we began to mount the range of hills which runs parallel to the coast all the way down to Melbourne, the same that we went up to at Sydney. Here they are not quite so rugged or high, but we got some beautiful views of great valleys of unbroken forest stretching away for miles. I rode most of the way in front of the engine, just above the cow-catcher; it is very jolly riding there, as one gets such a good view all round, and there is no dust.

*About 12.30 we got to the top of the range,
over 2000 ft I think, and stopped at a place
called Toowoomba for 2 hours to pay our
respects to the Governor, Sir Arthur Kennedy,
who lives the summer months there in a small
verandah-ed cottage. His household consists of
himself, his daughter and an A.D.C.; they were
all very courteous and civil; ... After leaving the
Governors we went on 3 more hours by train,
and got out at a little station, Macalister, in a
totally different class of country. Here we found
a 4 horse buggy to drive us 12 miles to Jimbour,
across a flat grass plain, the monotony being
only relieved by 4 gates in wire fences ...
Jimbour is a wonderfully well built house, one
of the best in the colony; in fact it was perfect
folly to waste so much money in such a
situation. It is just at the edge of some hilly
ground with open wood on it – where the two
sorts of country meet.*

Morris and Darwin returned to Brisbane on the
following day, and on 2 November the whole party
left for Jimbour. Charles Grover was responsible
for all Peek's equipment, which was removed from
the wharf in its cases on 1 November and taken to
the railway station in preparation for the journey.

*At 6 am next morning we left Brisbane. The
railway is a single line and after passing
through a good deal of scrub, with here and
there a little clearing and a settlers hut, it
begins the ascent of the mountains of the great
dividing range, making many a turn and curve,
and at times passing along a narrow shelf cut in
the rock with no protection whatever and you
can look out of the carriage windows down
precipices many hundred feet below, in other
parts the line crosses deep gullies on very
fragile looking wooden bridges, with the clouds
floating far below.*

Again they stopped at Toowoomba for lunch. This time it was Cuthbert Peek who had 'ridden the whole way up on the Buffer Beam in front of the engine and he said he never saw such magnificent scenery before'. Arriving in the late afternoon at Macalister station, the flat grass plain that Darwin found so monotonous Charles found 'a wonderful sight, almost as level as the sea and totally devoid of a bush or a tree, the eye can look round and see the clear circle of the horizon and the railway melts away in perspective, straight and level.' At Macalister Charles noted:

> *The whole establishment here consists of a woolshed, a small platform and station masters office, and of the wooden shanty in which that official lives, and he is the sole representative. Here we found five drays each with twelve horses for the transport of the expedition but it was too late to make any further advance that day. So Capt. Morris, Lieut. Darwin and Mr. Peek went on to Jimbour and I was left in charge of the instruments.*

Cuthbert Peek's letters home tell of his experiences of Jimbour – of this last stage of the journey he writes to his father on 5 November that 'We arranged to come in a four horse buggy while Grover and the gunner remained to look after the loading of the wagons' (an unusual mention of the all-but-forgotten assistant to Captain Morris and Lieutenant Darwin) – but Charles is expansive about life on the station in a way that he is not about life on board ship, and I think we can take it that he thoroughly enjoyed the place and the people, and that he was constantly fascinated by the country and by the natives about whom he writes somewhat ambiguously, sharing the general feeling of distrust towards them yet not unsympathetic to their situation, finding their way of life primitive and at times horrifyingly so while admiring their skills in surviving in inhospitable country. At Macalister:

After a refreshing nights sleep on a Tarpaulin wrapped up in a Blanket in the floor of the woolshed we were up by 5.30 am, and the Billy can being put on the fire and frying pan in requisition breakfast was the first thing, and to see these men put in a breakfast, a sackfull of loaves of bread, and nearly a quarter of a bullock from which steaks more than an inch thick were cut, about half a large loaf of bread and a vast steak washed down by copious cans of tea was each mans portion, no wonder they looked strong and hard as giants. Then they loaded up the drays, which took a long time as there were no appliances here for handling heavy goods, and by the time the 60 horses were captured and harnessed it was 3.30 in the afternoon. Our road lay straight across the great level plain, and so clear was the air that the great house and towers of Jimbour 12 miles away were quite distinct, but our destination was not so near as it looked. There was no road worthy of the name only a track on which the wheels of the heavily laden drays were often sinking a foot or 18 inches into the soft ground, so at sunset we halted, the Billy was again boiling, and as darkness came on and the fire lighted up the scene the transport train made a fine picture of Australian life. Again resuming our journey we came upon an object of great interest. There right on the great plain stood a large, new and valuable traction engine sunk into the soft ground over the middle of the wheels and the grass growing high around it. It appeared this fine engine, brought out from England at great expense was conveyed by the Railway to the Station and then the attempt was made to get it across the plain by its own stead. The soft ground proved too much for it and it got stogged [sic] and set where we now saw it with but little hopes of removal, no skilled engineers or powerful tackles being available to lift it from the spongy bed into which it was gradually sinking deeper as time went on. Leaving this behind we plodded on and at 1 am on Saturday November 4th reached Jimbour. Of course all the Station was aroused, there was a great commotion as the drays were drawn into the enclosure, the weary teams unharnessed and left to graze whilst we got a few hours sleep.

Charles Grover's sketch of Jimbour, 1 December 1882

Charles was enormously impressed by Jimbour – the house, the location, the sheer scale of the whole venture – but not all the party were as easily satisfied. Darwin noted on 8 November that McIlwraith's only answer to the question as to how the house was provided with the things that the party would need was 'that there was plenty of everything, and now we find there is plenty of beef and of nothing else; not enough sheets, tablecloths, towels, kitchen things; not much milk, butter, poultry; no mutton yet with thousands of sheep on the estate'. Sir Arthur Palmer was at the house to welcome them:

> which seemed a useless civility when none of the ordinary appliances of life was given us. He and Morris plainly disliked one another cordially, after a very short time; and he gave us all the idea that he wished he had not come. Whether Macilwraithe [sic] offered us the house without consulting him, or what the state of the case is we cannot imagine; but here we are and here we must remain, as we could not live anywhere else in the neighbourhood. From astronomical grounds I am sure we have done right in coming here, but from all other I would sooner be in Brisbane ... Sir Arthur Palmer and Mr. Mcilwraithe [sic] married sisters – if that is any clue to the mystery.

The Lieutenant referred to McIlwraith as 'rather a rough Scotsman' and to Palmer as 'a disagreeable old bear'. He also conceded on 3 November that: 'I see I have been abusing the only people I have written about, and this makes me wonder, as I have done several times today, whether my temper is getting bad too. But Mr Peek, who is as fat and good tempered as any man I know, feels just as much as I do about Morris and about this old wretch [Palmer].' On 3 December, recalling a later visit 'Sir Arthur Palmer ... was as pleasant as he could be. I hear, indirectly, that he is furious with Morris, and that was why he was so unpleasant when he was up here first; the origin of the ill feeling is a long story, about our Marine Artillery man, in which both Sir Arthur, and Morris, were in the wrong as far as I can make out.'

Mrs Darwin seems to have taken on the management of the house for the duration of the party's stay, but even she could not compensate for its shortcomings as described to Darwin's mother in a letter of 12 November:

> *The house is a very pretentious building, being built of cut stone, but it is badly constructed in many ways, and does not hold many people; the rooms are enormous, and as they are meagrely furnished, they don't look at all comfortable ... In front of the house we look out over the great grass plain, fifteen or sixteen miles wide, over which we get a good view as the house is a little raised above the level ... At the back of the house the country is covered with gum trees scattered about like an open orchard; this blocks out any distant view ... One always wants to know what is beyond the quarter of a mile which one sees through the trees, and the knowledge that this sort of country goes on for miles makes very little difference in the wish.*

The transit party at Jimbour. From left: Cuthbert Peek, Charles Grover (standing), Lieutenant Darwin (?), Gunner Bailey (standing), Captain Morris (?)

But not everything is negative:

The big bedroom in which Miss Morris and Miss Porter sleep, is about twice the size of the drawing room at home, with about as much furniture as would go in any of the bedrooms at home; the size has the advantage in that we can play badminton in it very comfortable [sic]; we had some good games yesterday, the ladies coming out in garments which certainly would not bear any further reduction ... in the evening light there is something very picturesque in this flat outlook, which I am surprised at.

The party at Jimbour. Standing from left: Cuthbert Peek, Leonard Darwin (?), Elizabeth Darwin (?), Captain Morris (?). Seated are Miss Morris, Miss Porter and probably Mrs Hume, the wife of the photographer, but it is unclear which is which

To Charles, 'Jimbour is a most important Government Station, on an elevation overlooking the great plain of the Darling Downs. The House one of the finest in Queensland, built of stone, with a colonnade in front supported by lofty pillars, and with fine gardens enclosed by a low stone wall. Being unoccupied at this time it was placed at the disposal of the British Transit of Venus expedition so we were very fortunate.'

Morris and Darwin, aided by the Marine Artilleryman, Gunner Bailey, and Peek and Charles began the erection of their portable observatories for the transit. The latter had a simpler job (and one can't help thinking probably also worked better together) than the official expedition members, and the hut and the telescope were both put up and fully functioning by the night of 6 November. Charles was 'pleased to find everything in perfect order, not a screw missing, and the clock and mechanism generally works as smoothly and accurately as in England'.

With Capt. Morris and Lieut. Darwin the case was very different. They had to put up a solid pier for a transit instrument and put up the Hut to cover it, to erect a sidereal clock, and to put up a 6 in equatorial, and a portable house for it. The Station was connected by telegraph to the Sydney Observatory, and the clock beats to the Standard Sidereal Clock there could be heard distinctly at Jimbour. They worked hard taking transits and exchanging signals so as to fix the position of the observing station with all possible accuracy. Needless to say this was a class [of] work which rendered interruptions by curious visitors impossible, so Mr. Peek was essentially the popular representative of science. Several newspaper men came, in among them the reporter for the 'Dalby Herald' for which I wrote a long article, giving a simple account of the phenomena [sic] of a Transit of Venus, and describing the Instruments and preparations of this expedition.

By 12 November, Lieutenant Darwin could write that 'We have had hard work so far in getting all the instruments up and in their huts, but now the bulk of that is done. We have to do a certain amount of observing every night, but when we are used to it I don't think it will take us very long.' He too mentions the press: on 27 November 'I heard the other day that we have a very bad reputation with the newspaper people: they think that we are proud and stiff, and none of them come near us. I suppose some of them have been to Morris, and have got snubbed, but don't know. I thought it better to propitiate them and have sent a little account of our doings.' It is a newspaper article – probably the one sent by Leonard Darwin – that describes 'four small wood and canvas huts ... three of these contain the equatorial telescopes, through which the three observers will watch'.

Lieutenant Darwin (observing) and Gunner Bailey in the portable observatory at Jimbour

Cuthbert Peek observing from the portable observatory at Jimbour; Charles Grover assisting

Cuthbert Peek and Charles Grover meanwhile occupied themselves with observations and in entertaining the people who came in from outlying areas to see what was going on.

We soon had striking proof of the purity of the air at this place over 1000 feet above sea level, and it proved an ideal place for observation, only two cloudy nights occurring during the six weeks we were here, which were occupied with observations of a large number of Double Stars, Nebulae and Clusters and especially of the nebula surrounding η Argus on which Mr. Peek published an interesting memoir on his return to England in August 1883. The planets Jupiter and Saturn were also much observed. Saturn in particular was seen with wonderful distinctness and it is not too much to say that all that is shown of this planet on the beautiful plates of De La Rue, the drawings of the late W.R.

Dawes, or the figures of the Washington observers with their great telescope were well seen with this instrument.

The arrival of the expedition at Jimbour caused a great sensation and people began to come in from all the country round to see the wonders of science, and as Mr. Peeks telescope was all in order and at work it was the centre of interest. At last visitors were so numerous that Mr. Peek arranged to have the observatory open for an hour or so after sunset, and crowds came to see the telescope and its mechanism by day and at night to gaze with wonder at Jupiter and Saturn and other celestial wonders. We used to shut up early and get a few hours in bed before midnight, when we began the regular work and kept on till the approach of daylight put an end to observations.

After weeks of sunshine and clear skies the observers' luck ran out. In Charles's words:

As the date for the transit of Venus drew near and the observations would have to be made when the Sun had risen but a few degrees above the horizon, we observed the Sun soon after rising on December 3, 4, 5 and 6th. The boiling of the limb and distortion was so bad that a solar spot that was on the disc was hardly visible, when an altitude of 6° was reached definition was better, and by the time 13° was attained a fair limb could be seen with 150, the power intended to be employed for the transit. Venus was observed at the same times without difficulty though getting very near the Sun, the crescent was very narrow and the horns extended like a silver thread nearly two-thirds round the planet, which of course now appeared at its largest possible diameter 66"5.

On December 6th after a fine morning clouds came on, with heavy rain, and on the morning of December 7th not a glimpse of the Sun or the transit of Venus was visible. Telegrams were received telling of similar bad weather at Brisbane and Sydney, while at Melbourne, Hobart and New Zealand the weather was fine. The day wound up with the heaviest thunderstorm I ever saw. Soon after sunset it became so dark, that objects even close at hand were quite invisible except when it lightened, when every tree leaf and detail was beautifully seen. The thunder was tremendous and the rain a perfect deluge, everything moveable was soon afloat. With the usual tantalising luck of astronomy the next morning was beautifully clear and bright.

And Lieutenant Darwin, on 10 December, whose letter implies that this expedition was his second attempt to see a transit of Venus:

We had four bright mornings before the Transit, and were up at 5 o'clock every morning to get everything right. Bee had been practising for many days counting aloud from the chronometer, and we had arranged the seat very nicely so that I could look through the telescope, be quite close to the chronometer, and that Bee could stand up the other side of it, and count aloud, or do anything that I might want. The weather seemed to have cleared up a little so that I managed to get observations of stars the night before. We got up at four, and found a dull curtain of clouds over everything; but went on making preparations just as if it was going to be fine for certain. We thought the sun might clear away the clouds, but when our final preparations were made, we became very hopeless. At 6.10 we were all sitting at our telescopes carefully pointed at where the sun ought to be, but the clouds were as thick as ever when we came out to tell each other that it was all over. It feels much flatter and duller than I expected it would; we have nothing to show for all these weeks of work ... there are few people

*who have been twice round the world to see a
thing without seeing it.*

The *Queensland News*, 'from our own
correspondents, Toowoomba, 7 December': 'In
consequence of cloudy weather and rain this
morning, the transit of Venus was not visible.
Heavy rain fell this afternoon.'

Natives and other Observations

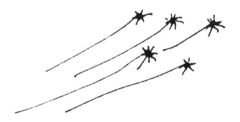

Aside from the central business of setting up the observatory for the transit of Venus, making observations and entertaining the public, there was time for Charles to see something of the life of both settlers and natives around the station at Jimbour. His attitude towards the Aboriginals is – as has been noted before – essentially that of a man of his time, but there is some ambivalence in his writing. There are skills that he much admires in the Aborigine, and on occasion he speaks to people and listens to their points of view. There is obviously much telling of tales and sharing of anecdotes, apocryphal and otherwise – perhaps around camp fires, perhaps watching the stars of the southern skies come up over the long veranda of Jimbour – of the devastation to lives and livelihoods caused by fire and drought, of the dangers of the outback, of the hazards of travelling with natives and the fears of travelling the unknown country without them. Charles has to find a point of equilibrium between the exploitation and maltreatment of the natives by early settlers, and what he and his time perceive as the blacks' own godless, primitive way of life; between the courage of the settlers exploring a new land and their own fears of the native peoples, the hostility and suspicion shared by native and settler of one another as the unknown. This is a part of his adventure that is included at length in his autobiographical fragment – in fact it brings the autobiography to a close – and is best told mainly in his own words.

The natives soon began to come in [to see the travellers as well as the observatories and the telescopes] and we had a good opportunity of seeing at close quarters what the native aboriginal of Australia was like, without a doubt they are nearly the lowest type of the human family. In their natural condition they wear little or no clothing, and never build a hut to live in, their only shelter is a few slabs of bark propped up by sticks, back to the wind.

These shelters – or 'gunyas' – were also remarked upon by Cuthbert Peek in his letters home: 'for tents they merely take the bark off a gum tree and put it up to windward, and when they leave the camp throw it down and leave it till they or some others come back again'.

they live on all sorts of the smaller wild animals which they very cleverly kill with the throwing stick or boomerang, we used to see whole families on the march. The man always walked ahead carrying his spear, axe, knife etc. The woman followed behind carrying a pot or kettle, a bag full of sundries and generally a baby was slung at her back. The rest of the children followed, always walking in single file. When they reached a spot where the man intended to halt or camp for the night, he would give a grunt, stop, and throw his spear etc. on the ground and then squat on his heels. The woman also put down her burdens, the children collected wood and a fire was soon burning, from the bag was produced generally an opossum, or some small animal which was put on the fire, skin, hair and all, and when it was well scorched outside, but barely warmed through the man took it up pulled it to pieces devoured the best parts himself, and threw the wife and children the rest, and they fed just like so many dogs, and then laid down to sleep. There are a few of them a little more enlightened, but they are fast dying out before the advancing white man and civilisation.

Aboriginal gunyas at Jimbour, around 1882

They used to bring in for sale nullah-nullahs [a kind of club with the handle end sharpened for digging, occasionally decorated with carving], spears, shields, boomerangs, opossum skins, native bearskins and many other things for sale and exchange for food etc., their notions of money were peculiar, a two shilling piece did not afford anything like so much satisfaction as four sixpences or eight threepenny pieces. I got into conversation with several of them to find out what ideas they had of things. A poor native woman called Mary used to help the cook and she told me in very broken English, 'You have no right here, this was our fathers hunting ground, where we did always hunt and fish, and you have no right to come and take away our country.' She evidently deeply felt the cruelties which had in former times been inflicted on her helpless race when they were wantonly shot down for sport just like so many rabbits, of which we heard many tales during our stay. Some of the old men handed down the tale of their wonder when the first sailing ships came up the Brisbane River. In those days vessels had to be well armed and a boats crew could only land with caution or they would have been certainly killed and eaten. The natives assembled in thousands shouting 'Chookie, Chookie' meaning Bird, Bird, they thought the ship was some monstrous sea-bird, and the sails were its wings. They surrounded it in their canoes till matters looked so threatening that the crew had to fire on them, at the report of the cannon and seeing the slaughter made, they put their fingers in their ears and fled, shouting, Devil, Devil, and their aversion to ships survives to this day.

One night a middle aged native man was brought into the observatory and Mr. Peek tried to get him to look at the moon through the telescope, he had to be held on the observing chair almost by force, and at a glance at the moon, uttered a loud yell of Devil Devil, broke away, and rushed off and never came near the telescope again. He was evidently thoroughly frightened.

Their senses of sight and smell are wonderfully keen and when marching through the bush they notice the most minute things, a little bent branch of a tree, a broken twig, a faint footmark of man or animal, all is observed and they can truly tell if man or animal have been that way and about how long before. If on the march with friends following they will let them know the route by breaking off the branch of a tree and laying it with the broken end pointing in the direction they have gone. This is done about every half mile, and the trail is rarely missed. I tried to find out their notions of a supreme being but they are very vague. They talked of the great Spirit, big fellow, strong fellow, and such like, but of religious ideas they had little or none. They had no marriage ceremonies but each man owned a gin or female who was more of a slave or a drudge than anything else, and for whom I never saw them show the slightest sympathy under any accidental hurt or illness.

A tribe of natives was encamped a short distance from the station. The chief named 'Cannon' was distinguished by a brass plate, suspended by a chain round his neck engraved in large letters 'King Cannon' of which he was very proud. He was an old man of great size, with a profusion of tangled hair, and seemed to rule his tribe with great severity. He was known to always carry poison, with which he did [not] scruple to quiet those who were in his way, but the day of vengeance came, and in a tribal fight, he was speared through the lungs and ripped open. Strange to say he was still alive and was carried on men's backs a days journey back to the camp, where he died on November 20th and the night was made hideous by the women, who chopped and hacked themselves in the most dreadful manner, and howled and cried for their departed chief.

They bury their dead with a post stuck in the ground, the foot of the post being close to the head of the corpse. Tobacco and a pipe is placed here so that when they awake they may solace themselves with a pipe, about half way up some money is deposited, while on the top some more tobacco and matches are placed so that they may start comfortable on their new career. Thus they show their belief in resurrection, and they believe the way to heaven is from the top of the Glass-House mountains, and they imagine a vine is let down from above on which the souls of the departed ascend to the celestial regions, which they fancy as affording fine hunting grounds and swarming with kangaroo.

During our stay on this elevated plain we found it very warm part of the time this being the Australian summer. Temperatures of 95° in the shade were common, and for a week together the solar maximum rose to 140° every day, and twice 160° was registered. The ground swarmed with Lizards, Snakes, Centipedes, Scorpions etc, and one day Mr. Peek shot a large brown snake over 6 feet in length, and the iron fence in the middle of the days was too hot to bear the hand on. We could well believe the tales we heard about bush fires, for everything was like dry hot tinder and a great fire would have started from a mere spark. We saw several large flocks of sheep on the Downs, one day 25000 were crossing the great plain, the heat was intense and several fell down panting and exhausted, while the birds of prey hovered over them waiting for the end as nothing could be done for them. The long droughts are the much dreaded scourge of the Australian Settler, and many tales were told us of rich squatters, owners of immense numbers of Cattle or Sheep who in a few short months or even weeks have lost everything. To provide better for the cattle wind engines are now being put up, and the tall triangular lattice frames carrying wheels of 12 and 20 feet in diameter are now familiar features of the landscape. They are very rarely still even in very light winds and are continually pumping water into a large concrete tank at the base of the tower. They require but little attention but where a considerable number are scattered over a wide district, a repairing gang is kept, usually four men with a waggon and team to carry the necessary tools and spare parts, a team of horses and a tent, with supplies of food etc. It is a rough and hardy life but they were a jolly lot of men and they came to Jimbour several times for supplies and outfit. It was quite a sight to see the Drays loaded up for a long journey into the interior, the Heavy goods were in the Bottom, then came on Sacks of flour, Bags of Sugar, a chest of Tea, Salt & Pepper, Matches, Spades, Crowbars, Screwjack, all that had to be remembered even to spare boots as they expected to be gone two months. Needless to say rifles and ammunition were included as they often depended on animals and birds for food. There were no roads, only a trail or track generally from one water hole to another, and the end of a days journey is managed whenever possible close to water, sometimes the track goes through miles of gum scrub where every tree is so like its neighbour that all notion of direction is lost and I used to smile at the tales of getting lost in the bush till it was brought home to me in a very simple manner.

I was out with Mr. Peek and a shooting party one day, and an old bushman promised to show them some snakes. We had not gone more than two miles before on turning over a slab of bark a perfect monster of a snake was disturbed, fully 8 foot long and as large as a mans leg, he soon showed fight, but a shot from Mr. Peeks rifle broke his back, in its dying struggles it lashed the ground with such force as to send a cloud of sand, stick and grass flying round and *was altogether a formidable looking reptile. The next day Jennings the Overseer of the station took me to see the dead Snake, and dragged it to near an Anthill, telling me that in a few days time the ants would completely clear out the inside leaving the skin intact, with the skeleton clear within. So a few days later I thought I would go out and find the snake which I thought quite easy to do as I had noted its position. I walked on about the distance as I judged but no snake could I see and after wandering around some time I started to return but soon found I had lost my bearings, so before I got too far away I gave a few loud Cooes the well known Australian bush call which I soon heard faintly answered and guided by the sound I soon reached the station, the old man smiled and said so you could not find the snake, now I will show you and he went straight to it at once. One has only to read the history of some of the early exploring expeditions to realize the horror of being hundreds of miles from any settlement, with provisions gone and no water and so being left to die of hunger or thirst. One of these men told me he was on the trail once with no food left but a little tea & sugar, and only three matches. When they halted at night a solemn council was held as to whether they should use one match that night or make shift without any tea as they were quite four days distant from any camp, and the last match was used the night before they got in. Here was clearly a case in which the native has the advantage for they can always produce fire quickly by the well known friction of two sticks or pieces of wood. These men evidently had no natives with them.*

When a party of white men are on the trail accompanied by natives, it is a wise rule to always make them march in front, not only as guides to show the way, but simply because you must never trust them to come behind you. Their nature is so debased, and they have little or no

*preception [sic] of right or wrong, they only
think of the strongest. Therefore the sight of a
gold chain, or a brass button, or silver
ornaments, and particularly a gun, knife or axe,
quickly excites the craving for possession and if
the owner is careless of his safety or is caught
alone or from behind, there is a sudden blow,
swift and sure and all is over. When several
white men are travelling with a number of
natives if prudent the whites never all sleep at
once, one at least is always on the watch, and
even then so noiseless and catlike are the steps
of the native, that the watcher can be struck
down in a moment. There is no doubt that
cannibalism was frequent among the natives
from time immemorial, and certainly some of
the earlier settlers fell victims to this custom.*

At this point in the script there is a digression –
'When I returned to England in 1883, and
mentioned the hideously debased animal instincts
of the Australian aborigines, my accounts of what I
had seen were received with considerable doubt,
but this extract from Pulman's Weekly News of
April 5. 1910 is complete corroboration, for
although this refers to a black boy there is no doubt
many a white man has fallen a victim to this lust for
human flesh, and women and children are an
especially tempting delicacy.'

*That cannibalism is still occasionally indulged
in by the aboriginal tribes of the Northern
Territory of Australia is generally accepted
among the white inhabitants of the country. A
trader named McPherson claims to have been
an eye-witness of a gruesome incident during a
recent trip down the coast. He states that while
trepang fishing at Rolling Bay, one of his crew
came off to the lugger with the news that a sick
boy had died, and that the body was being
roasted preparatory to a feast. He did not
believe the story, but to satisfy himself went*

ashore and visited the camp. Here he witnessed with his own eyes the roasted body being dismembered and eaten as calmly as if it had been that of a kangaroo. Why the natives should indulge in so horrible a practice in a region abounding with fish, flesh and fowl is a mystery. Mr. McPherson ascribes it to ingrained laziness rather than to any unnatural craving for human flesh. He is of opinion that the natives preferred to eat the food thus provided to their hand rather than go to the small trouble of spearing a few fish or a kangaroo.

Charles Grover's autobiography continues in somewhat melodramatic vein. But in spite of the horror stories that they shared, the settlers seem to have acted comparatively confidently – perhaps because that was the way that they felt; that the horrific possibilities that enlivened camp fire tales and sent shivers down the spines of visitors were hardly representative of everyday experience. It is also worth remembering that the newspaper report above refers to events following a natural death within the tribe; and that it is, effectively, based on a single claim.

The sight of a lonely white man, or of a white man with a woman and children, unarmed, and surrounded by a large number of natives is sure to arouse this instinct of the mere animal nature. And the carelessness of some settlers almost tempts disaster. I met a very intelligent man employed in the gardens at Jimbour, who owned a selection about 12 miles away. He had made a clearing and put up a wooden shanty, on four stout corner posts, the floor being about 1 foot above the ground. Here lived his wife and two children all alone from Monday morning to Saturday evening, as he went home every Saturday and returned on the Monday. She suffered agonies of fear, as the natives sometimes came up and looked at her through the window with hideous grins, and she rarely moved from the door of her hut while her husband was away, and every night well fastened up the Door and Window before she trusted herself to a little unrefreshing sleep, as she often heard the natives prowling around. One day to her horror the head of a large snake pushed up through a hole in the rough floor. She struck at it with a stick, and then set a Box filled with anything handy on the hole, and never opened the door again until her husband's return, when the snake was hunted out and shot. On Saturday afternoon about the time for the husbands return, she would say to the elder child 'now run along and meet daddy' and the little child knowing no fear would run along where the mother dared not go, though she never trusted it far out of sight for fear of its being lost in the bush, but the man was hoping for better times when he should have saved enough to enable him to stay at home and plant and work his own selection.

Another Character I met with was an old shepherd, he lived in the centre of what was called the 'Seven Mile Paddock', this was a square 7 miles enclosed with a very slight wire fence. The Hut was very simple, two posts about 12 feet apart were joined by a cross beam about 7 foot high, and planks were simply leaned against this and fastened by a few nails, at the ground it was about 6 foot wide, and you could just stand upright along the centre, a few rough boards formed the floor. Here lived the man, with his wife and a cat. They saw the boundary rider once a week, and once a month a dray called with supplies. At one of the corners, on a post a canvas bag was nailed, the post rider passing once a week left letters if there were any, and once a year the shepherd went into the town, which meant the township of Dalby about 25 miles distant. The woman told me, once she

never saw another white woman's face for 15
months. What wonder after a long term of such
isolation if when they find themselves in a town
they indulge in a little spell of dissipation.

There was a small mixed school on the station
and the schoolmaster showed great interest in
astronomy & the telescope. His house was a
wooden building of two rooms, on the ground
floor (no upstairs). One was the bed room, the
other the living room. The cooking was done at
a temporary fireplace out of doors, and owing
to the rule shifting schoolmasters every three
years, the furniture was of the simplest, as the
next move might be hundreds of miles, and the
difficulties and cost of transport enormous. I
was always a welcome visitor to his house, there
were only two chairs, the best armchair of
course for the wife, and the husband occupied
the other. A long packing case about 6 foot long
was turned bottom up and covered by a few rugs
forming a rough shake down if a traveller had
to stay the night, and on this I generally sat
when we had a chat about home and the Old
Country as they called England.

This was a fine place for sport, and Mr. Peek
sometimes went out turkey shooting. A drive of
about 15 miles in the Buggy was so arranged as
to bring us near to water, and while the
gentlemen went along the banks of the creek for
a shot, we made preparations for dinner. A fire
was quickly made and our bushman soon sets
about making johnny Cakes about 7 in diameter
and ½ in thick which were baked on the Hot
coals, and the billy can being filled with the not
very clean water of the creek was set on to make
tea, bye and bye the Sportsmen returning from a
long ramble have got a splendid appetite to do
justice to some of the sweetest cakes and best
tea we ever had. After a smoke and a look
around the traps are collected and stowed in the
Buggy, and a careful note taken of the storms
we see travelling round the timber belt on the

horizon, where a bright streak of lightning and a long heavy growl of thunder makes us shape a course for home. As we ride over the plain we have a fine view of the Bunya Mountains, the long undulating outlines of which are seen sharp and clear against the sky. Occasionally obscured by passing thunderstorms. Very curious effects of refraction are sometimes seen. The long belt of trees on the horizon appears considerably elevated and the outlines of cumulus clouds are seen below them, sometimes a sheet of ground mist looks exactly like a large lake or the ocean, and some distant object on the Horizon might be taken for a sail, and I often noticed one or two wisps of clouds, exactly like the smoke of a distant steamer. The thunder gradually got nearer and we reached home in a pouring rain and having handed over the results of the days sport to the cook, we were quite ready for a good meal and a rest.

Mr. Peek wished to visit the Bunya Mountains, and as they lay a long days march from Jimbour, it would be a three days journey. So preparations were made, a dray was loaded up with provisions, a tent etc and several men with an old bushman named Thomson in charge set out one morning for the mountains. The gentlemen intending to follow the next day. For obvious reasons no spirits were included in the baggage, but as they were starting Mr. Peek gave old Thomson a bottle of whisky as a little solace on the journey. No sooner were they got outside the gates than the old man pulled out the bottle, drew the cork, and drank the entire contents at once, remarking with a wink, 'That is much better carried inside.' The next morning Capt. Morris, Lieut. Darwin and Mr. Peek followed, and were about three days, and returned with two large kangaroo tails hanging from the Saddle. These were handed over to the cook, who was horrified and disgusted having never seen such things before, however one of

the men skinned & cut them up, and the cook
was bound to confess the resulting soup was
excellent.

Charles's retrospective writing has this expedition
somewhat confused. Peek's letter to his father of 10
December 1882 notes that 'Morris leaves on
Wednesday to catch the Orient steamer while
Darwin & myself remain to make a trip to the Bunya
Mountains.' (This provides Cuthbert Peek with
further opportunity to add to his substantial
collection of things to send home: 'I am told that
there are some very fine woods to be got in the
mountains which hardly anyone knows anything
about. I am going to see a timber merchant who has
lived in the hills all his life and shall probably send
home some specimens large enough to make
furniture of, if they come up to the description and
the freight is not too high.') Peek describes the trip
in a letter to his mother dated 18 December 1882:

we had to climb about 800 feet almost on our
hands and knees. The Bunya range divides the
tropical from the sub-tropical vegetation and as
soon as we got to the top of the range we came
across palms and other tropical plants ... On the
way up we saw the first native dog, they do a
great deal of harm among the sheep and 2/6 is
paid for every tail brought in. In the forest we
came across a good many parrots and cockatoos
but did not skin any on account of the difficulty
of preserving them from weevil and white ant.
Some of the pidgeons [sic] are very beautiful,
the wonga is considered the best for food and we
managed to get several of them. We also noticed
a good many bronze winged pidgeons but could
not get any as they are very shy indeed. On our
way down we saw a large number of kangaroos
and the first wild emus. The emus were very
tame but are rapidly becoming extinct in this
part of the country as they are shot for their

skins and oil, the latter is supposed to be a perfect cure for rheumatism etc.

Lieutenant Darwin also recorded the expedition in a letter to his mother of 21 December:

We had been planning an expedition to the Bunya Mountains for the whole party; the weather kept unsettled ... and after waiting for a day or two we gave up the idea of the ladies going at all ... Peek and myself determined to have a couple of days in the mountains, and we had a very jolly trip ... We took a tent with us, and camped out in a beautiful little patch of open country close to the tops of the mountains, about 3000 ft above the sea. The first day was a long ride there – about 32 miles most of it very uninteresting through the bush. We took all day about it going very slow, and reached the camp at nightfall, meeting there a rough old sailor, whom we had sent on the day before with the pack horses. We lit a fire, boiled some meat in a bucket, stood round the fire after dark for a little and then turned in ...

The country round there consists of beautiful semi-tropical forests with occasional open patches of rich natural pasture, looking something like the glades in an English park. From the tops, there are beautiful distant views across the forest and plain for miles and miles. The bunya pines, which the natives come up once a year to eat, make the forest very beautiful; the trees are very tall and stand up separately above the general level of the top of the trees in the forest, and stop the level monotonous look that the woods generally have when seen from above. We sent a native, who came with us, up one of the Bunyas to gather the fruit ... they are very large, about the size of one's head, and each of the seeds about the size of a chestnut, and with something of the taste. We did not want the fruit, but wanted to see him climb up the bare stem. He had a small hatchet, and made a few little steps about an inch deep, and 4 feet one above the other, and with these he climbed up like a cat very slowly and deliberately, he did not take all his clothes off as they usually do, and this may have made him go slow, but they are never in a hurry ...

We stopped on the way home at an out of the way timber cutter's house for lunch, which they seemed to take pleasure in giving. She was a nice refined natured woman I should think – a Scotch-colonial; she amused me by noticing how very sunburnt my hands were, and asking if I should not find that awkward if I went among gentlefolk. I saw one of her sons mounting an almost unbroken horse; he first put on the saddle in the stock yard and then let the horse loose and let it gallop round and round the yard till it had had its kick out; he then caught hold of its ear and was on its back without the horse feeling it hardly ... On the way home we were lucky in seeing all the animals of the country; first a bush wallaby (a sort of kangaroo), then a native dog, then about a hundred kangaroo, and finished up close to home with 2 emus and an iguana or sort of lizard about 3 ft long.

Cuthbert Peek 'left word to have some [bunya fruit] sent home' as 'they will be ripe in about two months'. Charles Grover recalls a scientific discovery recounted to him by Peek, but which neither Peek nor Darwin note: 'Mr. Peek said the Bunya mountains were wonderful ... and near the summit of the range was the remains of a forest, which had flourished in long past ages. The trees had fallen, and petrified into solid stone, long sections, several feet in length lay on the ground in which the grain of the timber and the rings from the centre showing successive years growth were quite distinct, but owing to their enormous weight could not be moved, and he had to be content with some smaller fragments.' An earlier shooting party may have been the occasion of the presentation to the cook of the kangaroo tails, recounted by Cuthbert Peek in a letter of 26 November 1882, to his father: 'The other day I went out walabi [sic] and kangaroo shooting ... By the Mansfield Act the Colony gives 8d for every kangaroo scalp & 4d for every walabi scalp brought in; in addition the station gives 4d and 2d respectively, making it up to 1/- & 6d; on an average day a man can earn 20/- which makes it well worth while hunting them. A kangaroo is considered to eat as much as 2 ½ sheep.'

The trip to the Bunya Mountains took place a few days after the date for the transit of Venus and amidst the packing of equipment to be transported home, or at least as far as one of the cities to be sold off. Charles Grover writes that 'by Friday December 15 all the instruments were securely packed for the return journey but no transport to the railway station at Macalister was available as this was just the height of the Haymaking season here.'

So it was on December 20th that we left Jimbour, after a stay of about seven weeks, which I shall always remember with pleasure, everybody about the place was so very kind, and the scenery and situation so beautiful, The semi-tropical plants, Georgious [sic] butterflies and birds, were all so different to what one sees in England. The most splendid peaches were as common as apples, and huge bunches of grapes weighing from 4 to 6 lbs flourished in the open air requiring very little attention. The sunsets were especially beautiful as the sun slowly descended to the horizon, the clouds were lighted up with a splendour and wealth of colour simply indescribable, and as night creeps on the stars shine out of the deep blue sky with a splendour never seen in England. At the same time I must confess to a feeling of disappointment at the first sight of the much vaunted 'Southern Cross', the stars do not form a true cross, and though the three stars α, β and γ Crucis are plain enough, the star δ makes a very small fourth, and it is a very small and insignificant asterism compared to our widely extended and conspicuous Ursa Major, the Great Bear of the Northern Sky. Neither is there any bright star near the South pole like α Ursa Minor, the Pole Star of the Northern Sky, a star which is constantly being observed for all sorts of purposes connected with surveying, navigation and exact astronomy. The attraction of the Southern Heavens is the wonderful brilliance and structure of the Milky Way, and the vast array of Clusters and Nebulae of which nothing like it exists north of the equator, a very large number of these and also numerous double stars, were observed under the most favourable atmospheric conditions.

As we could not leave Brisbane till January 3rd 1883, there was ample time for a good look round, this is one of the youngest of the Australian towns, and considering the few years that have elapsed since the site was only wild scrub it has made wonderful progress. Queen Street is quite a fine thoroughfare with many fine shops and large business premises where I found everything to be bought as good and as reasonable as in London. It leads straight up to the river which is crossed by a fine iron bridge, a section of which swings open for the passage of shipping. It was at that time the only iron bridge of any size in the colony and was regarded as a wonder, every stranger being sure to be asked 'have you seen the iron bridge.' This became such a bore that the Captain of a little craft trading on the river painted on the Sail in large letters 'All well, have seen the Iron Bridge.' The Electric light was then just introduced and was first turned on on December 23rd. A band paraded Queen Street playing favourite English airs with uncommon vigour, and the number of people was something wonderful. They had flocked in from all the surrounding country and as this was regarded as Christmas eve money seemed particularly plentiful. The Church 'Sometimes called the Cathedral' is a good looking stone building exactly like an English church at home. It has no tower, but a large and massive timber frame carried a peal of 8 bells, and I never thought church bells sounded as beautiful as when I heard this peal on Christmas morning, and the day was ushered in by the chimes playing the well known 'Hark the Herald Angels Sing'. The church was well filled at morning service, evidently a wealthy and well to do congregation, and being the height of summer and very warm a decided contrast to Christmas at home. The ladies dresses, hats and jewellery were quite splendid, and with the abundant floral decorations of the church presented a very beautiful scene. A considerable number of natives came into the town, and I saw one man with a large brass plate suspended round his neck by a chain, with the inscription 'King George and Queen Helena' presented by Jas. Campbell. His majesty was holding his hat for coppers, and the Queen with one of the royal children in a bag at her back stood close by. Her majesty was rather short and better looking than most of the black ladies, but yet by no means handsome, and her hair looked as if a comb had never been invented. The Kings suit was very delapidated [sic], in fact the pair were dressed in a few old clothes they had had given them. Among the people here I met several from Jimbour. One man told me he was employed with two others on a border station, during a whole year only two travellers passed that way, they never saw the face of a woman, and for five months had neither letters nor newspapers, and I met many similar cases. It often happens that a man and his wife are settled in a lonely *station many miles from the nearest habitation and the effect of this isolation is very bad for the rising generation, the children grow up without a sight or knowledge of anything civilised, they are regular little bushmen and women, strong, hardy, and expert in all that relates to bush life. Many girls I saw could ride a horse, catch fish or shoot as well as the men, and never having known any of the refinements or luxuries of life they never miss them.*

When Charles Grover returned from Australia he drafted a short article, dated March 1883 – which is unfinished and was probably never published – in response to 'numerous enquiries respecting the Australian colonies, more especially as regards their suitability as a feild [sic] for emigration and a future home for the working classes of England'. Here he gives outline impressions of the cities that he visited, describes a few of his own experiences, and rates – as he sees them – the prospects that might meet a young emigrant.

The first impression of an Englishman landing at Melbourne cannot fail to be one of surprise, especially when we remember that on its site only 40 years ago only two wooden shanties were to be seen, now we find a large and popolous [sic] city, the streets are wide and straight and laid out at right angles to each other, and the Buildings occupied as banks and the larger Commercial establishments, Hotels, etc. are solidly built of stone, and of magnificent architecture and ornamented with beautifully executed statuary so that they would be an ornament even to London, whilst the profusion of articles of Luxury and Elegance is not to be beaten even in Regent Street itself. The governors House is situated on an eminence just out of the Town & close by is the observatory from the tower of which you can see over the whole city, with the spires of numerous churches, the fine dome of the Exhibition building, the Picture gallery & Museum and beyond all the fine expanse of Hobsons bay in which the largest vessels can anchor in safety.

Sydney, though much older cannot boast of the regularity so apparent in the streets of Melbourne, neither is it so extensive, it can however claim to house the finest harbour in the world, with such deep water that large vessels like the Liguria drawing 26 ft of water can draw close to the wharf to unload. This is of course an immense advantage, and the water is always alive with vessels coming & going to all parts of the world. Here too they have the steam tramway in successful operation, and here is the most magnificent and commodious public library I ever saw. The Art Museum is not large but the examples of painting & Sculpture have been judiciously selected, and there are two of the marble figures here executed by a Sydney Sculptor, which for elegance of figure and graceful expression I have never seen equalled.

Mention must also be made of the Botanic gardens here, which are charmingly situated on the shores of the bay, and filled with the most beautiful tropical plants and flowers most tastefully arranged, these at the time of my visit were in full splendour, and the winding walks displayed new charms of nature and art at every turn.

Brisbane is nothing like either Melbourne or Sydney – it is however a busy place, and Queen St. the principal thoroughfare can boast of some fine shops, and a good display of almost everything imaginable for sale but nearly all as in the other cities brought out from England – the streets are laid out at right angles, but the Houses are mostly wood and built with no attempt at regularity and it has altogether the appearance of a city of the future. Here and there stone buildings of considerable architectural pretensions and solidity of structure are being erected, and there is every indication that in the future this will be a large and popolous [sic] place.

I have thus briefly sketched these three principal places, as they are the general landing place of people from England and the first thing which impresses one is that though he is on the other side of the world he is not in a strange land, everything is English, the people are of your own country and Language, the shops exhibit just the same things as in London, the Railway station at Melbourne has a bookstall after the W.H. Smith style – and here and at Sydney and even Brisbane you hear the too familiar sounds of the eternal street organ droning out the old familiar ditties of home.

Besides these are the three best (in fact the only) cities of any size round this side of Australia and the likliest [sic] places for mechanics and tradesmen to find employment, and employers of labour from all the up country stations are always on the look out on the arrival of every ship, to secure the men they require, in the Vicinity of these cities much building is going on and many factories, Engineering establishments etc. employ a large number of hands, and I came across several new arrivals while at Brisbane who found employment directly they landed. Brick-layers, Stone Masons, Carpenters, Painters and particularly all round handy men get plenty of work and good pay and as living is cheap they can do very well.

A man can board and lodge for 18/- a week and lodging houses are in every street – this means a comfortable bed, a good meat breakfast, a substantial dinner, and a good meat tea, in fact food here is unlimited, meat being about 3d a pound – a whole half a sheep 5/- and so on.

There are however two bad things about Brisbane, the water supply is so managed or *rather mismanaged that the fluid is of a thick yellow colour, and so suggestive of being filled with living matter as to require a great effort to swallow, in fact it is dangerous to drink much water here at all – and no doubt this is one cause for the large consumption of Alcoholic liquors.*

The Sewage is just as badly looked after, no proper provision is made for the removal of offensive matter – and this must be called a dirty town. This is remarkable in the capital of a large colony like Queensland, but it is comparatively young yet and no doubt these things will right themselves in time.

It is but right to mention that living is not so cheap in Melbourne & Sydney, and it is the height of imprudence to land in either of these places without a fair supply of those good friends of all travellers, viz. the English Sovereign, as in case of not at once finding the employment required the unprovided stranger would soon find himself, to use a common phrase 'on his back' or in other words helpless, and obliged to take anything which might turn up, and thus lose the advantage of a fair start.

There is one important piece of advice I would give to those who might be thinking of leaving old England – if you are a man of middle age, with a wife and family – and are settled in a fair and permanent position at home – don't leave it, you are best off where you are, but for those thousands of rising youngsters in England with smart heads and young blood for which the old country cannot find fair Elbow room then I would say be off to the new world, don't mind hard work and roughing it and you can assume yourself a position and a degree of comfort by the time you arrive at middle age which you could never acquire at home.

To the agricultural classes Australia is a veritable land of Plenty, but things are on a very different scale to what they are at home –

instead of the enclosures of a few acres, we here see paddocks & [?] extending for many miles, and it is no uncommon thing to see a wire fence 20 miles in length and you may ride 60 miles round one station, while the flocks of sheep & Herds of Cattle & Horses are simply countless.

When an Emigrant of this class lands (we will say at Brisbane) the agents of some of these up country stations are generally there looking for hands and a man of any ability soon gets an engagement and perhaps finds himself booked for a station 600 or 700 miles up country, and now begins his new experiences. He soon finds that either no railway at all runs his way – or if it does it only takes him on a very little way towards his destination, and the great means of locomotion is the dray.

Now an Australian dray needs a special description for it has to perform quite a different class of work to the Vehicle of the same name in England, for whereas at home a few miles is the extent of the Journey, here they have to travel for months together, and carry everything required for it is only at very distant intervals that a town or a few huts are met with, and supplies are not to be depended on, so rations have to be taken on and sufficient Beef, Flour, Tea, and Sugar for the distance of the first station which may be a fortnights march are packed on, as well as blankets for a camp out and many other things.

The Brisbane Railway station being the terminus of the Southern & Western Railway of Queensland is a rather extensive and busy place and one feels quite at home with the life & movement to which you are accustomed at home, but when you come to the end of your railway Journey and find yourself deposited at some little up country station, you begin to open your eyes. The Station at Macalister to which I was consigned consisted of a little office about 12 foot square, a scanty shed for passengers, and goods shed situated in the middle of the great plain of the Darling Downs. Here the line is so straight and level that you can see it melt away in fine perspective for 12 miles either way, and besides the Station Masters House no other building is within that distance. That official and a boy are the Staff of the place, there is no porter, no Hotel, no place of refreshment, in fact not even a tree for miles over the vast plain, so you many guess ones feelings on finding yourself left along with your luggage at this lively spot. Perhaps by a lucky chance the dray is there to take you on or perhaps not – if it is there they will not make a start that day – for there are only two trains daily on this section of the line, and the train which leaves Brisbane at 6 a.m. does not reach Macalister till 3.30 p.m. So you have to camp for the night. If your people are there waiting for you, you are lucky for you are sure of a good meal, if not you are likely to go hungry to sleep for you are far away from any place of refreshment, and the utmost extent of the Station Masters civility will be to allow you to sleep on the floor of the wool shed – with a tarpaulin doubled up for a bed and a sack or an old blanket for covering. This was my accommodation the first night of my arrival, but as the draymen were there to convey our instruments I did not want for food such as it was ... and when their hunger was appeased we sat round the camp fire listening to their tales of bush life and adventures, till the stars glittered thick above us when having to be up early we turned in, and probably slept better & more sweetly on the hard floor than some do on a bed of down.

From Australia
to Rousdon

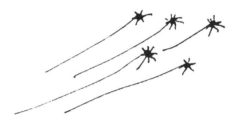

Although it seems an astonishingly risky thing for a
man in Charles Grover's position to have done, and
in spite of the fact that he appears, prior to 1882,
never to have been an especially adventurous
individual – doing well for himself through a
mixture of intelligence, good nature and perhaps a
judicious touch of subtle persistence – it seems
most likely that he signed on for the expedition to
Australia without there being any certainty as to
whether he would be employed at the end of it –
'being as I was comfortably placed with Mr.
Browning it needed a little thinking over ...
however ... I signed an agreement for the voyage in
July 1882'. His own unfinished article on the
prospects offered to men in Australia urges caution
on the middle aged with wives and families, and he
seems to have been fairly shocked by the hardships

endured by the settlers and in particular the sometimes fearful isolation in which women lived.

It is not known how Elizabeth lived between 12 August 1882, when the expedition left, and Charles's return at the end of February 1883. She may have been paid the greater part of Charles's remuneration as Cuthbert Peek's assistant – he would have had little use for money on the voyage and Peek would have met all the expenses of the travel in Australia. Their son George would have been with her in Wellington Buildings, aged 18, perhaps already teaching in some capacity, but certainly not earning a significant sum.

However, by the time the party reached Melbourne, Cuthbert Peek was writing to his uncle, the rector at Rousdon – 'I find the man I have with me a most useful fellow and if he is disengaged when I get back I shall begin to build a telescope; after a little practice it does not appear to be very difficult and will afford a good deal of amusement unless I am cured before' – and from Jimbour, on 12 November, he wrote to his mother: 'I find Grover a most invaluable man he seems able to turn his hand to anything and does not mind what he does to assist.' Because Charles Grover would be returning to England ahead of Cuthbert Peek it seems that Sir Henry Peek had to be assured of his usefulness and persuaded to formalise his future employment. On 10 December, again from Jimbour, Peek wrote 'As I said in my last I hope you will find something for Grover to do.' In a letter dated 3 January and written at Brisbane and marked, presumably indicating the date of its arrival, 'sent with Grover 5 March 1883', Peek writes to his father 'I have found Grover throughout the trip to be most useful and obliging. If you take him on his return you would find him ~~most useful~~ very handy in packing curios to send to Rousdon but he does not care what he turns his hand to. When I get back I want to learn from him how to build a telescope.'

Sir Henry Peek was plainly also conducting some investigation of his own into his and his son's current and prospective employee. He must have approached John Coles of the Royal Geographical Society – the man who had put Charles forward for the job of Cuthbert's assistant on the expedition – and Coles had shown him a letter that he had received from Charles, written from Jimbour on 9 November 1882. At the end of January 1883, Sir Henry asked to see the letter again. Charles writes, with evident enthusiasm and a real delight of the achievements of his side of the expedition, and in such a way of his employer as to melt the heart of any parent:

I have such pleasure in being able to tell you that after this long voyage we are very comfortably settled here and Mr. Peeks telescope is erected and adjusted and his observatory is in complete order – not a screw is missing – or damaged and even his delicate thermometers hang up here perfect. His telescope is put up and all in order several days before the others (for they are yet in a chaotic state) and the observatory is visited by all the people round – they come and admire the machinery of the telescope by day – and at night they wonder at the Views of Saturn and Jupiter, double stars and nebulae which are here seen in wonderful perfection.

Mr. Peeks observatory is evidently the most comfortable place on the expedition, and everybody comes here to see him and have a smoke and a chat, for we have two easy chairs and it is a regular drawing room – and what is more the people have seen through the other telescopes and the common verdict is that Mr. Peeks licks them all – so you will see we are alright.

Now a word as to myself. I can never sufficiently thank you for putting me on to this voyage. I have found that Mr. Peek is one of natures real gentlemen – and not one of the common order – I think we begin to understand

*one another now – and so far as my humble duty
goes I will do all that I possibly can to ensure
the success of this journey for he has shown me
an amount of consideration which I little
expected – what pleases me is that although we
have been here but 5 days Mr. Peeks is evidently
the leading place of the expedition, and attracts
an amount of consideration which quite eclipses
the others – we have quietly got everything in
the most beautiful order and adjustment and
can show our visitors anything whilst the others
are hopelessly struggling along behind.*

*I never forgot your latest instructions to take
good care Mr. Peek was first and it is done and
so far as we are concerned we are ready for the
transit tomorrow.*

Charles Grover embarked on the RMS *Merkara* on 3
January 1883 to begin his voyage home. The
Merkara was a ship of the British India Steamship
Company, and had been launched, together with her
sister ship *Dorunda*, in 1875. Like the *Liguria* the
Merkara was a steamship that also carried sails.
Because the ship was intended for trade in Far
Eastern waters where piracy remained a threat, it
was also fitted with guns.

On arrival in England Charles was to see to the
disembarkation of the transit equipment – with the
assistance of one of Sir Henry Peek's men – and to
call on Sir Henry in Eastcheap, presumably there to
hear what was to be offered him in terms of future
employment. It is hard to imagine that at this point
Cuthbert Peek had not been able to reassure
Charles to some degree as to permanent
employment with the family.

Cuthbert Peek accompanied Charles on the
Merkara as far as Townsville, between Mackay and
Cairns on the north-eastern coast of Queensland,
from where Peek was to set off for the remaining
part of his adventure into New Zealand. Lieutenant
Darwin was also on the *Merkara*, destined for
Singapore where he planned a stay of a few weeks

before returning to England, where, according to Cuthbert Peek, he had 'to join the Staff College at Aldershot in May'. Darwin wrote on 1 January that on 19 December

> *I was very busy finishing up everything, and they again made us feel rather uncomfortable in the grudging way in which they gave us wagons for our things. Mr. Wallace, the superintendent, is in many ways a good sort of man, but he has such an eye to business that as long as his hay was out he could not bear to let us have any horses or carts; luckily the hay was all in, and all the luggage was taken across the plain that day in two enormous wagon loads, with 10 horses to draw each. If there had been the least rain they would not have got there, and as it was some things were left behind; heavy rain followed and I don't know yet whether I shall get them in time to ship them on Wednesday 4th. We followed that day, rather glad to leave Jimbour, as in all directions 'relations had become somewhat strained'.*

As the *Merkara* made its way along the eastern seaboard of Queensland it took on cargo for the voyage to England. In a letter to his father, dated 6 January 1883, Cuthbert Peek wrote:

> *The wool trade is now in full swing, and this ship is taking home an ulmost full cargo of it. The noise of loading is almost deafening, at the present moment two steam winches are working just over my head and sometimes four are going at the same time ... I am sending home a lot of photos: taken at Jimbour please don't give many of them away as in the event of the negatives being broken in transit to England I could not get any more of them, the one with the telescope gives a very good idea of the observatory ... I expect that Grover will be home about the last day in February. The case of plants I am*

sending home by him seems to be very well packed and I have told him to follow the written instructions of the nurseryman. Several of the orchids are, I believe, new. He will call on you directly he lands but, as I said before, if Mr Gahen's agent were at the dock it might be of use.

There is little information on the voyage back on the *Merkara*, although Charles made a number of sketches that indicate that the ship took a route across the Indian Ocean, calling at Batavia before heading through the Suez Canal into the Mediterranean and on to England along the coast of Spain.

Charles was fortunate to have a clear run through the canal; on what must have been its next trip the *Merkara* ran into trouble of some kind. In early June of 1883, Cuthbert Peek wrote to his father: 'I see by the papers that the "Merkara" in which Grover returned has been in difficulties in the canal and that the Captain (Woods) is dead.'

On 20 May 1883, Cuthbert Peek wrote to his father from the Melbourne Club that 'I received a long letter from Grover in which he appears to be delighted with Rousdon and I think you will find him a most useful man in many ways ... The observatory [at Melbourne] is also very well managed and I have been going carefully over it in order to get some ideas as to what will be wanted at Rousdon.' A couple of weeks later, on 10 June 1883, he writes to his uncle, the rector of Rousdon: 'I suppose you have seen Grover ... He is a curious looking mortal but a very decent fellow.' Given the length of time that it would have taken the letter from Rousdon to reach Cuthbert Peek and even assuming that the writing of it would have been one of Charles's first acts on being settled in Rousdon, he must have made the move from London very soon after landing in London in March. It is also clear that Cuthbert is by this time thinking in definite terms of building an observatory, rather than the earlier suggestions that he might try and build a telescope.

Sketch made 9 January 1883 aboard the SS Merkara. Between Mackay and Brisbane. Curious wall-like rocks – arranged in a straight line – showing water marks on face – White Sunday Passage – E Coast of Queensland

We don't know whether before Cuthbert Peek returned from his own travels Charles Grover was, as his employer had suggested, kept busy with packing the artefacts from his travels to take down to the new house in Devon, but it seems likely. One of the roles that Charles was to undertake within the household at Rousdon was curator of the museum – and it was an extensive collection, even before Cuthbert's contributions.

One of Sir Cuthbert's children, Gwendolen Dalrymple-Hamilton (1890-1974), recalled the museum, which was split up and sold after the death of her brother Sir Wilfrid Peek in 1927. It was started by Sir Henry Peek in around 1876, soon after the construction of the house began. Sir Henry himself was not especially well travelled, rather he bought from an importing company, Messrs Jamrach, who specialised in oriental artefacts. There were brightly-coloured, life-sized figures from India, with arms upraised and of 'savage expression'; the entrance to the museum was 'guarded by 20 pikes, said to have been used at the Battle of Sedgemoor, but this was not substantiated'. To give an idea of the size of the collection, 'The walls of the Museum were covered by glass cases, about six feet high, containing many exhibits ... There were two which specially excited and interested the young, one portrayed in a very lifelike manner, the death by a thousand cuts, and the other of flagellation of soles of the feet'; and 'The centre of the Museum was occupied by waist-high exhibition cabinets, with drawers beneath them. These contained principally, the collection which Sir Cuthbert Peek made in New Zealand in 1883 ... The Maori wars had not long been over and European manufacturers had not been slow to imitate Maori implements. Sir Cuthbert Peek was luckily aware of this and all the green stone implements, stone and earthenware objects and a beautiful feather robe, were all guaranteed as genuine by New Zealand experts of the day.' Among treasures contained in a large safe were two wine cups set with turquoises that were supposed to turn green if wine in the gold-lined cups was laced with poison.

Where Cuthbert Peek's passion was for astronomy – hence the employment of his astronomical observer – Sir Henry's was collecting birds, for which purpose a taxidermist was among his permanent employees. His collection may have been the most complete in the country – at one time it was understood to include 301 of the 376 species of birds regarded as native to Britain at the end of the nineteenth century – certainly it was fairly comprehensive, including males and females in various stages of winter and summer plumage. Sir Wilfrid Peek added further to the general collection, introducing old and modern feather work from Mexico and multicoloured embroideries from Java.

The Peeks were a Devon family, Sir Henry Peek having formerly lived at Hazelwood in Kingsbridge, and the estate at Rousdon was acquired in the 1870s. In 1871 the population of the village of Rousdon was fourteen; soon these residents would be outnumbered by the establishment of the new estate. The site at Rousdon is magnificent, with sea views giving along the coast from Start Point to Portland Bill. Between the site of the mansion and the sea the gardens were carefully planted and landscaped to enhance the prospect. Whether or not any of the specimens or seeds that Cuthbert Peek had so carefully transported from Australia and New Zealand were transplanted or propagated in Devon with any success is unknown, but it is interesting to compare his ambitions with the achievements at Heligon – not so far away – where similar enthusiasm for plants from the other side of the world resulted in the jungle area of the now-transformed 'Lost Gardens'. The Rousdon estate – also like that of Heligon – was intended to be a self-sufficient enterprise. In 1891 the population of the estate was 58. There were farms, gardens and laundries, a gas works, and water works supplied by a pumping engine at the bottom of a hill. Sir Henry's philanthropic ideals dictated that the estate should be about pleasure as well as work, and the estate included a bowling alley, rifle range, archery lawn and tennis courts, as well, of course, as the beach.

Rousdon had had a chapel dedicated to St Pancras since the twelfth century. A document dated from *c.* 1155–57 records that Aldred (son of the founder of the chapel) had 'in the presence of his son (the incumbent) and the Bishop of Exeter, given St Pancras to the Abbey of Montebourg, in the Diocese of Coutances in Normandy'. It passed through the possession of the Abbey of Isleworth, the Crown, and down to the local gentry. A list of known rectors begins in 1279. It was a thatched building, simple in form, about 25 feet long and 13 feet wide and had fallen into disuse by the late eighteenth century. By the time that Sir Henry Peek bought the estate it was no more than a derelict farm building.

The new church of St Pancras was the first of the nineteenth-century estate buildings to be erected. Next came the school and the farm buildings, the stables and the lodges – three lodges at the points of the compass, north, west and east; the sea was to the south – and finally the house itself. In 1891 the school took about 62 children from the villages of Rousdon and neighbouring Combpyne and from outlying areas. It may have been the first school in the country to provide children with a hot meal – 'penny dinners' – at 5d per day for the first child in a family, 4d for the second and so on. Presumably it was a reasonable assumption that the larger the family the poorer the parents. A house was also provided for the schoolmaster. The school closed in 1939, and is now the Peek Hall.

The architect of the whole estate was Sir Ernest Green RA, who worked in partnership with a friend, Thomas Vaughan. In an article in *The Builder* in May 1921, 'An Architect's Reminiscences', Green recalled that Rousdon was 'the first work of importance'. In this same article he twice mentions Norman Shaw, which might give some kind of clue to the architecture that he admired and explain the eclectic architecture of Rousdon. For reasons that are not at all clear, the house is described in Kelly's directory for Devonshire of 1904 as 'in the Queen Anne style', but the exterior effect is more a kind of late-Victorian precursor of Arts and Crafts, with half-timbering, flint and dressed stone, a heavy entrance portico and mock-Tudor chimneys. The great hall is Jacobean in style, and there are a large tower and a small turret with conical roofs. There is one legend attached to the building: the white marble main staircase is rumoured to be made of Carrara marble retrieved from a ship wrecked on the beach below the estate.

Charles Grover lived in this benign community, in the East Lodge, from 1883 until his death in

1921. It was – and is – a pretty house, sharing the eclecticism of the architecture of the rest of the estate with again, half-timbering, and with the main upstairs window of leaded lights sheltered beneath a curved decorative plaster overhang. It was only a few years old, and by far the largest house in which he had ever lived – the newly-built two-bedroomed flat in London was probably the largest before the lodge – with a good-sized area of garden surrounded by an iron rail fence. By early 1884 a temporary observatory had been established in this garden, and throughout the same year the second-order meteorological station was assembled. The tower on which the anemometer and other instruments was placed was close to the temporary observatory, a short stroll from Charles's own door.

East Lodge, Rousdon, Devon. Charles Grover lived in the northern part of the house (here, on the left). Photograph probably from c. mid-1880s

The permanent observatory which replaced the early wooden structure at the start of 1885 was demolished in the mid-twentieth century, but the wooden shed is still in place, although very ramshackle. There is a separate panel evident on the roof of this structure – which luckily found a function as a garden shed – but no real evidence as to how this would have moved. It may simply have been a matter of climbing a few steps and lifting it free (an early photograph – below – shows what appears to be a flight of steps running up at one end of the building) or there may have been some kind of simple roller system that has long since gone.

The wind tower and the temporary transit observatory behind East Lodge. Towards the rear of the temporary observatory is the sliding portion of the roof. Photograph probably from c. mid-1880s.

It is possible that this structure is slightly displaced from its original position in order to forestall the problems of using a shed with a large concrete pillar sufficient to support a telescope mount in the middle of the floor, but if that is the case it is no more than a few feet distant.

Of the weather tower, like the permanent observatory, there is no trace. From 1 September 1883 Charles began making meteorological readings twice a day, every day, at 9 am and 9 pm. In the introduction to the *Meteorological Observations For the Year 1884, made under the superintendence of Cuthbert E. Peek, M.A., F.R. Met. Soc., F.R.A.S.* the instruments acquired and the dates at which they were brought into the observations are listed as follows.

On my return for the observation of the Transit of Venus, in Queensland, I resolved to establish a complete meteorological second order station, and procured from Mr. L.P. Casella the following Instruments:-

Standard Barometer, No. 1243, on the Kew principle, with Vernier reading to 0.002 inch, and attached Thermometer.

Pair of Maximum and Minimum Thermometers.

Pair of Wet and Dry Bulb Thermometers.

Symons' Snowdon Rain Gauge, 5 inches diameter, No. 6771.

Observations with these instruments taken twice daily at the usual hours, viz., 9 A.M. and 9 P.M., were commenced on September 1st, 1883.

The Thermometers at this period, were placed on a Glashier's Thermometer Screen, but before the end of the year I procured one of the Stevenson's Thermometer Screens, as last improved at the suggestion of the Council of the Royal Meteorological Society. This was placed in position on January 1st, 1884.

The Robinson's Anemometer No. 569 (also by Casella) has cups 3 inches in diameter, on 7 inch arms, and registers up to 505 miles; it was received in January, but as the Kew certificate showed rather large errors, it was sent back to the maker for adjustment, and afterwards to Kew Observatory for a new certificate, and was not received here till March; the wind velocity records therefore date from April 1st, 1884.

A sunshine recorder of the usual form, by Negretti and Zambra, is mounted 4 feet above the ground, the record commencing October 3rd, 1884.

A Kew Observatory Standard Thermometer, No. 598, is kept for reference, and the readings of the various thermometers are compared with it at stated intervals.

Great care has been taken to find a suitable position for these instruments. The barometer is placed in the sitting room of my assistant's cottage. The Thermometer Screen is at some distance North of the house, and the Earth Thermometers are planted at its foot. The Rain Gauge and Sunshine Recorders are close at hand, but well clear of all obstruction. The Anemometer is mounted on a pole, the cups being 30 foot above the ground, and in a fully exposed position

With regard to the routine of observations, it may be stated that the Rain Gauge and Earth Thermometers are read once daily, at 9 A.M. The Black Bulb Solar Radiation Thermometer is read, and the card of the Sunshine Recorder changed once daily, at 9 P.M. The remaining instruments are read twice daily, at 9 A.M. and 9 P.M.; at which hours are also noted the amount of cloud, direction of the wind, and the general weather characteristics of the time.

The Rousdon meteorological observations were published annually from 1884 at least until the death of Sir Cuthbert Peek in 1901. Whether publication continued into the twentieth century is uncertain, although there is little doubt that Charles would have continued to keep the records. In 1884 – perhaps in part because astronomical observations were hampered by the inadequacy of the temporary accommodation and the building of the permanent observatory – Charles took the time to make a comparison between weather forecasts and the actual weather experienced at Rousdon. From the point of view of south Devon the Meteorological Office forecasts were something of a misnomer, since they arrived by rail about 10.00 am in the morning after the day forecast. This enabled Charles to make his own observations entirely unconstrained by expectations. Once the observations were made his method was to draw them up in as near to the same form as possible to that of the Meteorological Office for the comparison. Total unreliability was unusual – at 16.6 per cent for the wind over the year, and 9 per cent for the weather – reliability was 61.6 per cent for wind, and 73.1 per cent for weather. Not, I suspect, all that different from the reliability of modern forecasts.

In the introduction to *Astronomical Observations 1882-5, Made Under the Superintendence of Cuthbert E. Peek, M.A., F.R.A.S.* (the observations are dated from 1882 because the publication opens with Cuthbert Peek's Australian observations of 'The Nebula Surrounding η Argus') the observatory and its equipment are described in detail.

As the building encounters the full force of the south and south-westerly gales which sweep the channel, it was necessary that it should be of a substantial character, a condition which is met by a construction of teak timber framing, filled in with cement concrete between the timbers, and resting on a base of stone with flint facing ...

The entrance is on the north side and opens into a convenient apartment on the west of the Dome, used as a Computing Room.

Beneath the Equatorial Dome is a circular chamber with no direct window light, and this forms the Photographic and Chemical Laboratory.

The observatory at Rousdon, built 1885, demolished mid-twentieth century

The Transit Room is to the east of the Dome, and is provided with the usual slit in the roof and opening on the south side, so that the meridian passage of all objects may be observed from the southern horizon, through the zenith, and to a considerable distance below the North Pole. The north and south shutters ... are worked by an arrangement of counterpoised levers, so adjusted that but little force is required to open and close them; they are found in practise [sic] to be perfectly water tight. The roof of both Transit and Computing Rooms are covered with lead.

A flight of steps from the Chemical Laboratory leads up to the Equatorial Room, a circular apartment, 16 feet in diameter, covered by a Dome constructed of sheet copper on iron ribs, furnished with a ring of rackwork and supported on 20 small grooved iron wheels, so that by a simple set of gearing, the Dome, though weighing nearly two tons, revolves with the utmost ease. A shutter, 1 foot 10 inches wide, opens from the horizon to a little beyond the zenith, and thus affords an uninterrupted view of any portion of the heavens. When the Dome was erected in the summer of 1884, I had reluctantly decided to paint it white on the outside, as a preventative of the intense heat which I feared would be felt under it during the summer; but in this I have been agreeably disappointed, as I find that on the hottest day [in 1884, 8 August, 79° Fahrenheit] the temperature of the interior never rises to any inconvenient extent. This is mainly due to the fact that the Dome is a few inches larger in diameter than the circular wall on which it rests, and so allows of a clear space of about two inches all round for free ventilation, it need hardly be said that this close equality of temperature greatly conduces to good telescopic definition. The copper plates are continued eight inches below the rail on which the Dome revolves, so as to prevent the insplashing of rain during heavy gales, and the experience of 18 months has completely proved its efficiency.

The transit instrument is by Troughton & Sims, and carries a telescope of two inches aperture and two feet focal length, the optical power suffices to take the passage of the brighter stars within one hour of noon, and is therefore ample for all rateing purposes. There are two direct vision and one diagonal eyepiece, with shades for Solar Transits, the usual vertical and horizontal adjustments, and a very sensitive striding level for the pivots.

The Setting Circle is five inches in diameter, divided on silver, with two verniers reading to 1' read by microscopes. The instrument is mounted on a stone pier, two feet square, the foundation of which is deeply laid in cement.

The Transit Instrument was installed in the new Observatory, January, 1885; it having been in use during nearly the whole year previous to this in a wooden building, which served as a temporary Observatory, a short distance north of its present position. A stout iron pillar about 10 inches diameter was firmly bedded in the earth to a depth of six feet and filled with cement, and on the top a slab of stone was bolted to carry the instrument, the floors being cut away round the pillar, and every care taken to ensure stability. Observations soon showed that the adjustments were continually changing, and both level and azimuth required constant correction. As time went on, the fact was surely established that the pillar had a daily movement by which it followed the sun from rising to setting. Thus, in the morning the western pivot would be high, at noon the axis was level, and toward sunset the eastern pivot would become highest, the level falling back to its normal position after sunset, so that the results of a series of transits during the evening would show a very fair agreement. These changes were greatest during the hot days of summer, and occurred with such regularity that it was almost possible to tell the hour of the day by the readings of the level. Under these conditions it was impossible that transit observations during the day could be of any value, and the result clearly shows that iron is of little use as a support for a transit instrument, and the stone pier was substituted.

There are two Chronometers by Dent. The Siderial, No. 226, is used for observations with the equatorial and general astronomical work, the other is a mean time chronometer, No.

2/24850, from which Greenwich mean time is given to the clocks of the parish.

A brick pillar, two feet square, built in cement, from a foundation deep below the floor of the Photographic Room, is carried up through the centre of that apartment to the Observing Room, under the Dome, and capped with a heavy slab of stone. On this is erected the Equatorial Telescope. [This is the same telescope that was taken to Australia for the observations of the transit, and it was used throughout the lifetime of Charles Grover at the Rousdon Observatory.] ... A very simple and well constructed clock movement carries the telescope with a motion so smooth and uniform that a star remains for a considerable time bisected by the micrometer wire, and by a regulating screw the rate can be at once made to coincide with Solar, Lunar, or Siderial time.

A set of five eye-pieces, giving powers of 64, 90, 136, 206 and 310, are those generally in use. There is a diagonal eye-tube for objects when at an inconvenient altitude, and a solar eye-tube for the study of sunspots, &c., with which all these powers are available. When higher powers are required they can be obtained by the use of a Barlow lens which furnishes a scale nearly double the above.

A very excellent Micrometer, by Hilger, has been recently brought into use. The Position Circle is divided on silver and furnished with two verniers; the micrometer screw head, also divided on silver, is furnished with a registering arrangement by which the number of complete revolutions is indicated. A considerable number of observations of star transits over the wires separated by given numbers of complete revolutions of the screw, have given very accordant values, also a series of measures of certain well-known double stars have shown by their agreement with the results of other

observers that the micrometer is a most
accurate and reliable instrument.

The contrivance for illuminating the wires, so
that they should appear as bright lines on a
dark ground, was very ingenious, and consisted
of a little bent vacuum tube, so placed between
the wires and the eye-piece, that when
illuminated by a coil and battery the wires were
clearly seen; when all was in good order this
arrangement left nothing to be desired, but I
found the electrical apparatus so uncertain in
action and so frequently out of adjustment, that
much valuable time was consumed in attending
to the coil and battery to the serious hindrance
of actual observation. I therefore procured
Cooke's usual Prismatic Illuminating Apparatus,
which I have applied to the telescope with
perfect success; with this arrangement the field
of view is illuminated, the wires appearing as
black lines on a bright ground. As a matter of
course the fainter stars are more or less
obliterated, according to the intensity of the
light employed. This, however, is brought
completely under control by a rotating
diaphragm pierced with a set of apertures of
different diameters, from 1/8 inch to 5/8 inch,
revolving over the opening which admits the
light into the body of the telescope. By this
means all superfluous light can be excluded, and
when faint objects are under examination, only
sufficient illumination is used to render the
wires clearly visible. A slide fitted with coloured
glasses allows the field to be changed to red,
white or blue, at pleasure, and I have found by
careful experiment that the definition of certain
stars is sensibly affected by the colour of light
employed in their measurement.

An observing chair is used with the
equatorial, which by a system of adjustable
seats enables observations to be made with
comfort on objects at any elevation from the
horizon to the zenith. A footboard can also be

placed where required, and there is a comfortable support for the back, as well as room for a chronometer and writing materials. The benefit of these arrangements is particularly felt during a prolonged scrutiny of the planets or micrometrical measures of double stars, in which a firm and easy position is almost essential to accurate observation.

So, slightly less than two years after Charles Grover's courageous decision to throw in his lot with Cuthbert Peek and cross the world to see the transit of Venus, Charles and Elizabeth Grover were established, with their son George, in a near-model community in a beautiful part of the country; well-housed, better-paid than probably Charles would ever have dreamed possible, and with a complete, well-equipped observatory yards from his house, under his charge, and almost entirely at his disposal. Even the comfort of the observer was taken into account – a far cry from the situation of the young brush-maker, observing in his spare time and at night with his home-made telescope, devising cheap alter-natives to the position micrometer.

It is I think, fair to assume that with his experience under John Browning in setting-up and assisting in a wide variety of private observatories Charles would have had a considerable input in both the design and the furnishing of the observatory; what his role was in the decision to concentrate observations on variable stars is less clear. He had been intrigued in 1866 by the appearance of a star in the Pleiades that he had not observed in 1861, when he had made a careful drawing of the cluster, but would not have had the equipment to embark an any systematic pursuit of the topic, even if he had been fully aware of the developments in the field of variable stars at the time. Already, in 1865, using his small telescope he was intrigued by double stars and by the variations in them, although again, the equipment that he was using would not have allowed for in-depth investigation – something that he realised; Charles often noted observations that he could not explain at the time, in the hope that later observations or reading would clarify what he had seen. In 1865 he is comparing his observations of a small pair of stars in Orion:

> *there is something curious in the colours of this pair and the following results of various observers would imply a change of tint in this pair, if it were not for the numerous sources of error to which such observations are liable, such as the state of the atmosphere at the time of observation, altitude of the object, correction of object glass, and not least among other sources of error are personal peculiarities of vision of various observers, and even of the same individual at various periods of life or under different states of health, here are a few comparisons*
> *1835 Smyth, A brilliant white B pale violet*
> *1845 Sestini, A yellowish B very white*
> *1850 Smyth, A pale white B flushed white*
> *1850 Webb, A white or pale yellow*
> *1866 Grover A faint bluish white B clear violet*

In 1867, in a note on observations of double stars with the 6 ½-inch reflector he writes of a 'faint pair *CB*' in Lyra: 'I had a strong suspicion that they are variable from the following observations'. This is followed by a list of observations for three nights in May, four nights in June, and again on 9 July and 1 October. In 1881 he revisits this pair on four occasions in September; and in 1882, 13 July, observes them again from the observatory of the Revd Canon Beechey, Hilgay Rectory, Downham, Norfolk. Before he has the reflector, where Charles notes magnitudes they tend to be ascribed to other observers – 'Note the various magnitudes, positions and distances of these objects ... are from Admiral Smyth – the colours and diagrams are from my own observations' – once he has the new instrument he is confidently assessing magnitudes as low as 13, and noting variations by as little as ¼ magnitude. In 1867:

May 19th *CB considerably unequal B the brighter by fully ½ magnitude*

    29 *very slight difference, if any C rather the brightest*

    30 *the same although they are both well seen, two excessively faint stars DE strongly suspected*

June 10 *C the brightest, when a triangular aperture is applied which extinguishes B, C is still seen*

    13 *superb definition, BC barely visible in strong moonlight, difference scarcely perceptible*

    23 *fine night BC well seen though faint, B plainly brightest, difference about ¼ mag*

    29th *fine night BC easily seen surprised at their brightness B considerably the brighter perhaps ½ mag*

July 9 *splendid night BC easily seen. B slightly the brighter but the difference is so small as not to be immediately noted and I notice a considerable difference in the appearance of the two stars. C though smaller than B shines with a more sharp and vivid kind of light and is of a lighter tint. B though rather the larger is not so well defined and more nebulous and is rather more steadily seen than C although by glimpses this appears as bright or even brighter than B.*

August 23rd *superb definition. BC well seen C the brighter by about ½ magnitude*

October 1st *well observed the same as on August 23rd*

In 1868, May 15: '*BC* very well seen with 220 B is rather brighter than *C*'.

And in 1881:

> *Sep 19th   CB very well seen. C is the brightest,*
> *   power 144 achromatic eyepiece*
> *   26th   very   little   difference   C   rather*
> *   brighter than B power 144 & 220*
> *   29th   C steadily seen with 220. B not visible*
> *   – very fine night*

In 1882 from Norfolk: 'July 13th observed with 10-in mirror at Revd Canon Beechey ... *CB* beautifully seen. *B* is rather the brightest.'

In 1844, only 18 variable stars were known, and it was not until that year, when F.W. Argelander called for more research to be focused on them, that they became a serious subject for study. The later nineteenth century was a turning point in the study of variable stars, with E.C. Pickering's work on the topic and his appointment as Director of Harvard College Observatory in 1876. Charles Grover would have seen Pickering's 1879 article 'Stellar Magnitudes: a Request to Astronomers' in which he invited assistance with a project to establish a standard method of estimating stellar magnitude and he would have known that his own perceptions of magnitude would have met Pickering's standards.

> *It is hoped that a large number of those astronomers whose experience has been sufficient to establish a definite scale for their estimates of stellar magnitude will consent to take part in the proposed observation, in order that the published series of observations may be complete enough to be of general utility.*

By 1890, the number of known variable stars had increased to 175. The Rousdon observations concentrate on 22.

The Rousdon observations were published annually from 1885, and continued to be published in the same form in the *Journal of the British Astronomical Association* under the name of C. Grover, Astronomer in Charge, until shortly before Charles's death: the last annual observations published were for 1920. Sir Wilfrid Peek was mentioned as the owner of the observatory, but there was no suggestion that he took any particular interest in the observations. However, in 1904, observations from 1885–1900 were gathered together and presented in book form, edited by H.H. Turner (Savilian Professor of Astronomy in the University of Oxford, and President of the Royal Astronomical Society from 1903–5) and published by the Royal Astronomical Society.

In his introductory note to the volume, H.H. Turner (in numbered paragraphs) clarifies the genesis of the observations made at Rousdon and sets out his initial reservations about the project in hand:

1. The observations of variable stars contained in this volume were made under the direction of the late Sir Cuthbert E. Peek, Bart., M.A., F.R.A.S., at his observatory at Rousdon, near Lyme Regis, in the years 1885–1900. The actual observations were made by Mr. C. Grover, but Sir Cuthbert Peek checked them frequently, and personally superintended the whole work.
2. In the early part of 1900 Sir C. Peek wrote asking whether I would help him with the editing and discussion of the results. He said that this request was suggested by the appearance of Volume LII. of these Memoirs, in which I had edited the observations of the late Mr. George Knott. I hesitated to undertake this new responsibility for two reasons: first, the editing of Volume LII. arose (as may be seen on

reference to the third sentence on p. vii) out of my work as Secretary to the Royal Astronomical Society; an office which I no longer held in 1900; secondly, I was fully conscious of the great disadvantage for such work of not having observed variable stars myself. But while the correspondence was proceeding Sir C. Peek became seriously and hopelessly ill, and this increased his anxiety that something definite should be settled about the observations, for the work of the observatory held a very prominent place in his thoughts. The reasons above mentioned were thus thrown into the background, and I undertook to do the best I could with the observations. I may add that before finally doing so I wrote to Professor E.C. Pickering, of Harvard, who had just published a volume [Harvard Annals, vol. xxxvii, Part I] of detailed observations relating to stars which are in great part the same as those observed at Rousdon (indeed, the Rousdon programme was adopted from Harvard), sending him specimens of the observations and some comments suggested by the brief inspection already made. He replied that 'the observations were even more valuable than he thought,' and urged the publication of the detailed comparisons. This opinion from such an authority had naturally great weight in determining the completeness of the discussion and the publication of the results in this form.

In his later discussion of the observations, Turner notes:

37. One point deserves emphasis. The observations were not only made with the same instrument, by the same observer, on the same plan, but with remarkable regularity and continuity. It is not often possible for an observer to work so uninterruptedly as Mr. Grover has done for the last dozen years: his holidays, for instance, have been of the rarest and briefest kind. Hence the observations afford a valuable medium for the comparison of the broken or short series of other observers.

There would have been, of course, simply nowhere that Charles Grover would rather have been; nor, except on the rarest of occasions, would he rather have been doing anything else. A digest of a year's work, dated January 1887, shows that observations were made on 146 nights throughout 1886, including observations on 19 nights in December, which was the clearest and, one might imagine, the coldest month. The dullest month of the year was February, when only five nights were clear enough for observations to be made.

Everyday Life in the Country

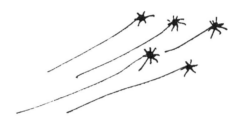

As well as his astronomical and meteorological observations and recordings, and in addition to his role as museum curator – both of which involved showing around a steady flow of interested visitors – Charles continued to write articles for journals, to correspond with journals and individuals, and, albeit with less frequency as the years went by, made regular visits to London. He also took part in the life of the estate and the village, which were inextricably entwined.

A number of reports exist of the Rousdon 'Annual Treat'. This is from the *Lyme Mirror* in January 1885 (so at a busy time, when the new observatory was just coming into use):

> *On Monday and Tuesday last the annual treat and entertainment, provided at the expense of Sir H.W. Peek, Bart., was given in the*

commodious school premises. The invitations to the festivities are issued on a very liberal scale, and include not only all employed at Rousdon and the immediate vicinity, but also the neighbouring farmers, their wives and families, and we believe almost the whole population of Combepyne [sic]. In order that all might be comfortably accommodated, the proceedings occupied two evenings, the first appropriated to Rousdon, and the second to Combepyne. We were privileged to be present at the Tuesday entertainment, which we understand was a facsimile [sic] of that given on the Monday. Shortly before 5 p.m. the guests began to arrive, and soon the school dining hall was well filled by adults, whilst the large Infants' School barely sufficed to accommodate the laughing, merry crew assembled there. A smaller room was set apart for other guests, and among these we noticed Mr. and Mrs. Sloman, Mr. and Mrs. Woolmington, Mr. and Mrs. Symes, Mr. Harris, Mr. Munro, and a number of other ladies and gentlemen. Abundance of rich cake, bread and butter, with excellent tea was provided, and in each case ample justice was done the same. At the commencement of the proceedings, the Rev. J. Curvengen read a note from the Rector of Combepyne, regretting his inability to be present, it was much regretted, too, that Sir Henry had been obliged to leave for London on the previous day. Tea being over, the party assembled in the large schoolroom, and here a varied and delightful entertainment was given. Mr Curvengen briefly introduced the programme, and for over two hours music, songs, and dissolving views entranced the attention of the audience. The programme was too varied to report item by item, but there were well-rendered songs by the schoolchildren; a capital variety of music by the drum and fife band (which, by the by, consists of about 30 instruments, and, if there was no other proof, would prove Mr. Burgess a master hand in the art of training); music by the Burgess family included a comic song by Mr. Burgess, song, 'Milly May' by Miss L. Burgess, a pianoforte duet by Master F. and Miss G. Burgess, and glees by the whole, assisted by Messrs. Curvengen, senior and junr.; a very amusing reading by Mr. Curvengen; a pianoforte solo by Mr. Curvengen, junr.; nor must we omit the nursery rhymes of the infants, which were wonderfully well sung and accompanied by suitable movements; such as the holding of the head when 'Jack fell down and broke his crown,' the emulation of the 'Cow that jumped over the moon,' 'Riding cock horse,' the sleepy 'Bo Peep who lost her sheep,' &c., &c., the droll mimicry causing roars of laughter, the musical accompaniment was played by Miss G. Burgess; the whole performance was crowned by a really splendid dissolving view exhibition, consisting of illustrations of the story of 'Hop o'my Thumb,' views in Egypt, a number of comic slides, chromatropes, &c., &c. The exhibitors were Mr. Grover, assistant observer at the Rousdon Observatory, assisted by his son Mr. G. Grover, whose apt and humorous remarks on the pictures added immensely to the interest of their exhibition. The lanterns were a pair of splendid instruments, projecting a disc of about 12 feet, and the pictures were thrown on the sheet clear and sharp. Towards the close of the exhibition a portrait was thrown on the field of view, which produced such a spontaneous hurrah as almost to lift the roof, this was no other than a life-like photograph of Sir Henry Peek, and the shout showed in what grateful esteem that gentleman is held; the next slide exhibited the National Anthem which, having been sung, the company separated. We should be neglecting a duty did we close this report without mention of those who are entrusted with the work of carrying out these annual festivities, and first comes Mr.

Burgess and his family, who, one and all, enter heart and soul into the proceedings, and although it must entail no small amount of labour to supply tea, &c., for over 200 people on each night for two consecutive nights, it appears to them a labour of love. The Rector too (Rev. J. Curvengen) is all alive to the occasion. The exhibitors and all concerned did their utmost to make it the success it undoubtedly was. What strikes a visitor is the profuse liberality displayed, for not only is there an abundance of provision, but, at the close, it is not one orange that is given to each, but three oranges; also the complete freedom of restraint is most noticeable; and while the people of Rousdon may be congratulated as to their noble and liberal-hearted employer, that employer must be congratulated on having those under him who endeavour honestly to carry out his intentions.

In the same month the *Lyme Mirror* carried a report of the festivities attending the christening of the heir to the baronetcy, Cuthbert Peek's first-born son Wilfrid. Cuthbert had married the Hon. Augusta Brodrick, daughter of the Hon. W. St John Brodrick, MP, on 3 January 1884, and the christening of Wilfrid took place on 21 December the same year. The christening itself was a comparatively low-key affair attended by family members only, but a party was laid on for the following Tuesday, 23 December, for all the estate employees and a number of other people from the neighbourhood.

the coach house had been transformed into a temporary dining hall; and a very pretty hall it looked with the tastefully arranged festoons of evergreens and the seasonable mottoes suspended from the walls. In fact had we not possessed some previous knowledge of the geography of Rousdon we could not have guessed that this pretty room was nothing more than the coach-house. Three tables stretched the whole length of the improvised banqueting-hall, and a fourth, across the top end, was set apart for the more distinguished visitors. The Rector occupied the chair at this table, while those who presided as carvers at the other tables were Mssrs Woolmington, Prosser [Clerk of Works at Rousdon; his wife Emilie was originally Silesian German], Ollerhead [gardener], Burgess, Grover Senr. and Grover Junr. ...

The dinner itself cannot be passed over without a few words. First came the fine joints of Rousdon beef, the quality of which reflected credit upon Mr. Woolmington who manages the farm on the estate. The amount of work which fell to the share of the carvers was in itself sufficient evidence of the appreciation of its excellence. Next came a bountiful supply of mince pies, which met with great approbation and disappeared accordingly. Then came some good specimens of good old English plum pudding, but the former efforts of the digestive organs were beginning to tell, and this did not meet with so sudden a fate as the things which had preceded it, and when the dessert came on the table it was a matter of difficulty to get people to eat it. Such facts as those speak well for the bounty of the giver of the feast; but there was more to come. The toasts were to be drunk, and drunk with wine such as rarely falls to the lot of those who do not keep a good cellar.

After the meal was over and 'grace had been sung' the house party came in and toasts were drunk and speeches given. Sir Henry himself made a speech in which he recalled a year of mixed joy – the marriage of his son and the birth of baby Wilfrid – and 'sorrow at a loss such as he hoped would not fall upon anyone present, for many years', the death of his wife in the summer. However 'He had been requested by Mrs. Peek to ask everyone to come into the Banqueting Hall, where they would find a

Christmas Tree and some presents prepared for their gratification and amusement.' During an interval when the tree was being prepared a great many more toasts were drunk and a few memories shared – including that of the party, rather like this one, held to celebrate Cuthbert Peek's marriage.

Everyone then adjourned to the Banqueting Hall, where an enormous Christmas Tree was groaning under the weight of numerous presents, candles, toys, bons-bons, &c. This was the work of Mrs. Peek, who had provided a ticket for everybody present, and a useful or ornamental gift on the tree, corresponded in number to every ticket. A chest containing about 6lbs. of tea fell to the share of every woman present, while the neighbouring farmers each came into possession of ferocious looking cudgels. Many of the labouring men were supplied with stockings or caps, or other equally useful articles, while those for whom it was thought such gifts were unsuitable, were provided with a handsome book, or some other present. The immense amount of work which this entailed may be imagined when it is stated that the number of tickets and presents was over one hundred and seventy, and every one was adapted for its recipient. Not one was omitted from the general distribution. The Hon. Wm. St John Brodrick became the owner of a large box of chocolate creams, which were speedily disposed of amongst the numerous children present, who also came in for all the small toys, &c. on the tree. When the distribution was over, tea and cake was handed round, in order that no one should go home suffering from the pangs of hunger (if such a thing were possible after the dinner of an hour ago); and then after some music from the Drum and Fife Band (another monument of Mr Burgess's energy and ability),

*and the Choir, the majority of the guests
returned home, after a very pleasant evening,
more pleasant perhaps than anything they had
before experienced.*

A few 'more favoured' guests remained behind 'and
enjoyed still further tokens of Sir Henry Peek's
good-will'. These would presumably have included
the Rector (although cards were played, whether or
not it was true that 'some gentlemen played whist
until their notions of trumps were rather hazy') and
Dr Bangay (whose late entrance to the party in the
coach house had been received with some
enthusiasm and the remark that it was hoped that
he would find little to do at Rousdon), but whether
or not the estate's astronomical assistant and
museum curator would have been included remains
unknown.

A report of a 'free entertainment ... the expenses
of which were defrayed by a gentleman whose name
must remain secret' in the *Lyme Regis Mirror* for 2
January 1886, noted that 'On Saturday evening last
a dissolving view exhibition was given in the
Assembly Rooms':

*The exhibition consisted first of diagrams
illustrative of the movements of the earth and
heavenly bodies and other astronomical
phenomena; secondly of views of some of the
wonderful places of the world; and thirdly, of
pictures illustrating Charles Dickens' well
known Christmas story of 'Gabriel Grubb.' The
first part was explained in a lucid and
interesting manner by Dr. Bangay, the
attention with which he was listened to evincing
the interest which he excited. The magic-lantern
operators were Messrs. C. and G. Grover, of
Rousdon.*

In 1886 Charles and Elizabeth's son George married
Mary Ann Collier, a gardener's daughter from
Rousdon, and they moved to live in London soon

afterwards. In the following year Charles's first grandchild, Percy Grover was born. In 1893, George and Mary Ann had a second son, Edward, but he died soon after birth. Their third child, Wilfrid was born in 1900.

In August 1898 the great era of Rousdon came to an end with the death of Sir Henry Peek. Cuthbert – then Sir Cuthbert – Peek died only three years later, on 6 July 1901, leaving a wife and seven children, the eldest of whom and the heir to the baronetcy, Wilfrid, was only seventeen, the youngest of whom had been born in 1900.

Charles wrote an obituary of Cuthbert Peek for the RAS *Observatory Magazine* (No. 308, August 1901). It says much for his reputation and the relationship that he and his employer enjoyed that he was the one to do this.

It is with deep regret that we announce the death of Sir Cuthbert Edgar Peek, Bart., of Rousdon, Lyme Regis, and 22 Belgrave Square, S.W. Sir Cuthbert, who was but 46 years of age, died on July 6 at Brighton, where he had been staying for about six months, suffering the greater portion of the time from congestion of the brain ... From an early age the deceased baronet was a zealous student of scientific and antiquarian subjects, and in 1881 made an extensive journey in the little-known parts of Iceland. On his return he established a small observatory in the grounds of his father's house at Wimbledon and worked with a three-inch equatorial ... In 1882 he went to Australia to observe the Transit of Venus ... The Transit of Venus was not seen, owing to clouds, but Sir Cuthbert often remarked that this caused him little regret, for he felt amply repaid for the journey by his observation of the wonders of the southern sky. After extensive travels in Australia and New Zealand, he returned to Rousdon in August 1883, bringing with him a considerable collection of curious and interesting objects, which further enriched the famous museum established by his father at Rousdon ... The Rousdon Observatory was erected in 1884 ... [it] was often open to visitors, and the genial baronet was never happier than when showing to delighted friends the wonders of the heavens, or explaining to interested enquirers the construction and working of the complicated meteorological apparatus in use for the weather records. Sir Cuthbert was a Fellow of the Society of Antiquaries, Hon. Secretary of the Anthropological Society, on the Council of the Royal Meteorological Society, and also on that of the Royal Geographical, which Society he has endowed with a medal for the advancement of geographical knowledge.

The Cuthbert Peek Award is still given by the RGS. In an obituary of Sir Vivian Fuchs, polar explorer and director of the British Antarctic Survey 1958–73, in 1999, it was noted that 'The Royal Geographical Society's Cuthbert Peek Grant in 1936 encouraged him to investigate geology further south, around Lake Rukwa.'

Charles continued his work as Observer in Charge at Rousdon after Cuthbert Peek's death, and the observations on variable stars were still published annually. By 1901 though, Charles was in his sixties, and, as letters written in the early years of the century demonstrate, thought of himself very much as becoming old, and perhaps a little more cautious – though not noticeably less enthusiastic – about long cold nights at the telescope.

On 27 July 1900 Cuthbert Peek had replied to a letter from a Mr Thomas Richards of Swindon (he may have been connected with the railway works because 'the Works' are mentioned one or two times in the correspondence that ensued and Swindon's fame certainly rested at that time on the Great Western Railway) on the subject of a photograph of an eclipse: 'I am most interested in the results you have got and should you be in this part of the Country <u>after Friday next</u> my assistant will be delighted to show you what we are doing and I shall be pleased to give you copies of any photos which have been taken here.' Richards was particularly interested in photography, and it is only in the letters to him that it becomes clear that photography was being carried on at Rousdon as well (although the observatory was equipped with photographic equipment at the outset).

The correspondence was taken up again by Charles Grover in 1902 and continued at least until 1910, the period covered by the twenty-four letters that still exist. The letters comprise the best record of Charles's life at Rousdon in the period.

He writes that 'I remember your writing to Sir Cuthbert as to seeing the observatory – but unfortunately I was then away for a few days and you returned to your duties the same day I returned here so it fell through. If I am here when you come this way in the summer I will show you anything I can of interest. I generally get a fortnights holiday but we shall see later on.' In the first letter – and this is very typical – he is offering advice on the setting up of telescopes – 'The new fashioned telescope illustrated is not worth considering and is wrong at all points. The six mirrors seem introduced to <u>prevent</u> the telescope being any good.' Later he offers condolences on the death of a Mr Richards (presumably related to his correspondent) of Seaton Gas Works who 'was well known to me and I was very much grieved to hear of his sudden death'.

In a letter of 8 February 1902 Charles confirms that 'Yes, I am the C. Grover of Mee's Observational Astronomy having corresponded with Mr Mee for many years.' Later he advises Richards that 'your 3 in Wray is capable of good work as you can go down to 10.5 mag with it, and remember what the preface to "Mee's" book says "much depends on the man at the small end"'.

Observational   Astronomy   provided   an
introduction to amateur observing. It was 79 pages
long and was published first in 1893 and in a
second edition in 1897. Mee was an enthusiastic
amateur observer, a founder member of the British
Astronomical Association in 1890, and the founder
of the Astronomical Society of Wales in 1895 and
the editor of its journal. In 1898 the journal was
replaced by the *Cambrian Natural Observer*, which
extended its coverage to other scientific areas, such
as meteorology and botany in order to increase the
range of the readership – although astronomy
remained at its core.

Charles may have met Arthur Mee while he was
working in London; or he may have been contacted
by Mee when Mee moved to Cardiff and set about
establishing an astronomical organisation of some
kind prior to the official establishment of the Welsh
society in 1894. Charles is listed as a member of the
Astronomical Society of Wales in 1903, and given
the organisation of the list – which is arranged
alphabetically in blocks, but within each block
appears to be arranged in order of membership,
with founder members at the top of each list and
those just voted to membership at the bottom – he
was among early members, if not one of the very
first. Plainly Charles's correspondence with Mee
was   significant   before   the   publication   of
Observational Astronomy; certainly enough to get
his name known in connection with the book.

Richards was obviously interested in finding a
model of the solar system, with which Charles was
not able to help: 'few people have an idea of the
scale and distance of the planetary bodies. I send
you a number of the Museums Journal showing you
some   attempts   in   this   direction   –   at   the
Geographical Museum, Jermyn Street, London they
have the Sun a globe 2 ft diameter, and the planets
are so small and distant you can hardly find them. I
have an old Celestial Globe dated 1801.'

One of the subjects of the letters is a series of
photographs taken by Richards of Charles Grover,

including – or so it would seem – the one of him at the telescope in the observatory, in his embroidered observer's cap, and another of him resting an arm on the stand of the celestial globe.

The photographs were taken at some time in late August or early September 1907, following a gap in the correspondence, for on 26 August Charles writes 'Dear Sir, [he would become 'Mr Richards' only following their meeting] I was very pleased to hear from you again and shall be glad to see you here and have a talk over astronomical matters'. Charles advised Richards to take a train on the Lyme Regis Branch Railway from Axminster to the neighbouring village of Combpyne – a journey of about 12 minutes – and sent him a map of the one mile walk from Combpyne to Rousdon: 'you will see a tall anemometer tower on the right when you get to Rousdon – that is my house'.

Apart from the taking of photographs and the inevitable astronomical discussions, tour of the observatory and sampling of the telescope, conversation seems to have turned also to spiritual matters. Charles writes, on receipt of the photographs and a variety of astronomical photographs:

> *Now to change the subject – thanks for your booklet on the Nature of Man. I never worry much about the future State for the good reason that of this we know nothing and never shall till we pass the line, and we have not one single Authentic incident of any who has returned from the life beyond to tell us anything. I expect our midnight thoughts are much the same as your verse from the 'Elegy' lets me know, for I often ponder over these things – we have a double nature – the Bodily and the Spiritual. The Body is the mere Shell so to speak – the Spirit the intellectual portion. How is it that when living, people of identical tastes etc can read each others thoughts even by a look – there is a response of mind, but the moment after death*

Charles Grover at the telescope in the observatory at Rousdon, August or September 1907

*look on your dearest friend – <u>they are not</u>
<u>there</u>. There is the body, the case so to speak of
the watch, but <u>that is not them</u>, they are gone,
that is the Spirit the intellectual portion is
departed. <u>Where?</u> We should all like to know a
little more about these things.*

The photographs seem to have caused quite a stir:
12 October 1907, 'Several of my friends having
greatly admired the portrait of me you took when
you were here – may I ask you to be good enough to
get me ½ doz cabinets printed from it – the <u>full</u>
face one is the best.' From 1907 onwards Charles is
gloomy – if philosophical – about his own chances
of surviving much longer. In November 1907 the
weather prevented him from seeing a transit of
Mercury and 'I shall not see another ... as the next
is in 1914 and by that time I shall have <u>crossed the</u>
<u>line</u>'; however he still has worldly concerns, 'I am
enclosing you a PO 5/6 as I want you to do for me
½ doz cabinets of my portraits which I want to send
to some of my friends between this and Christmas –
I have no objection to your giving any one my
portrait who is interested in Science.'
    The letters give an idea of Charles's continuing
writing and corresponding. In December 1907 he
tells Richards

*I replied to Col. Watson as to Hyperion in the
EM* [English Mechanic] *of December 6 and in the
EM of December 13 (letter no 482) a gentleman
makes out I have been seeing some of the
Martian Canals with a glass of much less than 8
inches aperture – I shall take care to correct
this error – I am glad you saw my drawing
when at Rousdon – and you know my views on
these matters. I presume you read the
correspondence in the EM on the British Astro
Association. I have never yet had the
opportunity of attending one of their meetings
as I live so far from London but I cheerfully pay
the 10/6 a year for the Journal and Reports of*

*Charles Grover with the celestial globe, August or
September 1907*

Everyday Life in the Country

*the sections. I am bound to say the Journal has
<u>not</u> improved of late and I am afraid the
Society has passed its Zenith.*

The cold weather at the start of 1908 is a hindrance
to observation and sets in train further thoughts on
mortality. On 1 January 1908: 'We are having real
winter now, first cutting cold NE winds then heavy
snow. No sight of sun for last 6 days, no observing
since Dec 23 – very poor for astronomy.' And on 9
January: 'What a snap of cold we have had, 17
below freezing – I tried to observe on Jan 3 but
Dome and Shutter would not work – all froze and
set, better now – but I believe more frost coming.
This cold was quite enough for us two old ones
nearly curled us up.'

In February 1908, Charles reported his visit to
an unusual natural phenomenon, the 'burning cliff'
near Lyme Regis: 'I went to see the Burning Cliff on
the 6th and have sent an account to the EM which I
expect will come out next Friday – it is an immense
body of Solid fire – <u>no flame,</u> and the heat is
intense – if I can get a photo I will send you one,
though there is not much to see only a little cloud
of Steam outside – the fire is within and the Cliff
too hot to stand on.'

The 'Burning Cliff', otherwise known as the
'Lyme Volcano', appears to have resulted from a
landslip – possibly provoked by the quarrying of
limestone at the foot of the cliff – and the exposure
to air of pyrite (ferrous sulphide) which, when
oxidised, 'is believed to trigger the spontaneous
combustion of bituminous shales'. The slip took
place on 8 January and smoke was first observed
rising from the mound created by it on 19 January.
A further slip in June seemed to extinguish the fire.
While there was no doubt that the outbreak of fire
was a natural phenomenon, there were those who
suspected human interference in the maintenance
of it as a tourist attraction. In a letter to the
Geological Magazine in February 1909, a Dr W.D.
Lang, writing under a pseudonym, 'Passer Veneris',

and with the caveat that what he related 'is only hearsay, and may be mere gossip' complained:

> *The cliff took fire in early 1908. Notices, descriptions, and explanations appeared in various papers, local and otherwise, and enterprising shop-keepers in Lyme took photos and exhibited them as picture postcards, which they sold as mementoes of 'the volcano'. The advertisement attracted visitors to Lyme, and evidently the burning cliff was a source of profit to the Lyme folk. In Charmouth, during April, 1908, it was common talk that when the 'volcanic' activity appeared to be subsiding, disappointed Lyme people poured paraffin on the cliff and relighted it. It is probable that, saturated with enough paraffin, any clay cliff would burn when lighted, and the effect would be commensurate with the amount of oil used. If the paraffin was poured on the burning part of Black Ven, it has made it impossible to judge the effect of the natural combustion and its effects.*

Whether or not the enterprising and over-zealous burghers of Lyme nursed the phenomenon of the burning cliff for profit or not, at the start of February, when Charles Grover saw it and made his report to the *English Mechanic* it was still, without doubt, an extraordinary natural occurrence. A few days after his first visit Charles sent Richards 'a print of the Burning Cliff – as I said before there is not much to <u>see</u>, but a lot to <u>feel</u> – the hole with the crow bar was made where the jet of steam is coming out just below the arrow, and the Cliff is inside a mass of dull red fire.' The print was from an old friend, Mr Down of R. Southwood and Co. in Lyme; perhaps it was one of those sold as picture postcards.

Early in January 1908 – an event not reported by Charles until a letter of 20 February – he 'received a visit by Prof Turner (Professor of Astronomy, University of Oxford) ... – he has just written me a letter in which he speaks in high terms of my work here and I have just sent the report for 1907 to the British Astronomical Association'. It is a passing mention, but such a visit does indicate the high esteem in which Charles was held among professional astronomers. At the end of March 1908 he sent Richards a copy of the observatory report (which he had promised earlier that he would send), adding 'I don't know if you saw the kind remarks concerning me in the EM for March 13. We have not been feeling very sprightly lately but am looking forward to the warm Summer to feel better.'

On 15 May, Charles wrote 'I had a fine time in London, Prof Turner asked me to attend the meeting and give some account of Recent work at Rousdon, and then I was invited to Dine at the Astronomical Club where I was most kindly received – and lots of good things said about me which I did not deserve. The Astronomer Royal and some of the Heads of the Greenwich Staff were there so it was a very interesting function.'

In fact, in a sense, this 'very interesting function' was the pinnacle of Charles's career as an observer, a formal recognition of his abilities and his achievements by some of the best-known and highest-placed figures in astronomy.

ROYAL ASTRONOMICAL SOCIETY OF LONDON

CLUB DINNER AT THE CRITERION April 10. 1908

PROFESSOR H. H. TURNER F.R.S. Chairman.

E. B. Knobel Esq. F.R.A.S.

Gentlemen,
    I rise to propose the health of my very old friend Mr Grover, whom we are delighted to welcome among us tonight. I was reminding Mr. Grover a few minutes ago, of a course of

---

*lectures on Astronomy which I delivered at the
Working Men's Institute, Great Ormonde Street
more than thirty years ago; and he brought to
my mind similar lectures delivered at Dulwich
College and at other places, where his skill with
the optical lantern considerably helped to my
success. We have just listened to his able
exposition of the work on the Variable stars
which has been carried on for the last twenty
five years at the Rousdon Observatory, and the
value of which has been spoken to by Prof.
Turner, and we sincerely hope that Mr. Grover
may have many years of health and strength to
still further enrich our science with his valuable
observations.*

Mr. Grover

Gentlemen,
*I am very much pleased with my kind
reception here tonight, though I feel I hardly
deserve all the good things said about me by Mr.
Knobel, whom I have known a great many years.
I think it was in 1872 that I brought to the
meetings of this society the model of Knobel's
observing chair and Knobel's triangular
aperture Astrometer which he invented about
that date. I am here tonight by the invitation of
Prof. Turner, and this gives me the opportunity
of expressing my thanks to this great society for
much kind help and encouragement from past
and present members during my fifty years as
an astronomer.*
*It is nearly half a century since I began to
study astronomy, being then a working brush-
maker. (Expressions of surprise). Yes,
gentlemen, I began the study of astronomy
without either books, instruments or money; but
fortunately I came under the notice of some
members of the Royal Astronomical Society, and
I gratefully remember good old Dr. Lee of*

Hartwell, the Rev. Cooper Key, pioneer of the silvered glass reflector, Mr. With, the celebrated maker of specula. Mr. George Knott, the well known double and variable star observer, the Rev T. W. Webb, and a host of others. From 1865 onward I wrote many letters and articles in the 'Intellectual Observer', 'Astronomical Register' and other publications, and in 1869 I was offered a position in the establishment of John Browning the eminent optician. The silvered glass reflector was then coming into favour, and during the next twelve years I had much to do with all the principal instruments of that kind, and became quite an expert in silvering specula.

I was a frequent attendant at the meetings of this society at the little room in Somerset House, the then Secretary being a short little gentleman, Mr. Williams. He was a wonderful Chinese scholar and an authority on ancient Chinese astronomical observations. I think he once read a paper on a great comet which appeared during the flood, and the only authentic observation of which was taken by Noah from the windows of the ark. (Cheers)

At one of the meetings, I think it was in 1873, a very young gentleman read a paper on the lunar theory. He arranged his papers with an air of great assurance, and, after going on at great length, looked down on the grey haired philosophers below him and remarked 'I have given great care and labour to this subject with the result that this important research is now nearly complete, and if any gentleman has any remarks to make, I shall be very pleased to hear him'.

Now the late Sir George Airey, the then Astronomer Royal, had listened to the young man, and now rose, and in a few well chosen words completely demolished his work, and finished with the remark, 'Our young friend has shown great courage, and expended considerable labour, for which he deserves some

amount of credit; but so far as I can discover,
he has left this great problem exactly where he
found it'.

Dead silence followed, and the eclipse of the
new exponent of the lunar theory was complete.

In the year 1882 I joined the late Sir Cuthbert
Peek in his Transit of Venus expedition to
Queensland, and, returning to England in 1883,
the Rousdon Observatory was at once
commenced. Of the twenty five years work there
I need not say anything now, only to refer to the
sad loss of our distinguished chief in 1901, and
to the great encouragement extended to the
work during the last few years by Prof. Turner.

Gentlemen, I thank you very much for your
kind sentiments expressed here tonight.

(Applause).

(The record of this occasion is two frail typed
sheets of paper, in a purplish-blue ink; it is
probable – given the interpolations of the audience
responses – that this comprises the formal record
of the evening, sent to Charles Grover as the
honoured guest on this occasion.)

On the subject of public observatories Charles
writes to Thomas Richards (suggesting that the
geniality that Charles always showed to visitors to
Rousdon was perhaps occasionally hard come by):
'Depend upon it public Observatories are not a
success – there [sic] only use is to give an
hardworking observer like yourself the chance of
using larger and better instruments than you could
otherwise get, in return for which you would be
appointed Curator and find yourself the servant of a
host of mere sightseers with an evening with
nothing to do, and you would be worked and
worried beyond endurance till the novelty wore off
and you would mostly find when something of
importance was coming on some busybody would
look in and just stop your work. I know a little what
this is by painful experience – better have a little 3

in of your own that you can use when you like –
than a giant telescope that you cannot use, only be
worried with.'

Charles claimed that 'I only stick to routine work
now, and rarely look at much else than Variable
Stars, except to show things to visitors. I have not
looked at the moon, but Venus has been a fine
sight. I have had her beautifully defined in daylight
with 300 several times about 6 pm. I looked very
carefull [sic] but could not see a ghost of a marking
on the disc, yet some people make drawings of
distinct markings and are sure of the rotation
period.' And in October, following another apparent
break in the correspondence due at least in part to
the wedding of 'Miss Margaret Peek – our eldest
Young Lady' he says 'I presume you have seen the
new comet – Morehouse – I first saw it Sept 24 very
faint in the Rousdon telescope'. In the same letter
he is anticipating the return in 1910 of Halley's
comet, currently 'beyond the reach of any but the
largest telescopes'.

The next winter sees Charles once again
anticipating his imminent demise: on Friday 15
January 1909 he writes 'we have both been very bad
this last fortnight and I have had a lay up in bed for
several days. The Dr says "Chilled Liver" and I have
had a very bad time – and of course quite unable to
look at astronomy as yet this year. Anyhow I am
about again, but far from well and I shall never
catch up our old friend Mr. Bickle [who died at the
age of 90 in June 1909] – this cold snap has carried
off a lot of old people and he is a miracle to be alive
... let me wind up by wishing you and Mrs. Richards
and family a happy new year for 1909 – myself and
Mrs. Grover are decidedly shaky but we may
perhaps cheer up as the Spring comes on.'

In March Charles advises Richards that a 'letter
on the Dumbell Nebula in last weeks EM though
signed Λ is really written by Mr. Edison Holmes
whose letters I expect you have often read in the
EM – he was a rare man to criticise and say
unpleasant things generally and at last got put

down by the editor so now he has written several articles signed A. I met him at Greenwich Observatory last June. I don't take any notice of his criticism of my notes of 1893, they are not worth it ... We have both felt this long winter very trying – we had heavy snow yesterday morning and it is very cold now, it has carried off a good many both old and young, we are about the same age as your father and mother. I was 69 on March 2nd [he was 67 on 7 March] and Mrs. G will be 70 next August, so we are getting on. There were several fine nights lately when the cold was so intense that nothing could be done, once it went down to 19 below freezing, and of course an old man like me has to be a little careful.'

By June, however, he had cheered up as predicted and on 5 June:

I was at the Greenwich Visitation ... and as usual there was much to see – a fine set of about 40 photos of Moorhouse [sic] Comet were a proof of how many midnight hours they work – more photos showing the movements of Jupiters minute distant moons, which so far as I know have never yet been seen visually, also photos showing several minor Planets, also new Photos of the Sun, Moon, Various Nebulae and fine Star fields, so the sky there cannot be so bad.

I met Mr. Holmes and had a long chat with him he is a grand old man notwithstanding his cranks and his articles on Nebulae etc in the EM lately show a wonderful research. There will be a great set to made on Mars when he comes round again in September and all the old Squabble about Canals etc will be fought all over again.

I also met Mr. Hardcastle the Sec of the BAA for whom I am doing some charts of Halley's Comet which will appear in the Journal. According to Mr. Crommelin [Andrew Claude de la Cherois Crommelin of the Royal Observatory, who led an expedition to Burgos in Spain in

1905 to observe the solar eclipse] they have got it well predicted and I have drawn the path among the Stars from Sept 12 1909 to July 1910. The Comet has not been caught yet but all the great telescopes will be turned that way in September. The Observatory is in splendid order, more than 60 persons are employed there, and it is certainly the leading observatory of the world.

The final result of the Eros observations was announced at the last meeting of the RAS, the parallax comes out at 8"803 which I take it is not far from the truth ...

We are both fairly well again now that Summer is come, and hope we may hold out for some time, it is the winter that gets hold of us.

(The asteroid Eros was discovered in 1898 by a German astronomer, Carl Gustav Witt, and the parallax results that Charles notes in 1909 would have been those calculated from observations and measurements made by Hinks in 1901.)

It was of course a sketch by Charles of the path of Halley's Comet that was reproduced in *Halley's Comet: With Plan of its Pathway in the Heavens and some Notes on Comets and Meteors* (London: undated, but certainly published by early 1910 because of its presence in Charles's birthday photograph), written by H. [Hester] Periam Hawkins, a woman who had come late to astronomy, after marriage to the Revd Joshua Hawkins – who himself joined the BAA in 1890 – and a career writing hymns and tracts. Allan Chapman describes the booklet as 'a largely historical work which presented a good account of cometary astronomy from antiquity onwards, and even corrected the bad Latin of "Isti Mirant [ut] Stella" which designates Halley's Comet in the Bayeux Tapestry'. (The Latin should have read 'Isti Mirantur Stellam'.)

The last letter is dated 14 May 1910 and is in reply to a letter telling of a new acquisition, a Browning 8 ½ inch silver-on-glass reflector of which Charles remarks 'I expect you are right and it is an old friend of my early days ... The book you mention is I expect the old "Plea for Reflectors" of which I wrote (and rewrote for successive editors) most of the astronomical portion ... I expected you had seen my notes on Halley's Comet in the EM. I got up at 2.30 on 16 mornings between April 14 and May 14, and on 12 mornings got good observation, and saw it turn the curve and change the direction of movement on April 25 ... Thanks for your good wishes we are both fairly well only a year older ... I expect to go to Greenwich for the Visitation on June 18.'

In 1916 Charles and Elizabeth's son George died in London aged around 52. At the outbreak of war Sir Wilfrid Peek left Rousdon for the Royal 1st Devon Yeomanry in which he served from 1914, and the estate would have lost numerous working men to the front line, many of them permanently. Like many other great Victorian establishments Rousdon would not recover from the loss of so many men in action nor the social changes that followed the Great War. In 1927, after Sir Wilfrid's death, the house was sold as a school, the contents of the museum dispersed and the observatory itself eventually left to fall into disrepair.

Charles himself was not to live to see the final dissolution of the place where he had spent so many happy and productive years. His final report on variable stars during 1920 appeared in the BAA journal for January 1921, and he died on 16 February 1921, at the age of 79, carried off by a winter as he had feared, and much mourned.

The *English Mechanic* for 25 February noted that:

We hear with regret of the death on the 16th instant of Mr. Charles Grover, of Sir Wilfrid Peek's observatory at Rousdon, Lyme Regis. Mr. Grover was 79 years of age and had followed astronomy for 62 years, his attention having been attracted to the science by the appearance

*of the comet of 1858, and since the year 1886
has observed variable stars of long period with
great assiduity and success at the Rousdon
Observatory, of which he has been in sole charge
in recent years.*

On 3 March, a further brief note outlined
something of Charles's early career:

*A little sketch of the life of Mr. Charles Grover,
whose death was mentioned in last week's
number, may prove of interest. He was brought
up, as he was always ready to tell anyone, to the
trade of a brushmaker, but he was of a scientific
turn of mind, and had a great liking for
astronomy. In the volumes of the 'Astronomical
Register,' as far back as the year 1865, there
may be found letters from C. Grover at
Chesham, Bucks, communicating observations
made with his telescope of 2-in. aperture, and
his name is frequently to be found also in
another publication of that time, 'The
Intellectual Observer.'*

A more detailed account of Charles's death – he
evaded the fate of 'poor Mr. Bickle. I hope I shall
not live to such a great age, as when mind and body
are so completely worn out it must be as the bible
tells us but labour and go now' – and of his funeral
appear in local reports, although some of the
historical details are inaccurate. (The source of
this is uncertain, but it probably comes from the
Lyme Mirror.)

ROUSDON
DEATH OF MR. C. GROVER
*A familiar figure has been removed from the
Rousdon Estate by the passing of Mr. Charles
Grover, at his residence, the East Lodge, on
Wednesday. Well known as a meteorologist
deceased, whose death we regret to record, had
for the last 39 years been in the service of the*

Peek family, as observer in charge of the Observatory on the estate.

The end came suddenly. About six o'clock on Wednesday morning, while in bed, he appeared to be rather restless, and his wife enquired of him whether he could sleep. He replied 'I shall get up when it gets light,' and thereupon, after breathing heavily for a few minutes, passed away. Dr. W. Langran (Axminster) was summoned and on arrival found that the deceased was beyond human aid. The sad occurrence was reported by the police to Dr. E.R. Tweed (coroner for East Devon), who deemed an inquest unnecessary. The sympathy of a large circle of friends is extended to the bereaved family.

Deceased, who was in his 79th year, was of a cheery and amiable disposition. By members of the Peek family, with whom he had been associated so long, he was held in warm esteem. To visitors to the mansion he was invariably their friend and guide. At no time was he happier than when escorting visitors over the Observatory where he had laboured for nearly 40 years, and explaining to them many interesting features of the instruments and of matters meteorological. For a lengthy period he contributed information records to Pulman's Weekly News, the last of which appeared a fortnight ago.

Astronomy found in the deceased a keen and persevering student and he was regarded as one of the greatest authorities in this country on variable stars. Shortly after he came to Rousdon he went on a world tour with the late Sir Cuthbert Peek Bart., when he gained considerable knowledge appertaining to the science of the stars. To astronomical societies he supplied from time to time valuable records dealing with celestial bodies. Henceforth the observatory at Rousdon will know him no more, *but his work will remain as a lasting tribute to his genius.*

THE FUNERAL

took place on Saturday afternoon in the little Churchyard at Rousdon. As the body was being borne away from East Lodge the coffin being surmounted by some beautiful floral tributes, the peacefulness of the countryside, bathed in warm sunshine, was only broken by the tolling of the church bell. It was difficult to realise that Rousdon Mansion would not see him again, he who with his geniality and kindly greetings had so many friends ... the little church was almost filled, and amongst the large congregation were the Hon. Dowager Lady Peek [widow of Sir Cuthbert], the Hon. Mrs Grenville Peek ... Mr. and Mrs. A. Wiscombe (the Mayor and Mayoress of Lyme Regis) ...

Charles was buried next to Sir Cuthbert Peek's grave close by the door of the little church of St Pancras.

In March 1921 the Rousdon parish magazine recorded Charles's death:

Charles Grover is dead, and if you put the forty and odd millions of Britishers of these Islands through a sieve it is improbable that you turn up anything like Charles Grover. He was unique and things unique seem ever to have found their way to Rousdon. One of the many gifts of the great Sir Henry was this, that he had the knack and the power of putting his finger on the very person or thing which he required. Hence Charles Grover, curator of Rousdon Observatories and Museum. For 39 years he was the round peg that filled the round hole which now no other peg can possibly fill. It was not only that he was good at his job – many are good at their job – but it was the delightsome way that he had with him when talking about it.

When he took one aside with his humorous little explanations so full of pith and point, and his climax laid so surely in the right place that an attempt at repeating it landed one in failure.

From childhood he fought this old world with his own resources and as he held his own with it he made it kinder and merrier to all of us. It would take a good deal more than our modest page can hold to mention any of the episodes of his 78 years. The Rector, alas, only knew him for 4, and being a regular attendant at the most distant seat in Church, having an ear not so keen as it used to be, the Rector found him a safe person to adjust his voice to.

His acquaintances are probably a great host, and the interesting pile of letters from all sorts of people, including men well known in the world of science, which have reached his devoted wife, are but a tithe of what they would be if her loss were universally known. And dear Mrs. Grover, if you have read so far. I have the assurance that all your friends and neighbours join me in offering to you from their hearts an overflowing tribute of sympathy, and sorrow for the loss of your good husband – their friend – my friend.

Various members of the Peek family attended the funeral. 'The coffin descended covered with wreaths and among them a tribute from Sir Wilfrid, *Hic jacet, C.G., R.I.P.*, buried by the express wish of Lady Peek close up to Sir Cuthbert, his master whom he faithfully served and passionately loved.'

Charles Grover's grave, Rousdon 1921

With strange synchronicity Elizabeth, who outlived Charles by more than six years, died on the same day as Sir Wilfrid Peek – 12 October 1927 – bringing the end of the Grovers at Rousdon into symmetry with the end of the estate. Effectively Charles and Elizabeth had lived the whole life of Sir Henry's dream. Because the family had changed – Sir Henry giving way to Sir Cuthbert, Sir Cuthbert dying comparatively young – the couple at East Lodge were perhaps the longest-surviving residents of the estate – over forty years their absences from Rousdon, added together, could probably still be counted in weeks rather than years – and as their arrival had coincided with the beginnings of Rousdon, so their passing matched its end. From the Rousdon parish magazine:

> *Dear old Mrs Grover passed away just 5 1/2 hours after Sir Wilfrid, and was buried while his body rested in the Peek Chapel, now she rests with her husband who lies next to his old master Sir Cuthbert, thus pass out the Grovers, two of the most striking personalities that we have seen here.*

Charles and Elizabeth Grover in the garden at East Lodge,
Rousdon

Speculation on
Two on a Tower

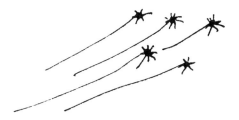

It should be said at the outset that there is no
concrete evidence that Charles Grover was in any
way a model for Thomas Hardy's astronomer,
Swithin St Cleve, in *Two on a Tower*; nor is there
evidence that the two men met. However, it is
possible to construct a compelling circumstantial
case.

According to Martin Seymour-Smith in his
biography of Thomas Hardy, the sources for *Two on
a Tower* include 'its author's reading, his
experience and his journeys into the countryside'.
Further 'the immediate and topical event which
caught his poetic attention was the possibility of
drawing symbolic capital from the transit of Venus
(Goddess of Love) across the face of the sun which
was due in December 1882, when the book would be
out in volume form'. Having moved from London to
Wimborne Minster in June 1881 the Hardys were

also delighted to see the appearance of Tebbutt's Comet from the windows of their new home. In his introduction to *Two on a Tower*, it is this event that Suleiman M. Ahmad pinpoints as the inspirational moment behind the conception of an '"astronomical" novel'. Like so many men of his time, Hardy had a long-term interest in science and, in particular, in astronomy. His family had owned a telescope, and there are references to astronomical subjects in a number of poems and writings before 1882. Ahmad believes that 'It would have been strange if Hardy had not written a novel in which astronomy was a strong element.'

Sources for Hardy's characters are – and always will be – a matter for debate. It might be supposed that in the same way in which he fictionalised the Wessex landscape and its settlements so he fictionalised and correlated characters and characteristics of people he met. Seymour-Smith wrote of *A Pair of Blue Eyes*, where the central character, Elfride, is closely modelled on Hardy's first wife Emma and the theme of the book is recognisably autobiographical (he met Emma while on an architectural tour of Cornwall), that 'his parents cannot be expected to understand the critical niceties of the relationship between characters in novels and their models from real life'; and in *Return of the Native*: 'Clym is Tom as he might have been had he not been gifted with a creative imagination ... Tom told [Sydney] Cockerell that he had portrayed his mother in Mrs Yeobright.' Similarly real events could provide the impetus for a narrative; the true story of the sale of a wife by her husband is the source for the story of *The Mayor of Casterbridge*.

Hardy's own knowledge of architecture underlies *A Laodicean* and is also present in *A Pair of Blue Eyes* which, as Hardy himself noted in the Preface of the June 1912 edition, was 'written at a time when the craze for indiscriminate church-restoration had just reached the remotest nooks of western England, where the wild and tragic features of the coast had long combined in perfect harmony with the crude Gothic Art of the ecclesiastical buildings scattered along it'. For *Two on a Tower* he had read Alfred Proctor's *Essays in Astronomy* (1874) and *The Poetry of Astronomy* (1881), and he applied to visit – and may have visited (the correspondence survives, but there is no sure evidence of an actual visit) – the Royal Observatory at Greenwich. At Greenwich he corresponded with Edwin Dunkin, then Chief Assistant at the Observatory – a post to which he had been promoted on the retirement as Astronomer Royal of G.B. Airy – answering a series of questions as to the intended purpose of his visit in a letter of 27 November 1881. Here he indicated that his 'particular object ... in view in desiring to see the Royal Observatory' was 'To ascertain if a hollow memorial pillar, with a staircase inside, can be adapted for the purpose of a small observatory, & how it can be roofed so as not to interfere with observations – etc. etc.' It is at this point that Hardy's research may have brought him into contact with Charles Grover.

The personnel at the Royal Observatory and the membership of the RAS overlapped to a considerable degree. G.B. Airy, who had been Astronomer Royal from 1835–1881, was an enthusiastic supporter of the RAS and had served four terms as President – 1835–37, 1849–51, 1853–55 and 1863–64 – as well as a period as President of the British Association (from 1851). Hardy's correspondent at Greenwich, Edwin Dunkin, had been Secretary of the RAS from 1871–1877 and would be its President from 1884–1886. The Secretary of the RAS in 1881 was Sir William Henry Mahoney Christie, who held the post from 1880–1882, and was Astronomer Royal from 1881–1910. From 1830 members of the RAS had been included in the Board of Visitors to the Greenwich Observatory whose role was to check the work and inspect the equipment of the Observatory.

Charles frequently attended meetings of the RAS between 1870 and 1880 'then held in a little room at Kings College, Strand. Long before the present palatial home of the Society at Burlington House was even thought of ... I think when I first went in 1870 the President was Mr. Warren de la Rue and during the succeeding years I saw there Airy, Adams, Lassell, Pritchard, Proctor and many other great astronomers of the day, and was an attentive listener to their papers and communications.' Part of Charles's job at these meetings was the presentation and demonstration of Browning's products: 'Micrometers, Spectroscopes, Astrometers and all kinds of astronomical apparatus'. It is impossible that over the years he did not come to know and – more importantly – to be known by some of the eminent scientists that he met there. And while he would have been known as a clever man and a good listener, his main reputation would probably have been centred on the work that he did and on his expertise with equipment and his knowledge – possibly unequalled at the time – of amateur observatories around the country, experience garnered through his 'many journeys to fix up and adjust equatorials etc.'

While there were undoubtedly many people in the astronomical world of the time who would have looked down upon a man who had started life in as humble a manner as Charles Grover, there were equally certainly others who had a far more egalitarian outlook. G.B. Airy – often dismissed as irascible and difficult – according to Allan Chapman held the grand amateurs 'in the highest respect' and believed that they were almost always the source of successful research: 'In short, it had been the Grand Amateurs who had spearheaded fundamental research in astronomy and its related sciences.' Edwin Dunkin began his professional life at the Royal Observatory at the age of 24 as a humble 'Supernumerary Computer', what Chapman calls 'one of the most evolutionarily versatile forms of astronomical life in Britain'. When Christie was

Astronomer Royal he even took the step of employing women on the staff of the Observatory. Christie also corresponded with an amateur from very much the same background as Charles Grover – 'John Robertson: the railway porter of Coupar Angus'.

So what is more natural than for Edwin Dunkin to delegate to Charles Grover, who is familiar to him at the very least from many meetings of the RAS at which Dunkin acted as Secretary and whom Dunkin knows will be able to answer any questions regarding the establishment of an amateur observatory, on or off a tower, the task of dealing with the questions of a novelist on astronomical topics?

Would it be reasonable to expect any meeting between Charles Grover and Thomas Hardy to have been documented? Probably not. As far as Hardy would have been concerned he would have been speaking to a man with a sufficient degree of expertise to answer his questions (and to give him a little more besides: Charles's obituary notes his delight in outlining the trajectory of his professional life at all opportunities and similarities between the background of Charles and the fictional life of Swithin St Cleve are the meat of the conjecture that the two men met) but effectively of no lasting consequence beyond that of a practical informant and perhaps the source of a few ideas for a character in a fiction (a subject about which Hardy was never especially forthcoming). Charles may or may not have heard the name of Hardy, but he only mentions scientific men in '50 Years an Astronomical Observer', and it seems quite probable that he never read a novel in his life. If he had, I doubt if he would have read a novelist such as Hardy, with his romantic themes and the whiff of scandal or impropriety about them. Like Hardy's creation, Swithin, who questioned by Lady Constantine as to what he had been reading in her library replied that he scarcely read any subject other than astronomy: 'In these days the secret of productive study is to avoid well.' Would they have got along? Is it possible to imagine a meeting between the novelist and the instrument maker's assistant cum amateur astronomer?

Hardy and Charles Grover were close in age: Hardy was born in 1840, Charles believed that he too had been born in that year. Both had learned to read prodigiously young – Charles 'never knew the time when I could not read or write' and Hardy described himself as 'able to read almost before he could walk' while others confirmed that he could read before he was three – both had attended British schools, and both were – to a degree – autodidacts, although Hardy's formal education went a lot further than Charles's had done. Martin Seymour-Smith's description of Hardy, the country boy come to London, could as well fit Charles Grover:

Tom may have been countrified, but he was no country bumpkin ... He carried with him an iron determination to succeed, and it is clear that those to whom he introduced himself, and who were to be useful to him, liked him ... The difficulties he experienced through his feelings of inferiority to those better educated than himself have been much exaggerated. More important was his private confidence in his abilities, and his determination to acquire sufficient knowledge to give himself, above all, an understanding of his subjects.

From 1876 Hardy kept literary notebooks in the same systematic way that Charles kept his observations book.

There is no doubt that Charles Grover would have been able to describe to Hardy a way in which the hollow memorial tower could be utilised as an observatory. Swithin St Cleve shows Lady

Constantine (Viviette) the arrangements that have been made and for which she has paid:

He brought a little lantern from the cabin, and lighted her up the winding staircase to the temple of that sublime mystery on whose threshold he stood as priest. The top of the column was quite changed. The tub-shaped space within the parapet, formerly open to the air and sun, was now arched over by a light dome of lath-work covered with felt. But this dome was not fixed. At the line where its base descended to the parapet there were half a dozen iron balls precisely like cannon shot, standing loosely in a groove, and on these the dome rested its whole weight. In the side of the dome was a slit through which the wind blew and the North Star beamed, and towards it the end of the great telescope was directed.

The 'great telescope' is the equatorial that Viviette has bought for Swithin.

Like Charles Grover, Swithin began his observations with a humble instrument, but longs for something better: on the first occasion that he and Lady Constantine meet, while he is telling her of his plans and ambitions, he also says: 'Ah, if only I had a good equatorial.' He is observing alone on the top of the tower in very much the manner that Charles Grover must have done in the nights after his work in the brush-maker's shop: 'Beside him stood a little oak table, and in front was the telescope.' Swithin St Cleve, like Charles Grover, is an orphan; his parents died when he was a child, and he has been brought up by his grandmother. Swithin wears 'a black velvet skull-cap', and while Cuthbert Peek's 'curious looking mortal' cannot compare with Hardy's 'guileless philosopher' 'in the shape of Antinous', his 'Adonis-astronomer', I suspect that Charles Grover's hair also curled beneath the edges of his velvet cap: 'a curly margin of very light shining hair, which accorded well with the flush upon his cheek'.

For two years Charles observed with the ship's spy-glass; Swithin thinks that with his small telescope he will obtain 'a practical familiarity with the heavens' in a year. Charles – admittedly not so unusually for an impoverished amateur of the day – made his first telescope, using a zinc tube. Swithin is making a telescope in his bedroom at his grandmother's cottage: 'In a corner stood a huge pasteboard tube, which a close inspection would have shown to be intended for a telescope.' Pasteboard may seem an improbable material for a telescope; Hardy may have been intending to point up the difficulties inherent in Swithin's dreams of astronomical fame and fortune – 'pasteboard' carries figurative connotations, according to the OED, 'Unsubstantial; unreal, counterfeit, sham'; but Charles could have told Hardy of the seventeenth-century telescope that he saw at Hartwell House, with the 10-foot vellum tube which would perhaps seem no more likely a material than pasteboard, or of his reading of the *Life of Faraday* in the 1870s and the description of Galileo's first wood and paper telescope that had impressed him enough for it to feature in his own brief notes on the book. Similarly there is a suggestion of vainglory in the scale on which this project is conceived. The object-glass that Swithin buys for the telescope – and that smashes, through his own carelessness, while he tells Lady Constantine the outcome of the errand on which she has sent him – is '... "a magnificent eight-inch first quality object lens – I took advantage of my journey to London to get it – I have been six weeks making the tube, of milled board; and as I had not enough money by twelve pounds for the lens I borrowed it of my grandmother..."'

It is this unfortunate accident and the emotions evoked in Lady Constantine by the distress of the young astronomer that determines her to help him by replacing the shattered glass and – when that does not work – by buying him an equatorial telescope; to protect her modesty she claims that she is buying the instrument for herself, although he will be able to use it whenever he so wishes. Charles did better than Swithin with his home-made telescope, constructed on a more modest plan, and he successfully purchased his first small telescope, but he was greatly helped thereafter by gifts and loans from wealthy patrons such as Dr Lee, the Revd Webb and, most notably in the context of comparisons with *Two on a Tower*, George Knott, who provided him with a fine mirror. 'The instrument which some kind astronomical friends have kindly furnished me with is one of the newly invented silvered glass reflectors ... this is mounted on a very simple but efficient equatorial stand'.

Swithin's ambition was to make a name for himself in the field of variable star observations; the same area that was chosen for research by Rousdon and in which Charles Grover had plainly had an interest for many years. He keeps the kinds of hours that would have been familiar to Charles: 'I observe from seven or eight till about two in the morning, with a view to my great work on variable stars.' Seymour-Smith notes of Swithin's talent that 'his creator credits him with drawing, despite his extreme youth, the same inferences about variable stars as the American astronomer E.C. Pickering made in 1880, and published in a paper in 1881'. Hardy was interested in science, but whether he would have been as up to date as Seymour-Smith implies here – that he would have been reading the latest astronomical journals – is a matter of conjecture. There is, however, no doubt at all that any informant recommended by the Royal Observatory would have been able to enlighten Hardy as to the latest discoveries and the most intriguing areas for present and future research. Swithin is:

preparing a work on variable stars. There is one of these which I have exceptionally observed for several months, and on this one my great theory is mainly based. It has been hitherto called irregular; but I have detected a periodicity in its so called irregularities which, if proved, would add some very valuable facts to those known on this subject, one of the most interesting, perplexing, and suggestive in the whole field of astronomy.

In order to pursue an errand for Lady Constantine, Swithin is prepared to give up several crucial nights' observation and to allow her to make the observation in his stead – poetic licence, I think – exhorting her in a letter: 'Please don't neglect to write down, *at the moment*, all remarkable appearances, both as to colour and intensity; and be very exact as to time, which correct in the way I showed you.'

Swithin's genius is to make the discovery that he is pursuing '"I have made an amazing discovery in connection with the variable stars!" he exclaimed': the dramatic outcome is that his achievement is eclipsed by an American astronomer and in his despair he succumbs to near-fatal illness. As he returns from his tiring trip to a main post office, to send off his paper – written in triplicate: a copy to a journal, one to the Greenwich Observatory, one to the Royal Society – in the cold rain, he reads the astronomical journal that he has picked up from the stationers. Here he reads 'a review of a pamphlet by an American astronomer, in which the author announced a conclusive discovery with regard to variable stars'.

Swithin is saved by a comet. As Charles Grover's ambition to be an astronomer was inspired by Donati's comet, and as he continued to be particularly fascinated by comets throughout his lifetime, and as Hardy may have been inspired to write a novel with an astronomical theme by the appearance of Tebbutt's Comet in midsummer 1881, so the maid Hannah's remark that '"Only that there's a comet, they say"' is the shot in the arm that the pale youth needs: '"A what?" said the dying astronomer, starting up on his elbow.' The comet of 1882, which Charles Grover first noted on 20 April that year and saw with the naked eye on 3 June, was Wells Comet: 'June 4th ... it appeared to the naked eye with a short fan shaped tail'.

While it may be no more than coincidence – Hardy drawing into his narrative another of the main events currently engaging the astronomical community – towards the end of the book, when the romance is unravelling, Viviette has discovered the error made concerning the death of her husband and it is clear that she and Swithin are not legally married, Swithin's astronomical enthusiasm is revitalised by news of the forthcoming transit of Venus. According to his letters, Hardy despatched the concluding part of *Two on a Tower* to the *Atlantic Monthly* on 19 September – two months after Charles Grover had signed for the RGS expedition and just less than a month after the expedition had sailed. Did Charles Grover's experience propel Swithin the same way? Did Hardy again rely on the life of his anonymous adviser for a dramatic purpose; that of putting Swithin fully out of communication and entirely out of reach?

Swithin has been to Greenwich; Viviette is concerned with the illegal marriage and with her discovery of Swithin's legacy (which he rejected, unbeknown to her, for their marriage), she is pale-faced, troubled. He greets her excitedly: '"I have so much to tell you about my visit – one thing is that the astronomical world is getting quite excited about the coming Transit of Venus. There is to be a regular expedition fitted out – how I should like to join it!"'

He is persuaded to go by Viviette's brother Louis, who is profoundly disturbed from the outset by the alliance between his titled sister and the impoverished parson's son who is eight years her junior, and by a letter and finally a face-to-face

interview with Viviette herself. To Louis: '"Then go
I will," replied Swithin firmly. "I have been
fortunate enough to interest some leading
astronomers, including the Astronomer-Royal; and
in a letter received this morning I learn that the use
of the Cape observatory has been offered me for any
Southern observations I may wish to make."' To
Viviette he replies: 'If you insist I will go.' And
then, at the last moment, rather than making the
proposed expedition to the Cape, Swithin finds
himself heading further south, to a more isolated
spot, altogether more closely comparable to a dusty
spread on the Darling Downs: Swithin's plans 'had
been modified to fall in with the winter expedition
formerly mentioned, to observe the Transit of
Venus at a remote Southern station'.

So Swithin, orphaned, brought up by his
grandmother, self-educated; who started observing
with a small instrument, embarked on the
construction of a telescope and was finally provided
with an equatorial through the magnanimity of a
wealthy benefactress; who gained the approbation
of some well-known and highly-placed astronomers,
ends the story on an expedition to see the transit of
Venus and to observe the skies of the southern
hemisphere. The observatory on the tower is roofed
over in model style, as would have been numerous
observatories familiar to Charles Grover and as will
be the observatory in Rousdon.

Postscript:
Transits of Venus

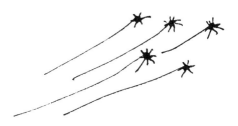

Transits of Venus take place when the planet comes into inferior conjunction with the sun almost at the precise point where the orbit of the planet crosses the orbital plane of the earth. Then the earthbound observer can see – projected onto a plane surface or, in earlier and more careless times, with specially adapted equipment such as graduated tinted lenses – the small black disk of Venus crossing the wide fiery face of the sun. They are rare and fascinating phenomena. Since observation of the first transit of Venus in 1639, there have been only five more, in 1761 and 1769, in 1874 and 1882 and on 8 June 2004. There will be one more in the twenty-first century, on 5-6 June 2012

Early on it was recognised that they would be immensely useful in the greater project of mapping the solar system, and most particularly in calculating the exact distance between the earth and the sun – the astronomical unit (AU). David Sellers, in a fascinating book, *The Transit of Venus*, notes:

> *Many educated guesses were made about the absolute distance [between the earth and the sun]. It was customary for these to be expressed in terms of the solar parallax. .. this quantity is actually an angle: the angle which would be formed between two lines, the one projected from an observer at the centre of the Sun to the centre of the Earth, and the other projected from the same observer to the outer edge of the Earth ... knowing the solar parallax would allow the distance between the Earth and the Sun to be easily calculated.*

The Copernican heliocentric view of the universe, allowed the theoretical possibility of transits of both Mercury and Venus, but Copernicus (1473–1543) himself, and Galileo (1564–1542), were of the opinion that the planets would not be visible against the sun. And although Copernicus proposed the heliocentric system – in which earth and the planets orbited a stationary sun – in published form in 1543 it was not universally accepted as any kind of blinding truth. There was fierce opposition both from the Church – for whom it contradicted doctrinal and Biblical truths – and also from the academic world in which questioning of Aristotle (or the Aristotelian model of the heavens) was tantamount to an academic heresy. It was Johannes Kepler (1571–1630) (who devised his own model of the solar system, closely resembling that of Copernicus) who accurately predicted the first transit of Mercury to be witnessed and sketched and who also made predictions for the transit of Venus, although here his calculations were less exact. In 1607 Kepler believed – albeit briefly – that he had himself seen a transit of Mercury. At the predicted time and date he had used a pinhole camera to project the image of the sun and had observed a black speck on the sun's face. Some years later, when Johannes Fabricius (1587–1616) and Galileo had discovered the existence of sunspots, Kepler was able to console himself with the thought that he had at least been the first to observe such phenomena.

Undeterred, Kepler continued with calculations for the next transit of Mercury and settled on the date of 7 November 1631. Although he was dead before the event took place, it did occur as predicted and was witnessed in Paris by the astronomer Pierre Gassendi (1592–1655), who thus earned lasting fame as the first man ever to observe a transit. Kepler's prediction for the next transit of Venus was also correct. He said that it would take place in December 1631, but as it took place after sunset for most of Europe it was not seen.

Kepler had also predicted that the period between transits was about 130 years, and that the next one would therefore not take place until the mid-eighteenth century, far beyond a lifetime.

The first observation of a transit of Venus came, therefore, at both an unexpected time and place.

Jeremiah Horrocks was born in Toxteth, Liverpool, in around 1619. His family seem to have been yeoman farmers and watchmakers – the latter skill perhaps offering a clue to a talent for astronomy – but they seem neither to have been particularly wealthy or well-connected. Nonetheless, Jeremiah was sent to study at Cambridge in 1632, when he would have been 13 or so. His comparative youth would have been less to do with his prodigious talent than with the general educational standards. Schools taught up to a fairly basic level beyond which universities provided what was probably closer to a modern sixth-form education than a degree. He went up to Emmanuel College as a 'sizar' or poor scholar, and did not take his degree, which is a further indication of poverty, since to take a degree of any kind was an expensive business.

After his time in Cambridge, it is known that Jeremiah Horrocks returned to Lancashire and that he lived in the village of Much Hoole. Local tradition says that he lived in a house called Carr House, owned by the Stone family, but it is not known for sure. Nineteenth-century writers also had him down as a clergyman or curate, but he would have been too young – deacons could not be ordained until the age of 23 and no one could be ordained priest until the age of 24. What is clear is that he had a fine mathematical mind, that he was well read in the latest areas of astronomical theory and that he was also an assiduous observer. He was in the habit of comparing his independent observations with the published astronomical tables of the time – particularly those of the Belgian Philip Lansberg (1561–1632) and Johannes Kepler – and he frequently found that the tables disagreed with each other and that they were wrong when compared to his own observations.

Comparing published tables in October 1639 he was therefore not surprised to see that there were wide variations and disagreement as to the date, time and position of Venus during the next inferior conjunction. His own predictions, based on his independent observations, were that the planet would pass directly across the disk of the sun, that Kepler had been right about the long period between the orbital configurations that produce a transit, but that such phenomena occur in pairs – approximately eight years apart. Horrocks therefore correctly predicted a transit of Venus for 24 November 1639 (6 December in the modern calendar), and that the transit in 1761 would be followed by one in 1769.

Horrocks set up a simple arrangement of a telescope (for which he says that he paid half-a-crown) and a sheet of white paper marked with a carefully graduated circle six inches in diameter. The telescope was positioned so that the sun's disk would be projected onto the paper to exactly fill the circle. Finally, after a generally dull day, at 3.15, only half an hour before sunset, the sun appeared and Horrocks was able to observe the dark shape of the planet moving across the bright circle on his paper. In that half hour he made three measurements, an apparently simple achievement that had momentous significance.

Horrocks wrote a treatise on his observation of the transit, which was published in Danzig in 1662 by the astronomer Johannes Hevelius. It was called *Venus in sub Sole Visa* (*Venus in Transit across the Sun*) and in the last chapter he tackled the difficult subject of the solar parallax, arriving at a new estimate of the sun's distance from the earth of almost 95 million kilometres (60 million miles). He was still a long way from the actual distance, but extended the estimate by four times the calculation made by Kepler, which, in its turn, had multiplied threefold the previous calculations. As the distance estimated grew larger so of course did the recognised size and power of the sun.

Jeremiah Horrocks' death is probably the best recorded element of his existence. His friend and astronomical correspondent William Crabtree noted it on the back of a bundle of letters – he died 'very suddenly' in the morning of 3 January 1641, at the age of twenty-two. In 1874, near to the time of another transit, a monument to Horrocks was unveiled in Westminster Abbey. The transcription concludes *'[he] predicted from his own observations the Transit of Venus which was seen by himself and his friend William Crubtree On Sunday 24th of November (O.S.) 1639'.*

In fact, Horrocks had exhorted both his brother in Liverpool and his friend Crabtree in Manchester to make efforts to see and measure the transit. The brother was thwarted by the weather, and Crabtree was so over-whelmed by what he saw – for no more than fifteen minutes before the sun finally set – that he failed altogether to make any useful calculations. In the Great Hall of Manchester Town Hall there is a mural by Ford Madox Brown – one of a series of twelve depicting key moments in

Manchester's history, from the building of the first fort by Agricola in AD70 to Dalton's scientific experiments – entitled *Crabtree Rapt in Contemplation*, celebrating Crabtree's almost spiritual experience of the sight of the transit of Venus. The projected light of the sun pierces the room like a supernatural beam. Crabtree gazes at the projection, a medieval saint transfixed by a beatific vision, while his wife and children pose as the awe-struck audience to his great revelatory moment.

The next 120 years saw a considerable refinement of the process of measuring the distance from the earth to the sun using observations of a transit of Venus. This time the young astronomer primarily responsible for progress was Edmund Halley (1656–1742) (whose name was to be immortalised in the great comet). One of a new breed of astronomers eager for adventure and to map new areas of the heavens, Halley and a companion sailed to St Helena in 1676 to observe and chart the southern skies. Dogged – as were so many astronomical journeys – by unexpectedly cloudy skies, Halley nonetheless achieved the identification and cataloguing of 341 stars. He also, and perhaps more significantly, observed a transit of Mercury. This event too was marred by cloudy skies, but he managed to observe both the ingress and egress of the planet across the sun and began to see a way in which the all important solar parallax could be accurately calculated.

The mathematics is complex, taking into account as it has to the rotation of the earth and its effect on the observation of a transit, but Halley's conclusion, essentially, was that if a number of observers situated at various points around the earth, as far as possible on the same longitude, but differing widely as to latitude, were to make observations focusing on the moments of ingress and egress of the planet across the sun and these were brought together and compared it would be feasible to make accurate measurements and achieve the understanding of the distance from the earth to the sun. He hoped that there would have been other measurements made in Europe of the transit of Mercury observed in 1677, which could have been used to test his thesis, but the northern hemisphere had been almost entirely cloudy on the day in question, and the only observations that had been made were unhelpful.

This technique had been mooted before, by James Gregory (1638–1675), a young Scottish astronomer, who noted in his *Optica Promota* of 1663 that observations of transits taken from places of known latitudes might be used to work out the distance of the sun; and the Italian-born astronomer Jean Dominique (Giovanni Domenico) Cassini (1625–1712) calculated the astronomical unit to within 90 per cent of its true value following a determination of the Martian parallax at opposition in 1672, with measurements made by himself in Paris and a fellow astronomer, Jean Richer (1630–1696) in Cayenne, South America. While Cassini's calculation was extra-ordinarily accurate for the time, his methods lacked conviction, and it was Halley who brought the idea into the light and who persuaded others of its feasibility.

It seemed clear to Halley that a far more accurate measurement would be obtainable from observations of the much rarer transits of Venus than from observations of Mercury, simply because of the greater size and proximity of Venus. Astronomical instruments, while constantly being improved, were also not yet at a sufficiently sophisticated stage for such natural advantages to be overlooked. Other essentials for the scheme were an accurate measurement for the radius of the earth – effectively the baseline for the greater measurement – and a means of ensuring that the observers were precisely placed for the observation of the event itself.

An Englishman, Richard Norwood (c.1590–1675) using two observations of the sun at midday on the longest day of the year, near the Tower of London in 1633 and in York in 1635, and a measurement of the distance between the two points made by using a chain and making the journey on foot, reached an estimate for the radius of the earth of 3983 miles. This he reported in a book published in 1636 and called *The Seaman's Practice*. In 1669, this was superseded by the work of a Frenchman, Jean Picard (1620–1682) who worked on a smaller scale but with greater accuracy and estimated the radius of the earth at 3955 miles. These are both remarkably close to the current measurement of 3963 miles and that of Picard provided an adequate base for the transit calculations.

The transit of 1761 was approached with enthusiasm by several nations. Astronomers were keen to see the phenomenon, and to record it with as much accuracy as could be managed, with a view to determining as nearly as possible the solar distance. The importance of this measurement is that it can be used to estimate distances throughout the solar system. The *relative* distances between celestial bodies had long been understood. Copernicus himself had worked out, through a mixture of observation and calculation, approximate planetary distances; and Kepler had proved mathematically the relationship between a planet's orbital distance and the orbital period. Kepler had provided the map, but it still needed the scale. Once the radius of the earth had been determined (as Picard had done) only one precise planetary measurement was needed to clarify the size of the whole system.

Halley presented a paper to the Royal Society in 1761 admonishing future astronomers to remember what he had learned and not to let the opportunity of viewing and learning from the next transit to pass, and while Halley's enthusiasm, and the respect in which he was held even after his death, were the motivating force behind British expeditions to observe the 1761 transit, there was equal commitment and interest in France where

Joseph-Nicolas Delisle (1688–1768) had devised a method of determining the solar parallax that did not rely on the same observer seeing both the ingress and the egress of Venus from the same site. Rather, the method involved comparison of pairs of observations made at different longitudes. Since *either* the start or the end of the transit was useful using Delisle's method, there was also less chance of observations being ruined by cloudy conditions obscuring a vital part of the whole transit. A number of prominent astronomers were among those sent out from France to distant points on the earth's surface, undertaking voyages that were at best perilous and that, in at least one case, proved fatal.

In England observing sites were selected in part following the work that Halley had done on the 1761 transit and in part following that of Delisle. Delisle had visited Halley in England, and Halley, in turn, had sent Delisle a copy of his paper on the transit. The Seven Years' War between Britain and France (1756–1763) had not put an end to scientific communication between the nations, and Delisle's *Mappemunde*, which showed the areas of the world from which the transit would best be viewed, had been presented at the Royal Society in 1760.

However, the war did have an effect on the parties sailing to observe the transit. The British expedition, which included Charles Mason (1730–1787), assistant to the Astronomer Royal, and Jeremiah Dixon (1733–1779), an amateur astronomer, on board *HMS Seahorse* was attacked in the English Channel by a French frigate, *le Grand*, and forced to turn back to Plymouth. After some wrangling with the Royal Society as to where the expedition should attempt to go next – the astronomers believing that its first port of call was now too far away to be reached in the time available – they set off once again for the original destination, Bencoolen, on Sumatra, in the East Indies. They did not discover until on their way that Bencoolen had been taken by the French: the alternative position agreed at the outset of the voyage was now unreachable in the time available, so they landed at Cape Town and made their observations from there. While conditions for their observations were, if not ideal, at least adequate, they pinpointed a particular problem – which also afflicted other observers – in achieving highly accurate measurements of the period of the transit.

From the same viewing position, the two astronomers' measurements varied from one another by a full four seconds. Both had been misled by the 'black drop' effect whereby Venus appears to elongate into a drop shape as it crosses onto the face of the sun. This can obscure the actual moment of ingress as, when the effect of the drop disappears, Venus can be seen to have made ingress and to be a discernible distance inside the circle of the sun – almost as if the planet had paused, then hopped on to make up the distance. Elsewhere, observers noted that the whole circle of Venus became visible as soon as the planet came close to the edge of the sun's disk. This 'luminous ring' effect was the first evidence that Venus might have an atmosphere, so was both interesting and valuable in itself, but it also served to blur the actual moments of ingress and egress and undermine the precision with which interim measurements could be made. The other British expedition could merely watch dense cloud cover as the time for the transit came and went above their temporary observatory in St Helena.

Nonetheless, despite the difficulties of war and natural hazards and the unexpected phenomenological complications to the observations themselves the figures produced following the 1761 transit allowed for a readjustment of the distance from the earth to the sun from Horrocks' estimation of 60 million miles to a more respectable estimate of between 77 and 97 million miles.

The astronomers and observers of 1761 were in a privileged position in that not only were they able to observe one rare phenomenon, but that they also had every reason to hope that they would be given a second bite of the cherry. The experience gained in 1761 was not to be passed to another generation who would need exhorting to undertake expeditions and observations, rather it could immediately be applied to the transit anticipated in 1769.

Nevil Maskelyn (1732–1811), who would be Astronomer Royal by the time of the next transit and who had languished under the grey skies of St Helena while the 1761 transit took place, was among those who believed that on the next occasion of a transit of Venus – only eight years away – measurements could be taken and observations made that would allow for the correct estimation of solar distance and for the subsequent mapping of distances throughout the solar system.

Maskelyn was also involved in the solution of another difficulty that had beset astronomers aiming for observations at exact locations (as well as mariners for centuries past), that of the calculation of longitude. Latitude could be determined from the stars, using a good star map, the provision of which had been a factor in the increasing tendency of astronomers to travel to far-flung places, but longitude needed to rely on comparisons made with known points at particular times. The longitude problem was thrown into sharp relief by the establishment in England of a Board of Longitude following a disaster at sea in 1707 when a squadron of Royal Navy ships led by Admiral Sir Cloudisley Shovel ran aground off the Scilly Isles, with the loss of almost 2000 lives. The Board offered substantial rewards to anyone who could solve the longitude problem; the incentives created considerable rivalries between astronomers – the venture was led by John Flamsteed (1646–1720), the first Astronomer Royal – and those such as John Harrison, a clockmaker and the eventual winner of partial prize money, and that handed over only grudgingly. Harrison's final design, a kind of large pocket watch that could be taken to sea and that continued to keep remarkably good time, was proved first in 1761 and then in 1764. Maskelyn was among Harrison's fiercest establishment opponents for the longitude prize, vigorously promoting his own 'Lunar Distance Method' of finding longitude using new tables by Tobias Mayer.

Although it would not prove problem-free – there were problems with the weather, astronomers died, the phenomena of the 'black drop' and Venus's atmosphere still introduced discrepancies and uncertainty into what had been hoped would be scrupulously careful measurements and observations – the 1769 transit was probably the apogee of such expeditions. Essential understanding of the diameter of the earth was established, sailing to a particular destination within a set time was becoming easier, 1761 had provided astronomers with first-hand, up-to-date information about the transit of Venus and its observations, and astronomical instruments were improving at speed. The stage was set for real accomplishment.

In the final analysis, too, real achievements were made. Once all the calculations had been taken into account, the distance of the sun from the earth was reassessed by Thomas Hornsby, Savilian Professor of Astronomy at Oxford University, as 93,726,900 miles. Hornsby took the average distance calculated from five observations. He used this to produce the most accurate estimates yet made of the distances to the planets in the solar system.

A side effect of the 1769 transit was the promotion and success of James Cook (1728–1779) – then only a naval lieutenant with no experience in either commanding a ship or in making long voyages – who became one of the best known British sailors, the man who 'discovered' Australia. His mathematical abilities had already come to the attention of the Royal Society in connection with calculations of longitude and observations of a solar eclipse, and mathematical ability was central to the role that he was being asked to play although an astronomer, Charles Green (1735–1771), was also on the expedition. Both men made measurements and sketches of the transit, and their observations, from Tahiti in the South Seas, were among those employed by Hornsby in attaining the solar distance in 1771.

Between the transits of 1769 and 1874 the figures for the solar distance were calculated and recalculated, with the resulting distance changing – in both directions – according to the data used. What became transparently obvious was that, as a tool for obtaining the necessarily precise measurements to work out an exact distance from the earth to the sun, transits of Venus were flawed. The black drop effect and the penumbra around the planet itself served to confuse the absolute moments of ingress and egress and did not seem liable to be overcome.

Other methods were searched for. Observations of Mars proved fruitful and 1862 saw calculations of solar distance come closer still to the modern figure of 93 million miles. Nearly 70 years later, in 1930–1931, the asteroid *Eros* was used to gain a precise measurement of the solar parallax, and the most accurate calculation of solar distance yet made. The 1930–1931 calculations were made by the Astronomer Royal, Sir Harold Spencer Jones and improved on those made by Hinks, based on the 1900–1901 measurements, and noted by Charles Grover in 1909. *Eros* had the dual advantages of proximity to the earth – and thus greater apparent movement – and very small size, so that it could be measured as a point of light rather than a less distinct ball.

However, the search for the solar distance – and hence the ability to measure the solar system – was only a part of the story of the transits of Venus.

While the usefulness of the transit of Venus as a tool for measuring the solar parallax was already disputed by the middle of the nineteenth century, they nonetheless remain rare occurrences; for many astronomers they offer a once-in-a-lifetime opportunity, for others there may be a chance to see two such phenomena; there is always the awareness that for many a sight of a transit of Venus will not come in their lifetime. By the late nineteenth century the lessons of Tycho Brahe (1546–1601) – above all else a great and accurate observer – were well learned: observation is at the heart of all astronomical knowledge and underlies all accurate calculation and all good models of the solar system and of the wider universe. Brahe's own observations were put to great use after his death by his one-time subordinate Johannes Kepler. Observations therefore are worth making in and for themselves. Not to make observations of a phenomenon that occurs at such rare intervals would be dereliction of duty as well as denial of the sheer pleasure that such a sight would bring. Further, of course, travelling to distant places enables observations of numerous other phenomena along the way; and transit expeditions presented some of the earliest opportunities of mapping the southern skies using the best equipment available.

Acknowledgements and Sources

The first people to thank are those descendants of Charles Grover who recognised that they had a forebear to be proud of and who kept photographs, books, notebooks, scrap books and press cuttings against the day when they could all be brought together. Jerry Grover made researching Charles a job of work, and discovered more about his background and – most particularly – unearthed his observations book, which was kindly returned to the family by Mike Hawker. Jerry also ensured the transfer of the archive on Charles Grover to the Science Museum in London. Dominic Sweetman and Carol O'Brien identified the Merz telescope that travelled to Australia for the transit of Venus in 1882, that subsequently served for all the Rousdon observations and that is also now in the Science Museum. Glenn Barrett read the manuscript and checked that the astronomical bits made sense and as a person with an interest in astronomical history was kind enough to say that he had enjoyed the book! Jim Sweetman of Courseware organised the printing of the book and the jacket.

The books I couldn't have done without were Allan Chapman, *The Victorian Amateur Astronomer: Independent Astronomic Research in Britain, 1820–1920* (Chichester: Wiley Praxis, 1998), J.L.T. Dreyer et al. (eds), *History of the Royal Astronomical Society, 1820-1920* (Oxford: Blackwell Scientific, 1987 reprinted for the RAS), Lucy Frost, *No Place for a Nervous Lady: Voices from the Australian Bush* (McPhee Gribble/Penguin Books Australia, 1984), Thomas Hardy, *Two on a Tower,* edited and with an introduction by Suleiman M. Ahmad (Oxford: Oxford University Press, 1993), Robert Hughes, *The Fatal Shore: a History of the Transportation of Convicts to Australia, 1787–1868* (London: Harvill Press, 1987), David Sellers, *The Transit of Venus: the Quest to Find the True Distance of the Sun* (Leeds:

MagaVelda Press, 2001), Charles and Hilary Maude Russell, *Jimbour: its History and Development, 1840-1953* (reprinted in 1989 by the *Dalby Herald,* Dalby, Australia), and Martin Seymour-Smith, *Hardy* (London: Bloomsbury, 1994). Thanks to everyone for loans of books. Information on Wellington Buildings came from the Peabody Trust, who acquired the buildings in 1968. Thanks are due to David Richards, great grandson of Charles Grover's correspondent Thomas Richards for copies of the letters sent to his great grandfather.

I would like to acknowledge the Syndics of Cambridge University Library for permission to quote from Leonard Darwin's letters to his mother MS.DAR.239.1:6; also, for their assistance in enabling me to read the letters.

Among a plethora of websites the most useful were as follows:

On Captain Cook:
http://www.captaincooksociety.com/ccsu4123.htm
John Browning and some of his instruments:
http://www.ex.ac.uk/nlo/news/nlonews/1995-10/9510-12.htm
The Great September Comet of 1882:
http://cometography.com/lcomets/1882r1.html
Grubb telescopes:
http://www.astro.ucc.ie/obs/grubbs/index.html
The Great Melbourne Telescope:
http://www.orrerymaker.com/OM_MelbOB.htm
and its loss:
http://www.abc.net.au/science/news/stories/S766412.htm;
http://msowww.anu.edu.au/fire/orchiston/telescope_loss_20 03.shtml
Peek Award (RGS): http://www.spri.cam.ac.uk/people/fuchs/
Lyme volcano:
www.soton.ac.uk/~imw/kimfire.htm
Magic mirrors: http://www.denverspiritualcommunity.org/ Wisdom/SeershipContents.htm
Charles Grover's articles in the Astronomical Register:
http://adsbit.harvard.edu